D0561080

WITHDRAWN

Conversations with Henry Miller

Literary Conversations Series

Peggy Whitman Prenshaw
General Editor

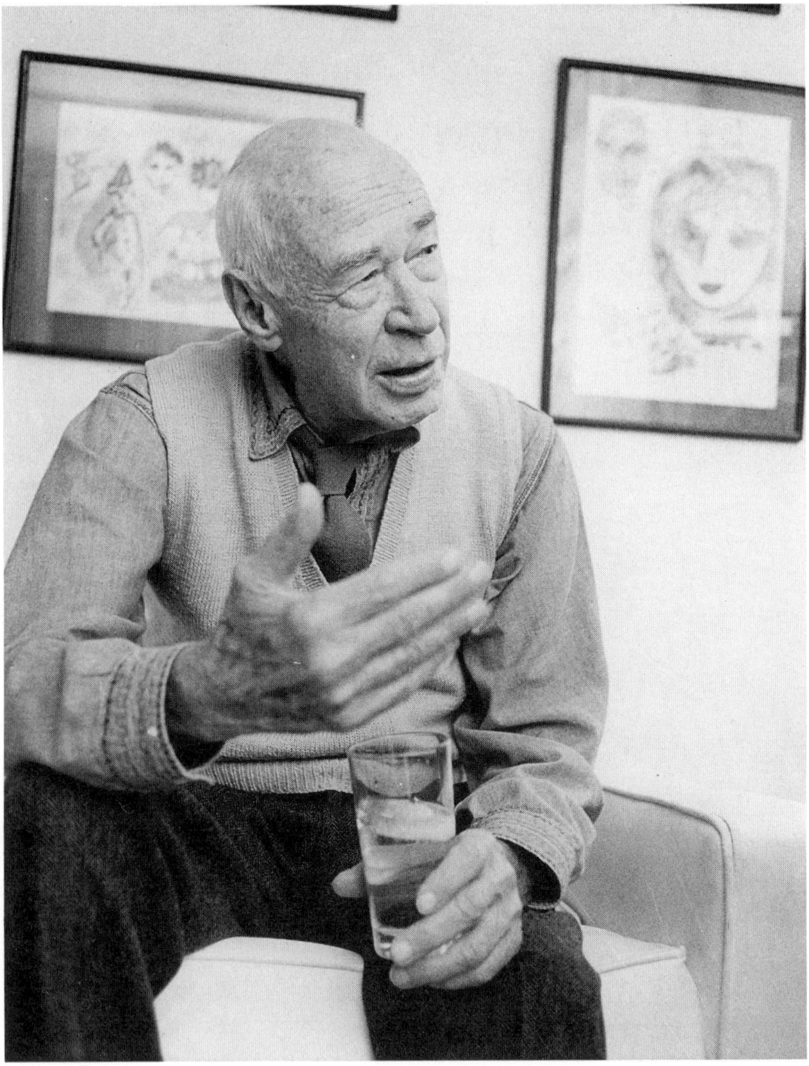

AP/Wide World

Conversations
with Henry Miller

Edited by
Frank L. Kersnowski and Alice Hughes

University Press of Mississippi
Jackson

Copyright © 1994 by the University Press of Mississippi
All rights reserved
Manufactured in the United States of America

97 96 95 94   4 3 2 1

The paper in this book meets the guidelines for permanence and durability of the
Committee on Production Guidelines for Book Longevity of the Council on Library
Resources.

Library of Congress Cataloging-in-Publication Data

Miller, Henry, 1891–1980
    Conversations with Henry Miller / edited by Frank Kersnowski and
Alice Hughes.
        p.   cm.—(Literary conversations series)
    Includes bibliographical references and index.
    ISBN 0-87805-519-3 (acid-free paper).—ISBN 0-87805-520-7 (pbk.:
acid-free paper)
    1. Miller, Henry, 1891–1980—Interviews.   2. Authors,
American—20th century—Interviews.   I. Kersnowski, Frank L., 1934–   .
II. Hughes, Alice.   III. Title.   IV. Series.
PS3525.I5454Z4625   1995
818'.5209—dc20   94-20382
                                                                      CIP

British Library Cataloging-in-Publication data available

Books by Henry Miller

Tropic of Cancer. Paris: Obelisk, 1934.
Aller Retour New York. Paris: Obelisk, 1935.
Black Spring. Paris: Obelisk, 1936.
Money And How It Gets That Way. Paris: Booster Publications, 1938.
Max and the White Phagocytes. Paris: Obelisk, 1938.
Tropic of Capricorn. Paris: Obelisk, 1939.
The Cosmological Eye. Norfolk: New Directions, 1939.
The World of Sex. Chicago: Printed by J.H.N. For Friends of Henry Miller. Ben
    Abramson, 1941.
The Colossus of Maroussi. San Francisco: Colt, 1941.
The Wisdom of the Heart. Norfolk: New Directions, 1941.
The Angel Is My Watermark. Fullerton: Holve-Barrows, 1944.
Sunday After the War. Norfolk: New Directions, 1944.
Plight of the Creative Artist In the United States of America. Holton: Bern Porter,
    1944.
Semblance of a Devoted Past. Berkeley: Bern Porter, 1945.
Varda: the Master Builder. Berkeley: Bern Porter, 1945.
Obscenity and the Law of Reflection. Yonkers: Alicat Book Shop, 1945.
Echolalia. Berkeley: Bern Porter, 1945.
The Amazing and Invariable Beauford DeLaney. Yonkers: Alicat Bookshop, 1945.
The Air-Conditioned Nightmare. New York: New Directions, 1945.
Men God Forgot. New York: Gotham Book Mart, 1946.
Emil White. San Francisco: Raymond & Raymond, 1947.
Remember To Remember. New York: New Directions, 1947.
The Smile At The Foot of The Ladder. New York: Buell, Sloan & Pearce, 1948.
Sexus. Paris: Obelisk, 1949.
The Books In My Life. London: Peter Owen, 1952.
Plexus. Paris: Olympia, 1953.
The Time of the Assassins. Norfolk: New Directions, 1956.
A Devil In Paradise. New York: Signet, 1956.
Quiet Days In Clichy. Paris: Olympia, 1956.
Bir Sur and the Oranges of Hieronymus Bosch. New York: New Directions, 1957.
The Third Eye. New York: Doubleday, 1957.
Art and Outrage. London: Putnam, 1959.
The Intimate Henry Miller. New York: Signet, 1959.
The Henry Miller Reader. Norfolk: New Directions, 1959.
Nights of Love and Laughter. New York: Signet, 1960.
Nexus. Paris: Obelisk, 1960.
To Paint Is To Love Again. Cambria: Cambria Books, 1960.
Stand Still Like A Hummingbird. Norfolk: New Directions, 1962.
Lawrence Durrell & Henry Miller: A Private Correspondence. New York: Dutton,
    1963.
Just Wild About Harry. Norfolk: New Directions, 1963.

Greece. New York: Viking, 1964.
Henry Miller on Writing. New York: New Directions, 1964.
Henry Miller: Letters to Anais Nin. New York: Putnam, 1965.
Order and Chaos. Chez Hans Reichel. New Orleans: Loujon, 1966.
Writer & Critic. Baton Rouge: Louisiana State University, 1968.
Insomnia or The Devil At Large. Albuquerque: Loujon, 1970.
My Life and Times. New York: Playboy, 1971.
Henry Miller in Conversation. Chicago: Quadrangle, 1972.
Reflections on the Death of Mishima. Santa Barbara: Capra, 1972.
On Turning Eighty. Santa Barbara: Capra, 1972.
First Impressions of Greece. Santa Barbara: Capra, 1973.
Walt Whitman. London: Village, 1973.
This Is Henry, Henry Miller From Brooklyn. Los Angeles: Robert Snyder, 1974.
Letters of Henry Miller and Wallace Fowlie. New York: Grove, 1975.
The Nightmare Notebook. New York: New Directions, 1975.
Books of Friends. Santa Barbara: Capra, 1976.
Genius and Lust. New York: Grove, 1976.
Gliding Into the Everglades. Lake Oswego: Lost Pleiade, 1977.
Mother China, and the World Beyond. Santa Barbara: Capra, 1977.
Four Visions of America. Santa Barbara: Capra, 1977.
My Bike and Other Friends. Santa Barbara: Capra, 1978.
Henry Miller: Years of Trial and Triumph, 1962–1964. Carbondale & Edwardsville: Southern Illinois; London & Amsterdam: Feffer & Simons, 1978.
An Open Letter to Stroker. New York: One Nine two Seven Press/STROKER, 1978.
Joey. Santa Barbara: Capra, 1979.
Notes on Aaron's Rod. Santa Barbara: Capra, 1980.
The World of Lawrence. Santa Barbara: Capra, 1980.
Reflections. Santa Barbara: Capra, 1981.
The Paintings of Henry Miller. Santa Barbara: Capra, 1982.
Opus Pistorum. New York: Grove, 1983.
Dear, Dear Brenda. New York: William Morrow, 1986.
Book of Friends: A Trilogy. Santa Barbara: Capra, 1987.
A Literate Passion. Letters of Anais Nin and Henry Miller. New York, San Diego &London: Harcourt Brace Jovanovich, 1987.
Henry Miller's Hamlet Letters. Santa Barbara: Capra, 1988.
Letters to Emil. New York: New Directions, 1989.
Letters from Henry Miller to Hoki Tokuda Miller. London: Robert Hale, 1990.
The Paintings: A Centennial Retrospective. Carmel: Coast, 1991.
Crazy Cock. New York: Grove Weidenfeld, 1991.
Moloch. New York: Grove, 1992.

Contents

Introduction

For modernists, such as Henry Miller, the self is potential, inconstant and inconsistent. It is not fixed. This is as much true for the lived self as for the self which produces and is a product of the narrative. These interviews record what Henry Miller says about his life and his works, not necessarily a description of either. They are, in effect, another narrative by Henry Miller, parallel to and different from the narrative of the books.

The earliest of these interviews was published in 1956, the latest in 1977. Here is the storyteller telling the story of his life and his works. The headlines are a good indicator of the perspective and the tone of the story they tell: "Getting Free"; "A Venerable Maverick"; "A World of Joy"; "A Mad Gaiety, a Verve, a Gusto." The headline of the last interview is a prefatory description by Anaïs Nin to Miller's first published book, *Tropic of Cancer,* used as a title to an interview by Kenneth Turan. *Tropic of Cancer* began the confrontational, often raucous, story of himself that Henry Miller told in his books, a story considered obscene by many readers and some courts of law. This story Miller mentions, but almost in passing in the interviews.

The story told to the interviewers is quite different, even though for them Miller and his works are fixed by the language which shocked and no longer shocks but still offends. Clearly, Miller wants to tell a story different from the one in the Paris books and *The Rosy Crucifix*. In the interviews, Miller mentions Chaucer, Villon, and Rabelais more often than June, his second wife about whom he wrote volumes. Miller sees his own work in the tradition of these storytellers. The outer life as it is rendered by these early storytellers, and by Miller, shocked and offended because it touched the nerve of the inner life, the life Miller, the self-described surrealist, the storyteller of dreams, tells in *Black Spring*. In an interview with George Wickes, Miller mentioned that he "loved" Lewis Carroll, making a connection between the two sides of the mirror Miller

describes as dadaism, "more important to me than SURREAL-
ISM . . . MORE TRULY REVOLUTIONARY." Such connections,
Miller makes repeatedly in these interviews, always stressing the
need to be free, to allow the spirit to grow. Seldom does he mention
the freedom his readers would expect from the writer of *Tropic of
Cancer,* a book banned in the English speaking world for almost
thirty years. Though living in America during the time these
interviews occurred, Miller most often speaks of freedom from
America's Puritanism and materialism, essentially freedom from the
America into which he was born and from which he fled when he
went to Paris in 1930 and fled from again on returning in 1940.

Henry Miller was born in Brooklyn, New York, on 26 December
1891, the son of second-generation German immigrants. His father was a tailor, as his father had been, which may well have been
the source of Henry's quite dapper appearance. His mother was
of sturdy bourgeois stock—strong, domineering and with a pro-
nounced Protestant work ethic. She and her son did not get along
well, and his resentment of her grew. In Robert Snyder's film *The
Henry Miller Odyssey,* Miller would complain that he never received
normal motherly affection from her. He would marry five times,
have intense affairs, and write about his life so frankly that his books
would be published in the United States only through the interven-
tion of the Supreme Court. Attacked and defended by protectors
of the public good (self-appointed and elected) and by literary
critics, Henry Miller's role in modern literature has undergone mo-
mentous changes. Liberals championed *Tropic of Cancer* when it
was published by Grove Press in 1961. Ten years later Kate
Millett, among others, would condemn and attack the book, Miller,
and much that he had written. In the interviews gathered here,
Miller repeatedly said he was unconcerned with either praise or
censure. In fact, when speaking with Julie Burns, Miller said: "I have
a contempt for all my readers and buyers." This is the same man
who received thousands of letters and answered many of them.

Miller moved to Paris in 1930. There he wrote and published
Tropic of Cancer because of the commitment of two women: his
second wife June who had encouraged him to stop working for
Western Union, and Anaïs Nin, who saw the novel through the

writing to publication in 1934. In her preface to *Tropic of Cancer,* Nin wrote:

> Here is a book which, if such a thing were possible, might restore our appetite for the fundamental realities. The predominant note will seem one of bitterness, and bitterness there is, to the full. But there is also a wild extravagance, a mad gaiety, a verve, a gusto, at times almost a delirium. A continual oscillation between extremes, with bare stretches that taste like brass and leave the full flavor of emptiness. It is beyond optimism or pessimism. The author has given us the last *frisson.* Pain has no more secret recesses.

In *Tropic of Cancer,* the first of three novels Miller would write during his self-exile in Europe, he established a reputation for dealing with the erotic in such a way as to cause his books to be censored. *Black Spring* and *Tropic of Capricorn* would maintain the reputation, as Miller shifted his subject from life in France to his earlier days in the United States. *Sexus,* the first volume of the trilogy Miller called *The Rosy Crucifix,* still shocks and offends. Through responding to the narrative itself, not merely the subject matter, so devoted a friend and admirer of Miller as Lawrence Durrell cabled Miller to withdraw the book from publication before it ruined his reputation as a writer. Miller rejected the advice and explained his novel. Later, Durrell would say, "I got my bottom spanked." Though Durrell's reputation was then in ascent, the Miller of the Paris days was still present. Then Durrell was in his early twenties and Miller, the accepted master, twenty years older. The two men carried on an extensive correspondence in which Miller wrote of books, friends, and his life with intelligence and without using the language that shocked so many readers of the Paris books and *The Rosy Crucifix.* The voice of Miller in the letters is the same we hear in these interviews, that of a well-read man secure in his understanding.

Miller's Paris was different from that of the Lost Generation, those writers who made exile fashionable before the Depression. The great cafes on Boulevard Montparnasse were still there, still meeting places for writers, though the writers had changed. Miller and Alfred Perles first met at one of the cafes. In *My Friend Henry Miller,* Perles said Miller could usually be found at Le Dome or Le Cupole, two of the great cafes of Montparnasse. Miller's friend,

Lawrence Durrell, retained Le Dome as his base in Paris. Inviting us to dinner, he said: "We can eat wherever you wish but brasserie food is quite good enough for me." The meal was excellent, quite good enough for anyone. So we have trouble accepting Merle Armitage's view of Miller:

> Actually, Miller was never in contact with the real producers of ferment. He did not know Pablo Picasso, or Braque, nor Gertrude Stein, Ernest Hemingway, or James Joyce. His intellectual pursuits consisted mainly of bohemian drunkenness and roistering with sympathetic whores. Many of his nights were spent under the arches of bridges on the Seine; he was never in the superior restaurants, nor had a bottle of great French wine.

Yet Miller knew and was written about by Man Ray and Brassai. And as he told George Wickes, he knew Sherwood Anderson, John Dos Passos, John Steinbeck, George Orwell, and John Cowper Powys about whom he said: "I was a midget and he was a giant." The contradictions in accounts of Miller occur throughout the interviews, largely because Miller accepted chance and accident rather than constancy and predictability as the determining forces in his life.

But that time in Paris remained a fixed point for Miller, as did his friendships, though they too would never be constant. With Alfred Perles (a displaced Austrian), Lawrence Durrell (a displaced Anglo-Indian), Miller (a displaced American) formed the Three Muske-teers. Their lives and loves were recorded in the diaries of Anaïs Nin, who also came of age as a novelist at this time. These were difficult days as Europe moved from the Depression to World War II, but an important literature came about before the war would scatter the writers. Central is Miller's use of unrelenting realism as a medium for an erotic mysticism.

Never again would any of these writers live close to one another. As in the world they wrote about, they had lost the old center and would have to fashion another. Miller chose to return to the United States, which had always stung him into writing. Alfred Perles mentioned in a letter to me that Miller and Durrell had an "odd eccentricity": they never spoke well of their own countries. Perles never returned to his; thus, he had less to complain about. Though Miller, as well as Perles and Durrell, made new friends in

their new homes, they were utterly shaped by that time in Paris.
Miller would only visit Europe after he left. Yet as he said to
Bernard Wolf about America, he is "*in* this country and not *of* it."

On his return in 1940, Miller rediscovered America by driving
through most of it for a year, as he gathered material about
Americans and America which he published as *The Air-Conditioned
Nightmare* (1945), a book that still irritates or delights readers.
He had already published *The Colossus of Maroussi,* the story of
his travels in Greece before he left Europe. He considered it his
best book; it has none of the eroticism for which Miller is known.
Having decided to live in America, he settled in California. He
lived at Big Sur during the time it was an artists' colony, but had
his last home in Pacific Palisades in what is usually described as
a mansion.

These interviews portray the mind and spirit of Henry Miller, not
the intricacies and excesses of his physical life. More accurately than
has been done in any biographical or critical study, Miller's own
words lead us to understand what has continued to attract new readers
and what captivated so many when he wrote. He was deeply
committed to freedom and liberty: intellectual, spiritual, and
physical. Never, though, did he become polemical or dogmatic. In
these interviews, he is "the Happy Rock" Lawrence Durrell
knew, a man fascinated by life, and omnivorous. He is a bibliophile,
a traveller, a nest builder, a writer, a reader, a talker, a painter.
He attracted the attention, both in adulation and condemnation, of
as varied a readership as any writer since Mark Twain. Yet of the
more than sixty books he wrote, few of his readers can name more
than a half-dozen. In these interviews, Miller mentions these
books no more often than *The Colossus of Maroussi* or *The Air-
Conditioned Nightmare* or *The Book of Friends* or *The Smile At
The Foot of The Ladder.* Merle Armitage is responsible for the
publication of *Smile,* which had been written at the request of Fernand
Leger to accompany forty of his drawings, as Miller mentioned in
the epilogue to the text and in his interview with Julie Burns.
Armitage mentions that he found the illustrations for the text but
not Miller's friendship with Leger and Miro.

Balancing Miller's popular reputation (a well-deserved one) as a
bohemian is Miller's interest in Zen and his devotion to a perhaps,

outmoded liberalism. Saying that he "loves women" or that feminists make the mistake of "trying to imitate men" when they should
"live like women," he does not intend to offend; he simply does
not comprehend that such words as *love, women, feminists* are
politically charged and have values other than what he assumes.
That Miller loved to talk and that he did so without restraint is
evident in these interviews, as is his generosity and naivety.
Whether or not we accept this naivety as a pose is problematical.

Miller liked to think of himself as "just a Brooklyn boy," part of
that wave of immigrants who came to America like Huck Finn
lighting out for the territories. They escaped the old world with its
castes and restrictions for a world in which they could live with
freedom. Of course, they brought with them old prejudices and
developed a few more as their traditional identities remained definite
in spite of the environment of the Melting Pot. Miller seldom
mentions those early days in interviews. In fact, he doesn't give much
biographical information at all in them. But then his books are so
autobiographical that for him to give details of his life in interviews would be redundant. What Miller gave instead in his interviews were direct responses to questions, frequently reiterated
rejections of pornography as of no interest to him and even more
frequently urgings to free the mind and body from the Puritanism
of America. Reversing the journey of European emigrants, Henry
Miller had gone to Europe.

Though he had written novels before he went to Paris, it was
there he found his voice in *Tropic of Cancer.* This voice he says
belongs to a thousand years of writing in Europe. What makes his
different, however, is that it is an American voice, rooted in that
culture. Necessarily, he would return. Inevitably, his writings would
become critical points in modern literature, though more often in
the rough and ready world of writers and readers than in the
academy.

Other works, though lacking the power of *Tropic of Cancer,* have
a warmth and tenderness that is endearing. *The Complete Book
of Friends* ends with this paean to Brenda Venus, who captivated
Miller late, revealing a Miller softer, though no less complex,
than his personae in the Paris books: "Where will this strange

creature lead me, I wonder? To what strange shores? I have put
myself in her hands. Lead me, O blessed one, wherever!''

Miller made the same request of many women—to his financial if
not artistic detriment. Miller's complex and contradictory personality caused him to seek and reject, praise and denigrate the same
beings or actions, seemingly without qualms. Exploitative of
women, he was exploited by them as well; inclined to reject fans,
he gave a great many interviews, many of which have disappeared. Of those which remain, we have included in this volume
ones in which Miller talked most substantially about his ideas and
writing. Some interviews with a more casual, even ephemeral, air
reveal a Miller whimsically able to laugh at himself, as in "Miller
Meets Bonaparte" by Dave Sheehan in *The Santa Monica Evening
Outlook* (22 May 1964): "That he still holds a strong sense of
unembittered humor was evidenced by the recurring merriment
coming from our corner [of the Restaurant Napoleon]; and too by the
format of his most prized work, a private printing limited edition
bound in gold gilded leather and entitled *What To Do About Sex
After Sixty* by Henry Miller. The two inch thick volume ostensibly
a collection of all the most erotically explicit wisdom and imagination
on the after sixty subject . . . is filled with nothing but big, blank
pages of white paper.''

The interviews and conversations in this volume are reprinted
uncut and unedited, and typographical errors have been silently
corrected. Miller was generally willing to be provocative. He remains so today, though his books are often classified under the
heading *Literature* in bookstores, which would have troubled him if
he were alive now since he believed "literature" was writing from
which life had been wrung. He would, without doubt, be pleased
that he has been portrayed in a film that extended the limits of
what can be seen, as his books extended the limits of what can be
read. Phillip Kaufman's *Henry and June,* the first NC17 film,
presents the life of Henry Miller, Anaïs Nin, June Miller, and those
around them, such as the great photographer Brassaï. Based on
Nin's unexpurgated and posthumously published volume of her
diary entitled *Henry and June,* the film portrays the complexity of
their lives, the uncompromised mixture of good and bad in Miller's
life, his obsession and casualness about his writing.

We owe thanks to many people for helping us with this collection: Seetha Srinivasan of the University Press of Mississippi for her careful monitoring; David Edwards for his reading and proofreading; Georges Hoffman and the Estate of Henry Miller for providing the permissions to reprint; and the librarians who helped us find items of considerable obscurity: Maria McWilliams of the Trinity University Library, Linda Coppens of Carmel Public Library, Polly Archer of Pacific Grove Public Library, the staff of Congressman Lamar Smith.

Many interviews, especially those in this collection, reveal Miller as so intensely committed to the practice of personal freedom that even the label anarchist would be unacceptable since it necessitated inclusion in a group, generally an anathema to Miller. He did, however, accept being one of the Three Musketeers of Paris: himself, Lawrence Durrell, and Alfred Perles. This book is dedicated to the memory of the three: Henry, Larry, and Joey.

FK
AH
March 1994

Chronology

invitation of Durrell; meets George Katsimbalis and
George Seferidades

1940   Returns to America; meets Sherwood Anderson and John
       Dos Passos

1941   *Colossus of Maroussi* published

1944   Moves to Big Sur and marries Janina Martha Lepska

1949   *Sexus* published

1952   Divorced from Janina Martha Lepska

1953   Marries Eve McClure

1956   *The Time of Assassins: A Study of Rimbaud* published

1957   *Big Sur and the Oranges of Hieronymus Bosch* published

1958   Elected to National Institute of Arts and Letters

1961   *Tropic of Cancer* published in America; divorced from Eve

1963   U.S. Supreme Court rules that *Tropic of Cancer* is not an
       obscene book; moves to Pacific Palisades

1967   Marries Hiroko Tokuda

1974   Receives French Legion of Honor

1980   Dies on 7 June

Conversations with Henry Miller

Getting Free
Ben Grauer / 1956

From *Life As I See It*. Offbeat Spoken Word RLP 4901.

Grauer: Is a man through with the joyous heart when he's settled into his forties?

Miller: I don't think so. I don't think he need be. I don't think that at all. Unfortunately, as I told you the other day, this is what I see around me all the time, that men at forty are saying they are getting old, you know, and they're settling down. They're already settled down, as it were. I have always reiterated, in writing, about the painters of France, that I found the older they were, the gayer they were, especially in their work, much more liberal in every sense and much more daring than the young painters, do you see.

Grauer: Certainly. Dufy, Bonnard, Matisse.

Miller: Matisse, Picasso. You can go right down the list. Even Leger.

Grauer: If a man has a good hold on life, the hold gets more assured and secure as he goes on.

Miller: That's right. Then things should become easier for him. The problems of youth are the problems of awkwardness, aren't they. There's the awkwardness of technique, in meeting life, in social life, in combatting their medium, working in their medium. All these are technical barriers, you know, which make them stumble and falter.

Grauer: Then what did Wilde mean by saying youth was so wonderful it shouldn't be wasted on the young or "Tell me not of names great in story; the days of our youth are the days of our glory?" I think that's a bad translation of Goethe? Isn't there a certain elixir when you think the world is your oyster?

Miller: Yes, yes. There is, there is. The only thing is, I don't think youth should be defined in terms of age. Youth can only be defined through spirit, by the measure of spirit in a man, so that when you meet a man sometime of eighty you can still say, "There is a youthful spirit." Do you see. And you meet a man of

3

thirty-five and he's finished, do you know, isn't he, he's a crater already. So it has nothing to do with age really.

Grauer: Well, let's take Henry Miller, age mid-forties, right?

Miller: Yes.

Grauer: You found a kind of renaissance. You'd been hacking it out in a routine job. What happened?

Miller: Well, I think that was a combination of things. First I'd found my own voice in the writing.

Grauer: You hadn't written before?

Miller: I had. I'd been writing for ten to fifteen years before, but not finding my own voice as I say. This was a most important thing, do you see? And then as I told you, another great thing happened during that period when I analyzed my dreams and began to get a glimpse of the pattern of my life. I saw the errors I had made and assumed full responsibility for everything. You know instead of being a man who would say well it's a rotten system we live under and griping about politics, economics and the social condition, I said despite that all I could have acted differently, I could have come out, do you see. And I saw that as being the fault of my own nature, character, and temperament. I accepted it, and once I did that a great weight fell off me. I was liberated. I was able to really enjoy myself, no more recriminations, no feelings of guilt, and remorse, and regret, do you see. Life begins anew, all over again. Each day is a fresh new day to live and enjoy, you know. Yes and then a third, maybe, the fact that I was cut off from America and thought I would never return. That buoyed me up tremendously. I had never wanted to return to America. I was completely identified with France and thought I would even become a French citizen. And the fact that I thought that I had burned my bridges behind me and it was irrevocable was another great factor. Yes.

Grauer: You were completely on your own.

Miller: Yes.

Grauer: It was here you go.

Miller: Yes responsible only to myself, so to speak, yes.

Interview

Rochelle Girson / 1956

From *Saturday Review*, 39 (May 5, 1956), 15. Reprinted by
permission of *Saturday Review*.

Henry Miller was in New York recently, on a visit from his present
home at Big Sur, California. Rochelle Girson had a long and pleasant
chat with him during which he told her:

I didn't begin to write until I was thirty-three. If I were ever
counseling anyone I would say delay as long as possible. Unless
you are a poet. A poet can begin at any age; he doesn't need any
knowledge of life.

The fact of being censored acts as a boomerang to the censors.
Instead of my books being killed off by that it only brought them
more and more to the attention of people, and all the young people
going to Europe look up my books. That business of banning
books here only made them go all around the world. And of course
they were sneaked in here—many thousands. . . .

The first book which aroused so much attention was *Tropic of
Cancer*. It was about my immediate life in Paris, which was then
the life of an exile living on the French without money, who had to
use his wife to live, which brought me into contact with the
strangest people. They were all kinds—rogues, prostitutes, wastrels, people whom you wouldn't meet if you were living an ordinary
life; and in talking of them I would transcribe their language. I had
reached a point of desperation when I wrote that book. I had
written three that weren't published and was finally at the end of
my rope. That was how I got my start, by being completely
defeated, and then I found I could write; I found my own voice. . . .
No, I wouldn't [eliminate the obscenity in *Tropic of Cancer* to get
it published here], because it is so integral a part of the book that it
would destroy the whole value of the book from a literary standpoint. It doesn't stand out like expletives, coarse words, but in the
characters' talk it comes out continually—well, I don't know what the
book would look like without it. . . .

I am considered quite a realistic writer because I am writing about living people and today and so on, and yet I don't consider myself a realist at all because I employ every device. I use dream sequences frequently and fantasy and humor and surrealistic things, everything and anything which will deepen and heighten this thing called reality, because what people call reality is not reality in my mind. I am not only telling the truth; I am telling the whole truth, which is in your whole being and not just the surface truth, do you see? I don't like the realist writers at all—the journalistic writers, so-called hard-boiled writers. We are being cheated by them, because we are many things; we are a great universe. Just to describe our acts, our sexual life, our conflicts that are external, that's nothing. There's the inner force, which is so much more important. There's no such thing as an objective view of things which is the truth. It is all colored by one's own vision.

I hope to go off the deep end, and by that I mean that I am going to write, if I wish, absolute nonsense, you know. I love a man like Lewis Carroll. *Alice in Wonderland*—what a delightful thing and how great it was! I believe that when you write freely and easily and joyously, even if it doesn't make sense, that you do more good than when you write seriously with all your heart and soul and are trying to convince people. We have underestimated humor as a leavening, as something to loosen people and make them think.

The Miller of Big Sur

Lawrence Clark Powell / 1960

From *Books in My Baggage*
(New York: World, 1960), 56–62.

Sooner or later everything comes in and goes out of a university library: books on French roulette and the dynamics of turbulent flow, on vector analysis and psychoanalysis, books of missals and on missles, on flood and drought, law and disorder, books for and against, of good and evil, all free to all, a storehouse as powerful as any uranium stockpile, each volume awaiting the touch of hand, the sight of eye to release its energy.

Into this magnetic field there came one day in the spring of 1941 a small, erect man in conventional garb, carrying a checked cloth cap, who approached my desk and said, "I am Henry Miller. My publisher told me when I reached L. A. to go out to UCLA and see Larry Powell, a librarian who reads books."

"Guilty," I said. "And sometimes on company time."

"Do you have any books by Jakob Boehme?" was Miller's first question.

"We'll go into the stacks and see," I said.

So into the great central bookstack we went in search of the German shoemaker mystic of the 1600's, whose books influenced English mystical thought from William Penn to William Yeats. Our quest led us to the second underground level where, like an ore deposit, we found solid shelves of books on religion and philosophy, and one book in particular with a title Yeats thought one of the loveliest ever conceived—Boehme's *Aurora, or the Morning Redness in the Sky*.

I have never seen a man change so fast as Miller did when I put that book in his hand. He settled down on his haunches on the floor and began to leaf through it, read phrases, and talk more to himself than to me. Up to then he had been rather insignificant as a person; now he began to fill out and expand, to communicate and radiate energy.

7

"Somewhere in the Southwest I found myself wanting to read Boehme," he said, "and of course there was no library en route that would even have heard of, much less have Boehme on its shelves. It is worse than being without water, not to have a book when you want it. When are you through work? Four-thirty? Good. Come back for me then and we'll go out for a cup of coffee."

So I left Henry Miller reading on the cold floor, and when I returned two and a half hours later, he was still there, like the Buddha, smiling and joyful. And in the years since then our friendship, rooted in mutual bookishness, has flourished like the coast live oak, green the year round.

We had met ten years earlier on the staircase in the Faculty of Letters of the University of Dijon, where I was a graduate student and he a teacher in the Lycée Carnot, suffering the exile from Paris so painfully described in *Tropic of Cancer*. Two people who passed on the stairs, neither making an impression on the other. No true meeting, perhaps because there were no books on the stairs.

During those years after his arrival in Los Angeles, Miller lived near us in Beverly Glen, a Bohemian backwater in the Santa Monica hills a mile from the university. Commuting back and forth, I ran a bookmobile service for him, fascinated by the variety of his interests, dropping off a book about the headwaters of the Blue Nile, picking up one about the guild of medieval cathedral builders, today books on bristles and Balzac, tomorrow a biography of Colette or a book about Chartres. Either we had them or we got them for him, which is what a librarian is supposed to do.

We rendered a bit more than bibliographical service for Miller. *The Colossus of Maroussi,* his exuberant book about Greece, had appeared in the beautiful Colt Press format, and he wanted it translated into Greek. There was a Greek girl working in the library. When she and Miller met, it was combustion rather than translation that occurred.

When Miller moved to the Big Sur, we continued to give him help by mail. He made the library the depository for his manuscripts, papers, correspondence, and ephemeral publications, and there was commenced what has grown into the Henry Miller Archive, a vast collection documenting his transformation from Brooklyn intellectual to Paris Bohemian to world celebrity. Along with Mark

Twain, Jack London, and Upton Sinclair, Henry Miller is one of the widest read of all American writers.

Books were ever and always the bond between us. One night when we were driving from his home on Partington Ridge to the nearest telephone fourteen miles down coast at Lucia, I asked Miller if he would write a piece on the importance of books and libraries in his life which I might have privately printed as a Christmas keepsake. He examined the idea with a few questions, punctuated by that characteristic meditative sound he makes—a cross between a groan, a grunt, and a sigh—and said he would have a try at it.

I returned to Los Angeles, and then I learned the way Miller works. An idea rises in him like the headwaters of a river, first the merest trickle, gradually increasing to brook to stream to river, and finally to confluence with the sea. A page or two arrived, a few more, a chapter, another, and then, page after page, chapter upon chapter, the torrential manuscript which was to become *The Books in My Life*.

I was appalled by the prospect of my private printing bill. Likewise Miller was troubled by the thought that I would print only a few copies of this work which, rightfully, should reach the widest possible audience.

"Would you mind," he finally queried me, "if we made this manuscript available to my publisher as a regular trade edition?"

I got off my own hook by replying, "Good Lord, no!"

And so the book took shape and the mail sacks between Westwood and Big Sur bulged, as Miller asked for a thousand and one references and confirmations. I accepted the ultimate dedication of the book on behalf of the entire library staff, who toiled to keep the furnace stoked.

There is a dichotomy, but no contradiction, between Miller the writer and Miller the man, between the violence of his view of life as re-created in his prose and the gentle manner of his actual way of life. "Live like a lamb," Flaubert said, "so that you can write like a lion." This has been Henry Miller's way, at least in the years I have known him. If he had not been fated otherwise, Miller would have made a good reference librarian, with a passion for knowledge, a sense of order, and a desire to communicate.

"Artesian" is an adjective I have always applied to Henry
Miller—free-flowing, abundant, without need of pumping. So
many writers are stingy-dry, selfishly working their talent, giving
out only when they are getting in. All the years I have known
him, Miller has been generous to the point of prodigality, giving all
to anyone in need, whether it was literary aid or the money in
his pocket.

Passing by his place one day in the Glen, with our younger son
Wilkie in the car with me, I stopped to see if Miller was in need
of books. It was at the time of his "Open Letter" in the *New
Republic,* calling for donations of money, food, and clothing, in
return for which he would send the donor one of his water-color
paintings. A variety of clothing arrived, including an incongruous
tuxedo which Miller spread like a scarecrow on the picket fence.

We found him at his easel, and after an exchange of greetings he
observed my son, age seven, eyeing pennies on the table.

"Like money?" Miller asked.

Bug-eyed, Wilkie nodded.

"Take those pennies then."

Wilkie carefully gathered them.

"Want more?" Miller persisted.

The child nodded his head.

Whereupon Miller began to light up and come to life. He turned
his pockets out.

"If you like money, you shall have money," he cried, throwing
coins on the table.

"Take it all!" and he swept the money into the lad's eager hands.

It added up to seventy-six cents. Wilkie, starry-eyed, ran outdoors. It was the most money he had ever had at one time.

"It's every cent I have in the world," Miller said to me. "A
useless sum to me; a fortune to him."

After that Wilkie had understandably to visit Miller. Cash windfalls never recurred, but there was always some kind of abundance
lavished on him by Miller. Keys, watches, colored shoelaces, all
given in the spirit of, "You like it? Well then, take it!"

Carried over into the field of correspondence, this prodigality has
become a problem to Miller, as people write to him from all over
the world to ask help of various kinds. The problem is one of time.

How apportion it between the needs of others and the need to write his own work? Too many people seek to go beyond a writer's work, fasten on the man himself, and suck him dry. Nevertheless, at nearly seventy Henry Miller is still flowing, and I expect he always will be. He has a capacity for lasting friendships and with a variety of people such as the late Emil Schnellock, Anaïs Nin, Alfred Perlès, Lawrence Durrell, and his long-time publisher James Laughlin.

A meal at Henry Miller's is something of a religious ceremony, the food by candlelight, with Henry's outflow starting slowly, waxing stronger as the intake of food and drink warms the blood. He is one of the world's great talkers, and the greatest perform-ances come at mealtime when the Staff of Life, the Meat and Wine, the Fruit and Cheese, have made the old master glow and radiate heat. Suddenly a key word triggers him and he launches on a *tour de speech* more pyrotechnical than any Royal Fireworks.

Once in the Glen, at a dinner cooked to perfection by my wife, the trigger word was *Marseilles*. Miller took it the way a trout takes a fly, and away he went, first talking at table, then rising and pacing the room, glass in hand, recalling the glories of France—people, food and drink, the river-sweet ambiance of Paris, talking several parts in turn, questions and answers, an antiphonal monologue, his own delight mounting as he saw the pleasure in the others' eyes, an essentially impersonal performance, spokesman for life itself, focused and finding expression in the Boy from Brooklyn, the most original American writer since Walt Whitman and whose fame will eventually permeate his native land.

If an astrologer had told Henry Miller thirty years ago in Paris that the crowning years of his life would be spent on an isolated stretch of the Central California coast, he would have changed astrologers. Nothing seemed less likely. And yet it came to pass that in 1945 Miller quit smog-blighted southern California for the clear air of the Sur Coast, settling eventually in a cottage on Partington Ridge, high above the wind-blown Pacific. Fifty miles north, on Carmel Bay, lives Robinson Jeffers, the greatest poet of his time. It seems to me no accident that these two writers should have been drawn to this wild and beautiful coast. I can very well understand the reason: it is a creative region, where strong forces are available to those with the necessary transformers.

There in the company of this vital man and his wife Eve, loving, beautiful, and wise, I have found surcease from too much city; eating by Millerlight, talking of life, love, and learning—and of books, of course, those honeycombs of all three.

One need not go to Big Sur to partake of Henry Miller. There are his books, overflowing with the man himself, and immortal as man is not. The *Tropics* are generally unavailable in the lands of his native language but enough has been legally published, and now this third paperbound selection, to satisfy readers' desire for writing that is strong, bold, personal, refreshing, and nourishing. Henry Miller belongs to the Unbeat Generation. Old-fashioned now, per-haps, yet joined with such outspoken men of good will as Rabelais, hands across the centuries, timeless, lifegiving, and free.

The Man behind the Smile:
Doing Business with Henry Miller
Merle Armitage / 1961

From *Texas Quarterly*, 4 (Winter 1961), 156–61.

Early in the 1940s, as I recall, Henry Miller established himself on
Partington Ridge in the Big Sur, a magnificent region where the
mountains come precipitously down to the sea, and where primeval
forests still cover the mountains. The name Big Sur designates a
river that winds through the canyons to the sea. This region, now
well known, is approximately thirty-five miles south of Monterey on
the California coast. Miller's place was atop a plateau which is at
least 2,000 feet above the sea, and provides a view of the rugged
coastline for many miles north and south.

My first contact with Henry Miller came about when I answered
an advertisement which Henry had run in one of the little literary
magazines. He had asked for money. It was a unique sort of
advertisement and its candor was appealing. Henry needed
money for food, so that he could continue to write. Would people
please send him some? The very directness of this appeal must
have stirred many others.

On one of my frequent trips to San Francisco by car, I made it a
point to stop and see Henry Miller. Leaving the coast highway,
the very steep dirt road winds up a series of hills, and eventually
comes to a Y where roads to other houses branch off. We took
the one that said *Henry Miller* and after several rather hazardous
turns found ourselves in a parking area at the end of the road.

Miller came out of his studio, a small white building where he
worked. I was not sure he was Miller, for coming towards us was
a small man, with a quizzical, friendly grin. His face was slightly
oriental, yet his whole posture and appearance suggested an
assistant cashier in a small city bank. His welcome was exaggerated,
we must come and stay, stay, stay! How wonderful it was to see

13

us (Mrs. Armitage was with me) and he could easily take care of us for a week!

Thinking the Millers would be unprepared for guests, we had brought salad and other luncheon material, so after assuring him we would be able to stay only for lunch, we began an inspection of his place. Mrs. Miller was very cordial. At that time the children were babies, and we were concerned about their safety. About fifty feet from the house, the land simply ended, and it was an abrupt descent to the sea far below. They assured us that the children never went close to the rim. It seemed an odd assurance.

Miller's studio was a single-room, wooden affair, and its one striking feature was an old upright piano which had been painted white. On it Miller and his friends had pasted nudes and other photographs from various periodicals, and there were painted statements scrawled on the case, which had all the weird connotations of an instrument in a college fraternity house. Miller thought it was grand.

The house where they lived was immaculate. There was a tiny kitchen, a refrigerator on a slight porch, a living and dining room in one, a couple of bedrooms, and a sun porch. Several pictures painted by Miller hung on the walls, and they seemed to be an odd mixture of what might be produced by a Paul Klee influencing a Gauguin. They were free and tight at the same time, an expression of a man who wanted to portray many things without an adequate technical equipment. But colorful, and right for this place.

Miller and his wife planted many flowers and small trees about their tiny area, and part of it was fenced off. Altogether a spectacular place with the benign sun shining on the glittering Pacific, attaining a dark blue in the vast distance.

At lunch Miller plunged into an interrogation of who I was, what I was, what I did, and what were my interests. This caused Mrs. Armitage to say, "This is the first time I have ever seen Merle on the witness stand." This embarrassed Miller, who explained that I was a new type of American to him, and he was deeply curious to find out what made me tick. It was an amusing conversation. When I explained that by profession I was an impresario, Miller just would not believe it. "There is not a single thing about you, except your authority, that says *impresario*," he maintained. "Where is your

florid attire, your big cigar, your arrogance?'' In spite of my
assuring him that I had plenty of arrogance and that I had been
managing concert and opera celebrities since I was about eighteen
years old, Miller refused to be convinced. But what were my
hobbies? Collecting modern art struck him as a complete contradiction of his image of a young, prosperous American. "Don't you
play golf, or drive a sports car, or *anything*?'' he asked.'' No, just
collect Chagall, Braque, Picasso, Klee, and others going back to
Gauguin,'' I assured him. "But I have heard that you were a
writer. Who told us that?'' he asked his wife. Then came a long
explanation of my premise. I was a writer simply because no one
was writing about certain modern men and women who interested
me, Stravinsky, Martha Graham, etc. . . . If the truth were
known,'' I continued, "I write books so that I will be able to design
them.'' What did I mean by that, Miller insisted. "Does a book
have to be designed?''

I assured Miller that most books were *not* designed, which had
resulted in a monotonous string of look-alike books flowing from
our presses. "The cookbook looks like the novel, the scientific
book looks just like the book on history, and a book on philosophy
cannot be told from one on modern warfare,'' I replied. "Would
you accept a theatrical series where Shakespeare, Noel Coward,
and Rogers and Hammerstein were all presented in the same decor?'' That seemed to stop Miller, and he begged me to send him
some of my books. "A book is a book, and I don't see how you can
do much about it,'' he said finally.

A few weeks later Miller wrote me. He had received copies of my
books on the U.S. Navy, Martha Graham, Picasso, and the first
Edward Weston. "I do not know what to make of them, they are so
crisp and definite and compelling,'' he wrote. "I like European
books, they are mellow, and more decorative and have the feel of
old castles and tradition. Your books have no tradition.''

My reply of course was my stand-by answer to all persons who
will not give up yesterday, no matter how obsolete the plumbing,
the roof, the architecture, and the ventilation. "These books are an
attempt to represent today, plus the subject they convey,'' I
assured him. "Today will be tomorrow's tradition, provided we do
not imitate the past,'' I went on. "If every generation imitated

the past, there never would have been any of the great periods when
architecture, painting, music, and literature sprang forward, to
enrich the world." But Henry was not convinced. They were
strange and compelling, those books of mine, but they did not
look European. This curious preoccupation with Europe of course
is the key to Miller and his confusion. He does not really understand the past, else he would have a much clearer understanding of
the present.

The next time I called on Miller he was in a panic. He was heavily
in debt, he had used up his credit at the grocery. He had sold
nothing in the past six months. No one had responded to his
advertisements.

"Look at this manuscript," said Miller. "It's been to seventeen
different magazines, and it's produced seventeen rejection slips.
That gives you a very good picture of your stinking, bourgeois
magazine publishers." He went on to explain that because of the
rejection of all his short stories he was going to mortgage his
wonderful Big Sur place. Immediately I argued against this.
"Somehow, you will manage to eat," was my theme, "and as long
as you have this place you will make out. But if you lose this place,
then where are you with no food *and* no roof over your head?"

"Well, there is nothing else I can do. The only trouble is I hate to
see about a loan. I hate bankers."

While he had been raving against American publishers and bankers, I had been glancing over his manuscript. It was a short story
titled *The Smile at the Foot of the Ladder*.

"Let me take this manuscript and see what I can do with it," I
suggested. "How much do you want for it?"

He had offered it for $500, he replied, but no takers.

Then I unfolded my proposition. I would write him a check for
$500, take the manuscript, and if able to do anything with it, he
would have any additional money it might earn. "Armitage, you are
a fool," Miller said, his face wrinkled in one big smile, "but I
love you."

Coming back down the coast, I stopped to see my old friend
Edwin Corle, the novelist, in Santa Barbara. Over a highball, I
outlined my plan for Miller. "Let's you and I get Miller out of
bondage and give him a little security," I suggested. Corle was

enthusiastic. My plan was to have Miller write an epilogue. I would illustrate it with paintings of clowns by great masters—Toulouse-Lautrec, Picasso, Klee, etc. Then if Corle would write an introduction about Henry Miller we would have, by setting it in large type, enough text to make a book. A Merle Armitage book distributed by Duell, Sloan and Pearce. For the next six months I worked with museums getting the photographs of the paintings, with the printer, and on design details. Miller gladly wrote his epilogue. For end sheets I used red vertical stripes reminiscent of carnival tents. My design finally jelled into a book. The text began with a large red disc of the sun. It ended with a black similar disc, as the hero goes down to defeat. Related here, this sounds rather obvious, but in the book it happily takes its place as a component in the design.

Duell, Sloan and Pearce were enthusiastic with the result, and the whole edition was sold out within a year. As I recall, the exact total we were finally able to send to Henry Miller was $1,685. This was his unsold, $500 manuscript. Stinking American publishers, indeed!

Here is a verbatim copy of the letter Henry Miller wrote me the day the first copy of his book, *The Smile at the Foot of the Ladder,* reached him in his Big Sur retreat:

Big Sur—May 18th, 1948

Dear Merle,

I got the book (five of them) only yesterday and am writing you immediately to tell you how very, very pleased and grateful I am for what you did with it. As I wrote friend Corle just a minute ago, it should win you an award. If not, it will certainly win you many new friends, of that I am certain. I'm more than amazed that such a book can be put out for five dollars a copy. My only regret is that you didn't issue ten thousand at once. For a long time now I've lacked enthusiasm with the appearance of a new book. When the "Tropic of Cancer" came out I was dazzled, of course—it was my first published book and I had waited almost four years to see it printed. With this one of yours, that same unforgettable thrill shook me. I actually had tears in my eyes turning the pages. Of course, I shall never forgive you for not including one of *my* clowns, but the ones you chose are superb, and I must thank you again for having made such a selection. I think the two that come off best are the Picasso and the de Segonzac. (At least, little Val thinks so.) She also loves those big moons. That was the first thing she spotted— "*Moona!*" she said, clapping her hands with delight.

The book is beautiful from beginning to end, Merle, and how you managed to do it with all the preoccupations you then had, beats me. Well, you were not an impresario for nothing! I wish some of those grand old friends of yours—out of the now "antique" world—could see the book. I only wish Satie, Max Jacob, Nijinsky and some of the others were alive. As I told Corle, I want to have a copy put in Charlie Chaplin's hands. He ought to appreciate both the form and the contents. (I'm taking care of this, so don't worry.)

An excellent and surprising touch was the signatures. Yours resembles that of the great painters—did you notice? Almost Chinese. It tells us more about you than your wonderful voice does, and that's saying a great deal.

Yes, Merle, this is one of my prize possessions. I am confident it will be read and go into many editions. Sometimes I am ashamed of the prices asked for my books, a matter usually beyond my control. This time I think the price is far too low. For once, I feel that I don't want to give copies away.

I sincerely hope that your new job will not deter you from making more books. We need your talent, believe me. Lepska joins me in all this praise and thanksgiving. She is practically speechless. Just says over and over—"Beautiful! Wonderful! Very Wonderful!" and so on.

Well, good cheer, good luck, and blessings on you!

Your friend ever,
Henry Miller

After receiving one of the checks Miller wrote: "I feel guilty in accepting money from you for the Smile."

There were many more trips to the Big Sur and Henry Miller. On one occasion, I remembered his timidity about bankers and discussed it with him. "I just cannot go into a bank," said Henry. "Once I had eighty dollars in the bank in Monterey. I was out of money, needed ten dollars for food. But I could not face going into the bank and writing a check. I walked past the bank a dozen times, but I never made it. I went on down the street and borrowed ten dollars from a cobbler who works on my shoes!"

Believing America offers the most to the largest number and that this country despite its imperfections (which are the failures of man) is a sort of triumph, Miller and I of course had many conversations, and arguments. It is obvious that Miller will equate all of America with a small section of the city of Paris, and draw some ridiculous conclusions. America to him is commercial, provincial, materialistic, and unfortunately was not organized as the home for artists. Europe

(translate *a section of Paris*) is where an artist feels at home,
where so-called intellectual anarchy is not only tolerated, but insisted upon. Actually, Miller was never in contact with the real
producers of ferment. He did not know Pablo Picasso, or Braque,
nor Gertrude Stein, Ernest Hemingway, or James Joyce. His
intellectual pursuits consisted mostly of bohemian drunkenness and
roistering with sympathetic whores. Many of his nights were
spent under the arches of bridges on the Seine; he was never in the
superior restaurants, nor had a bottle of great French wine. A half
hour talk with him is convincing. Here is a case of arrested mental
development, a man who has short-circuited the true and vital life of
any country.

He will give on no point. He insists that environments be made to
order for *him*. He asks that all America be reconstructed to be
sympathetic to the artist—his kind of artist. You speak to him of
the narrow provincialism of smaller French cities and he will not
discuss the matter. Paris is Europe, and Europe is Paris, with the
possible exception of Greece. But Greece is not *quite* perfect!

On one occasion I met Miller's friend Alfred Perlès in the Big
Sur. Perlès is a gracious little man who worships Miller but feels
that the best thing about him is his Americanism. Perlès says:

> It is ironical that in his ravings against America, Henry Miller himself
> always emerges as an American. His enthusiasm, his exuberance, his
> childlikeness, are essentially American. No European could write or talk
> thus. And of course, he makes no attempt to conceal the fact that he
> *is* an American; subconsciously, I suppose, he is proud of it.
>
> Throughout our long friendship, I have had innumerable glimpses of
> his splendid Americanism. His naiveté and generosity always gave him
> away immediately. I have seen him bestow royal gifts on casual acquain-
> tances who come to him with sob stories. . . . He never made any
> distinction between the deserving poor and the undeserving ones. The
> Lord giveth and the Lord taketh away. It was as simple as that to him.
> Henry had thought up the Lend-Lease idea long before President Roose-
> velt or General Marshall appeared on the scene. He is an American
> through and through, and a most representative one, no matter what his
> countrymen may say of him.

Miller fights everything American. In *The Air-Conditioned Nightmare* he not only exaggerates, but he indulges in the most remarkable
fabrications, lies, and misrepresentations. It is the amusing attitude
of a very bad boy, bent on vengeance.

One of our conversations concerned advertising. "American advertising really is excrement," said Henry. Knowing he would not listen to me, I let the matter drop, and later wrote him a letter. This letter is reproduced in Annette Kar Baxter's book on Miller, titled *Henry Miller Expatriate,* and published by the University of Pittsburgh Press. I quote:

> . . . in your disgust with so much in America (which I share to a degree which would surprise you) you have apparently included all advertising. That is unfair and unjust and lacking in discernment . . . provided it's true. Notwithstanding the fact that the advertising artists must please the advertising agency, the man who pays for the job, and eventually the public, some of the most individual art that has been created in America has come from the advertising or commercial artists. Compared with many of the commercial artists, many of the so-called *fine artists* are anemic, derivative and without personality or indigenous style. American advertising, notwithstanding its flamboyant and often crass results . . . is in a class by itself. . . . There is simply nothing like it in the world.

But one learns that logic or truth have no receptivity in the case of Miller. It is particularly true in his writing. No man can write with more facility, style, and descriptive richness than Miller. He can astound you with his virtuosity. But he never knows how to stop and he never knows how to edit. The *Colossus of Maroussi,* for instance, is brilliant for the first half. Then it declines into repetition, warmed-over enthusiasm, and overdecoration. This holds true in many of his books and articles.

Few men are so unable to see the truth, or face it.

Part of his hatred of America, indeed the real basis of it, is that he was published first in France, while America ignored him. Actually, not one regularly established publisher in Paris would touch his *Tropic* books. They were published by a man in a completely different line of business, who saw a chance to make what we Americans call "a fast buck." In the cheapest possible editions, full of typos, and with newspaper stock and flimsy bindings, his books came out in France. The audience? American GI's who bought them for their pornographic content! Ironically, then, it was America which gave Henry his start! And for years the money for the sale of the books piled up in France. French laws made it impossible for Henry to get a cent. That inspired the little advertisements in American literary magazines, asking for financial help. But was Henry angry with France for not giving him his rightful royalties? Not at all, France was a civilized country. So Americans who helped him with checks in answer to his pleas were uncivilized. But France, which held and drew interest on his money, was civilized. There you have Henry!

The Smile at the Foot of the Ladder began to be published abroad. Henry sent me editions of the book brought out in Japan, Holland, France, Germany, and even back of the Iron Curtain. From many of these he received either royalties or fees. Yet when Henry brought out an edition of *The Smile at the Foot of the Ladder* a year or so ago, with a New York publisher, it was as a first edition of the book. It was reviewed as a new Henry Miller book, since the generation of book reviewers who had been so generous about our first edition had passed to other occupations or were deceased. In this new volume, Henry, with studied indifference, never even mentioned Edwin Corle, this writer, the first edition of the book, or the editions that had been published abroad. A very endearing character.

But possibly the most revealing and amusing incident occurred after the publication of *Big Sur and The Oranges of Hieronymus Bosch*. In this book, Henry devotes a big part of chapter three to a discussion of my daughter Chama, plus my concert activities. The Chama sequences are charming fantasy which she as an adult will someday read with surprise and delight.

One of the memorable chapters in this book concerns a European friend who came to visit Henry for a few weeks, and remained over a year, much of the time as an invalid, and a disagreeable one at that. As Henry had always been hospitable to every crackpot, moocher, and panhandler that turned up at the Big Sur, it seemed that this was some sort of justice. Flatter Henry, and he will feed and sleep you forever!

Planning a trip to Carmel soon after receiving his letters complaining about his "guest who came to dinner," I wrote Miller that I would stop for a chat, or possibly would bring the luncheon material. This was a sort of standard procedure which we had enjoyed innumerable times. To my astonishment, I received a post card from Henry, saying that if I were truly his friend, I would not bother him! He was busy.

Henry Miller: Interview

F. J. Temple / 1962

From *Mercure de France*, 345 (May–August 1962), 184–85.
Reprinted by permission of F. J. Temple. Translated by Alan
Astro.

*In 1934, Miller moved once again into the Villa Seurat. Fraenkel
greeted him with open arms. As luck had it, an apartment was
vacant on the floor above. Among the many artists living in the
same small street were Chagall, Lurcat and Gromaire. This was
to be Miller's residence until 1939, and it was there that Blaise
Cendrars came to see him after the publication of* Tropic of Cancer.
*That visit marked the beginning of their friendship and mutual
admiration. In February 1961, shortly after Cendrars' death, I invited
Miller, then in Hamburg, to speak of Cendrars in Montpellier. He
responded in these terms:*

No, I cannot do what you ask of me. Sorry. I have an instinctive
repugnance for ceremonies of whatever kind. It would be impossible for me to speak of a man whom I admired and cared for as I did
Cendrars. You must know that he is the contemporary writer I
felt closest to, that I always revered his name, that I have never
ceased to speak of his works and that I cannot forgive the French or
especially the Americans for having displayed so little interest in
him during his lifetime. It is revolting and typical of the Europeans
to wait for a man's death to pay the homage due him. What I
despise above all is that they do not even wait for his body to be cold
to sing praises to his glory. Whoever has true depth of sentiment
ought to wait a while in respectful silence, before drowning a
dead man in encomia and panegyrics. I have thought of Cendrars
practically every day of my life since our first encounter. I lived
with him in spirit, with devotion, as a disciple lives with his master.
Now that he is dead, I cannot bring myself to deliver a eulogy. I
wish to live silently with the memory of the man I revered. What I
would suggest to the French, if they truly wish to honor him, is
to choose a day when every man in the nation would cease all

activity for five minutes and bow his head in deep silence. In my
opinion, that would be more forceful than all the grandiloquent
phrases soon to be uttered by eminent writers. I hope that, when I
die, I shall be quickly buried without flowers or tears: no speeches,
and no tombstones with Latin or Greek inscriptions. What *we* want is
a reaction now, while we are still possessed of flesh and blood,
when it would mean something. To hell with posterity!

*Nonetheless, on April 12, 1969, while Miller was in Montpellier, I
got him to come to the radio station for an interview. I caught
him off guard, as it were, in the midst of a conversation on other
matters, by suddenly mentioning Cendrars:*

FJT: Henry, will you finally speak to me about someone who was
your friend . . .

HM: I told you, once and for all . . .

FJT: . . . and who is remembered as having composed a famous
phrase about you: "Let us hail Henry Miller. An American writer
is finally born unto us." That was more or less as it went. How did
you meet him?

HM: Indeed, it was about the time he wrote those words, or a
little later, that he came to see me at the Villa Seurat, unan-
nounced I believe. Yes, I think he just showed up, knocked on the
door, along with the editor of a small magazine. What was
it called?

FJT: *Orbes, Orbes* magazine.

HM: *Orbes,* yes . . . No. I believe he came alone that time. Yes,
I recall, and he stayed the whole afternoon, discussing everything;
he was fascinating. Perlès was with me that afternoon. Finally,
Cendrars said: "Let's go out and have dinner somewhere." We
turned red because we were broke; we hadn't a sou. Thereupon,
Cendrars claimed that he had just received an unexpected check
that afternoon, or morning. It was a lie. But he took us to a
restaurant in Montmartre and we spent the rest of the night with
him in the bars there.

FJT: And you saw him often after that?

HM: No, I can't say often. I don't know why. But from time
to time.

FJT: No doubt because he traveled a lot.

HM: Yes, at that time, indeed.

FJT: And you remained in correspondence for a long time, until his death.

HM: Ah yes, yes.

FJT: I know that he had a great deal of affection for you.

HM: Yes, but my feelings for him went beyond that. It was he that I came to admire most as a writer and as a man.

Miller then spoke of another writer, John Cowper Powys, whom he claimed to admire as much as Cendrars. The topic changed. A few minutes later, we were discussing Powys' "paganism" and D. H. Lawrence's religiosity. Abruptly, I brought the next question back to Cendrars.

FJT: Was Cendrars a pagan?

HM: It's hard to say. I can't answer that. Certainly, he wasn't religious, he never spoke of morality, but . . .

FJT: Father Bruckberger, with whom I once spoke, told me that Blaise was a deeply religious man.

HM: That could well be the case, indeed. That's why I was reluctant to respond. Cendrars always had a secret side. Things that he cared about deeply, he spoke of only in general terms. He would keep them to himself.

Up to the very end, Cendrars remained for Miller a model and an object of admiration. Not only was Cendrars the first to acclaim Tropic of Cancer, *not only were his literary positions close to Miller's, but their attitude to life and to current affairs had much in common. Miller would always display deference and admiration for Cendrars:*

I bow before you. Not being your equal, I hardly feel I have a right to acclaim you. It pleases me more to remain your fond and devoted disciple, your spiritual brother *in der Ewigkeit.* At the end of each of your letters, you extend to me a "friendly hand." I seize your warm and vigorous left hand, I squeeze it joyfully, thankfully, and from my lips pour forth words of gratitude that know no bounds.

An Interview with Henry Miller
Audrey June Booth / 1962

From *Interview with Henry Miller*. Folkways Cassette Series 09724. The Smithsonian Institution. Reprinted by permission of the Smithsonian Institution.

From June 3 to June 7, 1962 Henry Miller was in Minneapolis, Minnesota to meet members of the Henry Miller Literary Society, and during his stay he spent many hours discussing a wide variety of subjects with, among others, Edward P. Schwartz, the president of the Society, and Thomas H. Moore, the Secretary. He also talked informally with radio interviewer Audrey June Booth, with Mr. Schwartz and Mr. Moore in the studio with him. The interview was a particularly illuminating one and Mr. Miller referred to it, in a letter to the Society, as "Probably the best interview I have ever had." It is here included in its entirety, with the exception of Miss Booth's introductory remarks and the closing comments of Mr. Schwartz and Mr. Moore.

Q: How long have you been in Minneapolis, Mr. Miller?

A: Just three days.

Q: Three days, and you're en route to Big Sur, California?

A: No, I'm en route to the penitentiary at Jefferson City, Missouri. To see a—

Q: Just a visit, I trust.

A: No, to see a friend who's a lifer there, who is one of my fans, if I may call him that.

Q: Yes?

A: I got into correspondence with him through his reading my books, and I paid him a visit a few months ago on my way to Europe, and I'm hoping that I can get him out on parole soon.

Q: Oh, that would be wonderful, wouldn't it?

A: Ah, he's in for life, plus, I think, 18 years.

Q: Do you quite frequently meet and become friends with the people who do read your books?

A: Oh, yes, naturally, I mean, how can you avoid it, ha, that is, they are coming to see me, don't you know, or if I'm traveling, they're sure to meet me somewhere, you know, in a public place,

Q: (Your paths do cross.)

A: —even on the street they come up, don't you know. Just in Berlin recently and every day there were students running after me in the street; "Aren't you Henry Miller?" You know this happens everywhere, mm.

Q: This would be a wonderful—

A: So I get some idea of who my readers are. Sometimes I'm very disappointed.

Q: Are you?

A: Oh, yes. I mean not in general. I make exception for the young people. I think young people are the better readers, my best readers, more intelligent, more alert, more alive, more full of knowledge, more hope in them than, say, the adult even the learned adult, you know, like a professor, do you see. He, I have less in common with him, less talk, less to say to him, than I have with a boy of 17 or 18 who happens to read me.

Q: Why do you think this is? Do you think that the—

A: Because the old—by the time a man gets to be a professor— ha—35—he's already half dead, do you see, (laughter) and he's stuck in his profession and stymied, do you know? Caught in a trap. Whereas the young are open; they don't know where they're going yet, and they're curious about everything, and enthusiastic, and their eyes are not blinded, blindfolded, you know, hah, yes.

Q: Do you think then that the reader today is more receptive to your books or do you think that the younger readers have always been receptive in this, than legally that your books have not been accepted?

A: Oh, there's never been any question about that, that the legal thing is a completely false thing, do you see, and deprive people who—I would have been read by millions of people had it not been for the censorship.

Q: (Yes.)

A: I know I have millions of readers in America. Do you see?

Q: Of course you have.

A: And yet, until recently I was hardly known, you might say.

Q: Because the books had to be smuggled in?

A: Yes, yes.

Q: And weren't available on the open shelf.

A: And then known for the wrong reasons, don't you know?

Q: Yes. A—mm. Well, I'm interested to learn something about whether when you're traveling, as you have been in Europe, you write on a regular schedule, or whether you travel, absorb, then come home and write.

A: That's right. When I travel I have an empty head. I can't do anything, except sponge in things, do you see? Absorb, as you say. No, I can't—I have—if I settle down for a while in a place, say I know I will be three weeks or a month, then I might do some short writing, not a book, do you see, but I've written many things while traveling, largely prefaces for other books, you know, or some little thing for a paper, you know, but I would never be engaged on a long work while traveling.

Q: Would you write something like your delightful stories, "Nights of love and Laughter," while you're traveling?

A: No—do you see, I think those were all selected from books, those the—I think so. I don't think I wrote anything like, aa, those things while traveling, none at all, no. I remember I wrote, writing one thing I told Tom here. "My Life As An Echo." I wrote that in a hurry, in a few hours, in Berlin in a hotel room because I had a cablegram; I had to do something for my Italian publisher. He was just bringing the "Tropics," the two "Tropics" out in Italian, and it's a very delicate situation. The authorities are against it, and he was hoping I could give him something that he could give to the papers and magazines, you know. So, I wrote this thing, (laughter) "My Life As An Echo," which is a steal from a Yiddish writer, who, by the way, never, I don't think he ever wrote the book. He's credited with it, but I'm dubious if it ever existed.

Q: Who was that?

A: I, I forget his name, at the moment. Yeah, Moishe Nadir, like nadir, you know, the lowest point. (**Q.** Yes.) A Moishe, pseudonym it was. I think he's dead now, but I had a good friend who had told me all about it, and the whole thing intrigued me. It's a funny story about him acting the part of an echo in some hotel (laughter) for the tourists, do you see? They'd go to a certain place, and it was said that if you went there you'd get the echo, and it was him always echoing back. (laughter)

Q: Well, now, you do have a new book coming out soon, don't you?

A: Yes, the New Directions book, "Stand Still Like The Hummingbird," which is a collection of things, mostly things that have not appeared in book form, ever, only in magazines, do you see.

Q: And when will we expect that?

A: That's the end of this month.

Q: The end of this month.

A: Mhum. Yes.

Q: Well, a, do you have a favorite book? Most authors do, and sometimes the particular book that an author will choose isn't the favorite book of the public.

A: Mm, I have many favorite books.

Q: Do you really?

A: Many.

Q: Which ones?

A: Well, to name, I'll name just one tonight, because I got it for Tom today, he didn't seem to know it. *Siddhartha,* by Hermann Hesse. You know this name, don't you? Hesse.

Q: Yes. Yes.

A: Hesse, *Siddhartha.* It's one of my very, very beloved books. I think there's a great, great message in it. You see, I think it's a—it's a very slim volume. It's in the form of a story, and yet this is to my mind the essence of Zen Buddhism without ever mentioning the word, do you see. It's about a, a Siddhartha, an enlightened one, like a Buddha, and then the real Buddha also comes into the picture; and for me, the other Buddha, the one called Siddhartha, is better than the real buddha. This is an extraordinary book, written in the early 1920's, I believe, and only brought out in English recently, through New Directions.

Q: And you yourself are interested in Zen?

A: Yes, very much.

Q: I was thinking, Mr. Miller, of one of your own books.

A: Yes.

Q: Are, are you—(a, oh, ah) do you have a favorite (A. Yes, I do.) Or do you have many favorites in your own selection?

A: There I have—I have one partic—the one I like the best of all, and I'd like to be remembered by, of all them is a, *The Colossus of Maroussi,* my book on Greece.

Q: And do you think, that this is one that has been a favorite with the public?

A: I know that, I know it has. Yes, I know that, very well. There are two books of mine, only two, that I know of, about which there seems to be unanimous approval, and acceptance. All the others are, aa, provocative, they are divided in opinions, you know.

A: Yes.

Q: But *The Colossus of Maroussi,* chiefly, and then a tiny little book called *The Smile at the Foot of the Ladder.* No one ever has a word against those books, do you see? They like them; they love them. I think.

Q: And isn't it strange that probably the books that you will be remembered for, are the controversial books?

A: That's right. Yes, yes, although who knows? Who knows? (**Q.** Yes.) One never knows.

Q: In the long run, and this is what is important to you, I imagine.

A: Mm, yes. Well, I tell ya, it isn't important, because once I'm dead, what do I care?

Q: You don't care?

A: No, what do I care? I don't care what people think either now, or afterwards, really. I'm just telling you this as a fact; you asked me did I know or did I believe. This I know. But what I, what people should or will do doesn't interest me, really, no.

Q: Is the important thing to you the writing of the book, (**A.** Yes.) the communication, or don't you really care what the reader thinks or what he's inspired to do because of the book?

A: No, it's for me, I, it's for my own sake, my own pleasure, do you see. And whatever happens, well, that's interesting; but it isn't why I do anything. But how can I tell? How can anyone say he's doing this for this and that reason, or he hopes to accomplish this? It's a gamble. Nobody knows the effect of anything that he does upon the world. Do you see what I mean? (**Q.** Well, this—) Wouldn't you think, for instance, that Jesus, who came to save the world, don't you see, would have had a profound effect, that we would all be Christians? Where are there any Christians? Are there any?

Q: Only those who profess Christianity.

A: That's what I mean. But is there anyone like Jesus, who followed in his footsteps? St. Francis is probably the nearest one, hah—St. Francis. In fact, I love him much more than Jesus, do you see. Yes. But that's it. One or two, hah, you know, or three or four, no Buddhas are there, no. (**Q.** Unfortunately, not.) You see no Socrates. Yes. These men struggled, didn't they, to make the world aware of their thoughts and their ideas, and their principles, and so on. And what is the end result? The opposite, it seems to me. The opposite, everything turns into a parody, a caricature, do you see?

Q: Then the truly creative spirit, you feel, doesn't care?

A: Well, I don't know. I can't talk about others.

Q: You can only talk about yourself?

A: Yes, really, I wouldn't set up to say what creative minds have in mind, do you see? (laughter)

Q: Well, I understand that you do have a book which didn't sell but which has provided quite a bit of fun in your life.

A: Yes.

Q: A book that you and Alf Perlès published.

A: A book we published together? Or do you refer to a magazine?

Q: About New York. It has New York in the title.

A: Oh, yes. It's called *Aller Retour New York.*

Q: Well, now, that that, intrigues me. What does "aller Retour New York" mean?

A: Well, it means, it should be aller, accurately. It should be "aller a Retour," which, when you ask for a ticket, both ways, going and coming.

Q: Oh, going and coming, New York.

A: Yes. And it's in the form of letters, do you see. My letters to him. Yes.

Q: Well.

A: That's a, that's what that is, that was—

Q: What happened to this book?

A: Well, that book has been printed in English. Let's see, did it, did it, was it printed by the Olympia Press? (TM. Well, no.) It

was printed privately in Chicago (Note: New York—TM) by Ben
Abrams, (Note: Abramson—TM) a book seller, and he didn't give
his name as publisher; he put something else down. He was afraid
the book might be censorable. It had first come out in English.
Yes. It first came out in English in Paris because I had made my
trips to New York twice, during my ten year stay in Paris. I made
two brief trips to New York, and this—the first occurred maybe
after four or five years in Paris; the whole of America, New York
especially, was like a foreign world to me. I had already become so
thoroughly imbued with the French spirit and way of living, don't
you know, that my own country seemed very bizarre to me. I saw
it with new eyes, and it looked bad, very terrible to me.

Q: I can well imagine. (laughter)

A: Yes. This is rather a cruel book, in a way. It's exaggerated. It
isn't a true picture of America; it was primarily of New York City,
I think.

Q: But it was true at that time, it was the way that you saw.

A: It's the way I saw it. Of course, in a sense, all my books are
this way. They're all entirely personal, subjective, biased and prejudiced, do you see. I don't profess ever to be saying what's true or
what is, you know, only what I see, what I feel.

Q: The way that you perceive.

A: Yes, yes. ahah. That's my truth. (laughter)

Q: Well, Mr. Miller, when you judge the books of other people,
now you recently judged a contest in Mallorca, and I understand
that you're going to Edinburgh next fall to judge another contest,
and are in great demand there as a judge. What are you looking
for in the work of other people?

A: Mm. That's very difficult to answer. That's very difficult. I
think that rather than the—than the book, I judge the man. You
know, this is the one difference. I said it the other night, to
someone, between Europe and America as regards literature, I think:
how we feel about literature. That in Europe it's the man, the writer
who is accepted. And once he's accepted, he's accepted, he remains
so. I mean he remains a part of the body of literature, and he's
always highly considered. Whereas here we can drop a man over-
night. We take a book of his, and it's a great sensation. Tomorrow
if he happens to write one that the public doesn't care for, he can

be forgotten, or annihilated, do you see. There isn't this loyalty to
the man, the writer, I don't think.

Q: Reputations rise and fall on the individual work.

A: Yes, I think so. I think so. Well, now, as to how do I judge a
book, once again because it pleases me, don't you know? I don't—
same with paintings. I don't pretend to know the value of them, but
I certainly know the effect that they have upon me. And it's from that
that I judge, do you see?

Q: Yes.

A: I don't know what others may think, and I don't know where
it belongs in the scale of values, but I will say it's a great book, if
it happens—you know, if I happen to feel that way about it. Frankly,
I think that all criticism boils down to this, to your feelings about it,
an emotional thing, rather than a rational thing, do you know?

Q: Yes. That's why you can't sit down and add up numbers and
make them come out to a hundred.

A: No. No. ha, ha—

Q: It's a feeling that you have about a certain product. (A. Yes,
yes, yes.) But do you agree with other judges in this respect? Is it
always easy for you and the other judges to see (A. Oh, oh.)—this
man should be awarded the prize? (A. No, no, it isn't.)

A: Naturally—well, I haven't had much experience, you see.
Mallorca, fortunately I was in bed, (laughter) I was taken with the
chills and fever, and I was spared this whole discussion. I was only
there the first day when they discussed several French authors
and Italian, and my choice was the English—or the Welshman,
rather, whom I do think is one of the greatest living spirits today. A
man whose name should be on everybody's lips, as, just as Picasso's is, or Einstein. John Cowper Powys. Do you know
that name?

Q: No, I don't.

A: You don't.

Q: No.

A: There you are, you see; very few people know of him. He's
got quite a range of books. He must have about 15 books, at least,
to his credit, some of them quite huge, and particularly—let us,
there are two books of his that I consider, what, without equal
almost. One is his *Autobiography,* to my mind greater than any

autobiography that I have read, and that goes way back to St.
Augustine, you know, when I think of autobiographies, and the
second is *A Glastonbury Romance.*

Q: Now are these books available here?

A: Yes. I think that they were, the *Autobiography* was published
by Simon & Schuster, and has been republished by New Directions recently. Maybe in a paperback. (**Q.** I'll watch for that.) I
heartily recommend it. The other, I'm not so sure; it would exist
in the English editions—England, he has a publisher there. All his
books are current in this English edition. Yes.

Q: Well, did did, the other judges agree with you about his—

A: Oh, not at all, no, because nobody knew him in the first place,
hardly any, only one French woman knew him, and made a
wonderful, eloquent speech for him, and I had sent from, down
from my bedroom a little note about him, do you see. But I knew
it was hopeless, but then how could I—they asked me who is the
man—I think that was my man. They want somebody contemporary. He's a he's a man, you see in his nineties. Yes. Yes. (**Q.** I see.)
Let me add that he spent 30 years in America, bringing culture to
America, as he flippantly would say.

Q: Which part of America did he—

A: All over. He's been in every town, village and hamlet in
America in those 30 years. Did nothing but travel around. And he
would lecture for absurd sums. I used to listen to him for ten cents
at the Labor Temple in New York.

Q: And I suppose that he wrote quite a bit about America in his
autobiography.

A: Yes. In the *Autobiography* he has a wonderful account. And
he loved America, I must say that, yes.

Q: Well, what author was chosen at Mallorca.

A: Oh, a German, a young German, fairly unknown, called Ewe,
e w e, I think. I don't know if that's how you pronounce it,
Johnson. And, God, I even forget the title of his book, that he.
(laughter) You see, I hadn't, I hadn't read it.

Q: You hadn't read it?

A: No. It hadn't been out; it isn't out in English even; it had to
be read in German, you see. Another Italian girl won the prize.
There were two prizes, you see. One that the publishers judged, in

manuscript; and then the authors judged only published works, and it had to be within a three-year period, the last three years. Well, that's very difficult.

Q: That is very limiting and confining, isn't it?

A: Yes, sure. The man I had thought as a second choice was Saul Bellow. I loved that *Henderson The Rain King*.

Q: Oh, yes, of course—

A: I loved that book.

Q: We like to claim him as a Minnesotan because he has taught here, he's worked here, I've interviewed him. (**A.** Indeed.)

A: I didn't realize that. Is that so? Yes. I see. Well, he would have been second choice. Yes.

Q: Well, we're very happy to learn that. Well, what young American authors besides Saul Bellow do you admire? Now, (**A.** Yes.) we should probably say then since you consider that as in Europe you should judge by the man, rather than the individual work.

A: Yes, yes. I don't have any that I think of offhand. I have been fascinated by Kerouac, I must say. Very uneven writer, perhaps and I don't think he has yet shown his full possibilities, Kerouac.

Q: He's too young. He hasn't—

A: But he has a great gift, this great verbal gift like Thomas Wolfe had, you know, and a few others. Tremendous gift I think, but to me rather undisciplined, uncontrolled, and so on, but I am fascinated by one book of his called *The Dharma Bums*. I don't know if you know that, do you?

Q: No, I am not familiar—

A: Yes. That's a beauty, in my mind, and is, and has more— better grip on his subject too, than the other books, less loose, and, you know, it's more contained. Wonderful subject, wonderful theme he's got, wonderful characters in it, and I love his writing there. Wonderful writing. Yes.

Q: It seems to me, Mr. Miller, that in writing, as probably in composing, that the maturity of the man is something that a, is, is all, that you mentioned Kerouac. He can keep maturing—he has the possibilities, the potentialities. He can probably at 90 write.

A: Yes.

Q: —more beautifully than at any other time of his life, if he lives to be 90.

A: Yes, but he doesn't have to wait that long. You know. (laughter) (**A.** Yes.)

Q: No, I don't mean that you can't produce earlier, but I think that it's one thing where they they will not say a man is too old, he's reached his prime, (**A.** Yes.) and he can no longer produce because—

A: Well sometimes—excuse me for interrupting you—I think that when one has this gift as I call it, that it's a handicap. Do you see, the facility overcomes or is at odds and mitigates against the good writing. (**Q.** Mhm.) You know, it just flows out too easily, therefore there isn't enough struggle. I think there has to be a great element of struggle, always. I think when one is a bad writer to begin with it's much better than if one is a good one immediately. Do you see?

Q: Yes, you feel that you have that struggle yourself?

A: Oh yeah, I think I did, I think so many had and I think even a man like Picasso, and so you might say, aa, people may deny that. I don't think he was—I can see in his early work how very derivative he was, how much he was influenced by other men, how imitative he was. I don't give two cents for a lot of his early things, do you see. Umm, and I think it's been that way with most men. You can see the seeds. Well, we all—none of us start—none of us are originals, by the way.

Q: No.

A: Do you see, we all derive, we all stem, we all have had our what shall I say—our gods, our idols, whom we modeled ourselves upon, do you know? Now, mine I've always mentioned Dostoevsky was my great passion, surely, but actually, from the standpoint of writing, the way of writing, the style, and so on, hardly anyone knows that it was Knut Hamsun who was my—the man I was trying to model myself upon. Knut Hamsun. Do you know his name?

Q: No, I don't.

A: The Norwegian, who won Nobel prize, lived to be 90 also, who was—don't you know? He wrote *Pan,* he wrote *Hunger,* he wrote *Mystery,* he's written a whole what—thirty books, I suppose. Novels and novelettes.

Q: I've never read any—

A: No, really, really?

Q: Now, when did you discover him?

A: Very early, in my early twenties I would think. In that period, in the 1920's, the publisher in America called Knopf published wonderful translations of all foreign authors, many foreign authors, the best he could get, and Hamsun was one of them, do you see. Yes.

Q: And he's the one you feel had most influence on you as a writer.

A: From the sheer writing standpoint, do you see. From other standpoints, Dostoevsky was the god, the real one, you know, the all, mm, but to write like Hamsun is what I wanted. That style—I even studied it, paragraph by—line by line, to find out where is the secret of this?—of course you never can, there's no way of taking an author apart and discovering how it is he does it, and so on, the magic there is a secret thing, do you know?

Q: Once again, it's that something that you feel.

A: Yes, yes.

Q: The person feels as he reads it and some other author just doesn't have it.

A: That's why I also think, you know, I don't know whether it's relevant what I might say right now; but I also think it's a very great waste of time to go through a course of how to write, do you see. I don't think anyone can teach anyone how to write, anything about it at all. Do you see what I mean?

Q: Do you—you don't even feel that you could give advice to young writers?

A: Yes, you can give advice; but how, will they follow it? Can they follow it? Does anyone follow advice anyhow, don't you see? Advice is always wasted, in my opinion. It's no use giving advice.

Q: Should they follow it—advice?

A: No. (**Q.** They shouldn't.) I don't think they should either. No.

Q: I thought you'd say that. (laughter)

A: No, I don't think so. The only thing one can do is follow himself, do you see; dig in, discover what he is, and who he is, and reveal himself. We're all interested in in everyone because he's unique. Everyone, the humblest to the highest, do you know?

They're all interesting, and the more they are themselves, the more interesting they are. People become uninteresting when they become like everyone else, which is what America does to everyone, try to make them like one another, do you know, like buttons in a button mold.

Q: Do you think that all over the world people are emulating us, and that people are becoming more conformist?

A: That's yes, that's very true, although—yes, I have reservations about that, that is to say they may follow us in matters of technique, you know, how to manufacture things, how to what, do all the things that go on in the world of activity, of business, and so on, but; in the way of life, the daily pattern of life, how they eat, how they regard woman, how they philosophize about life, there, I think, it's gonna take quite a while. You see what I mean? The imitation that they, what we see is—superficial, it's a surface thing, right. It's got largely to do with security and economy, you know. How to get along better. How to live better, in, in a material way, do you see. (**Q.** But—) Which, but that doesn't affect them profoundly, I don't—

Q: They won't, they won't change inside?

A: I don't think so, no. I don't think, for example, the Chinese, for all the radical changes they've made you know, by legislation, decree and so on, I don't think that that it's gonna be a great, profound change in their nature, in their thinking.

Q: Though, I don't believe that you could really change centuries of Chinese thought and philosophy.

A: No, no, no old peoples, no, no. Now the Israelis, of course, have made startling changes, it would seem don't you know?

Q: Yes.

A: And yet, in a sense, don't they more and more seem like the Jew of the old testament at their best, when they were at their heights, you know, a the a fighting, warlike a dominant a people who are agrarian, you know, who could do things with their hands and so on, than the Jew that we know through a the ghetto period, you know, the dispersion, do you see. (**Q.** They've gone back to their dreams.) In a way, that's right, they've recaptured the essence of themselves, you might say. Hah? Yes, I think so.

Q: Well I noticed, Mr. Miller, that you were quoted as having

said that a you felt that the old Chinese and Hindu cultures were
closest to reality and that this is where we in America and also this
was a world trend, where we fail today, that we were living in a world
of illusion.

A: Yes. Yes.

Q: Now, we were just talking about China, do you think that
the—the new China—you said you didn't think that the new
China would have lost this completely, you said they concentrated
on the fundamentals; now I wanted to ask you a question, what
do you consider the fundamentals?

A: Mm. I think the fundamental probably would be, let's say,
one's attitude toward the cosmos, how you relate to mm God, for
lack of a better, you know—(Q. I'm going to let you) call it whatever
you wish, and that, well, the Chinese are not supposed to have
bothered much about that, as Hindus have, for instance, isn't
that so?

Q: That's true.

A: Yet, there is something marvelous about the—how shall I
say—the aa philosophy of the Chinese. The greatest book in the
world probably, in my opinion, is, one of the smallest books that's
ever written, and that's that—the *Tao Tā Ching* by Lao-Tzu isn't that
so? (Q. Yes.) Condensed to, what, how many pages, 50, 60 pages?
And what, what is greater, what has been more wonderful than
that book. It seems to contain everything. Unfortunately, the Chinese didn't follow after him, do you know? They went rather the
way of Confucius, let's say, and as the other aa one, aa the ethical
way, whereas his was of the Spirit. This is what I am talking
about. It's the a—the sense of whether life is a thing of Spirit.
Spirit, Spiritual has a poorer cast when you use the adjective, but
Spirit, everyone knows what it is. This is the essential thing, I
think, the knowledge or the awareness of Spirit and its domination
of all life, do you see. I think in America we are hardly even aware
of it, do you see.

Q: Well, don't you think that the first Americans, the Indians,
had this sense of Spirit?

A: Ah, yes, that's another thing. We forget them, we don't think
of them as Americans. Here they are. You're right, of course,

absolutely. I agree with you. Surely. That's why they're still so powerful. They may outlast us, I always say. Do you know?

Q: There a man couldn't attain his manhood without knowing who he was (**A.** Yes.) and what he was (**A.** Yes.) and how he related to the universe, the cosmos.

A: That's right. And there, that's there again that's a—you see we have education, don't we? We have these great universities, can they ever give what those men received, the boys through their invitation, do you see? What they got from the elders? We aa, have no—no counterpart to this in our life. In the whole educational life, the best you get is a what is called religion, and this religion, whichever it may be, you know, is a watered down thing, isn't it? hah? It hasn't much effect upon us, you know. No. And then too, (**Q.** No, because it's something that.) we don't relate whatever we adhere to, to activation, to living, to living it out. Do you see what I mean?

Q: Yes. It's something that's imposed upon us from the outside, it really doesn't have any relationship to us. We never, instead of having it come from within.

A: Yes.

Q: So that we relate.

A: Yes. Yes. Yes. Right. I know.

Q: This is a very sad thing. But what can we do about it? Now, I was a (**A.** Yes) little bit disappointed when I read a part, paragraph farther in the article about you and it said that there was hysteria in the world today and you said there's no way out of it, we simply have to live through it, and yet I felt—I don't really believe if Henry Miller had thought about that, that that's what Henry Miller would have said.

A: Yes. Well I'll tell you (**Q.** Because I don't think you feel that way.) myself, I personally don't feel this way, but this is the way I look upon the world. I consider myself a a fortunate man in that I'm a happy man, that I've accepted the world and life, do you see, even the atom bomb and the total destruction if you like. Do you see what I mean? (**Q.** Yes.) But, other people, the most of the world, is concerned, and is worried, but is incapable of doing anything about it, do you see, they're very—fear and anguish is what prevents them from doing anything. As soon as you give way

to fear, I mean, do you see, you become the victim. It dominates
you, you cannot do anything then, to overcome it. You're the slave
then. You've got to be detached. You've got to get detached, do you
see. Let's say indifferent, if you like, which is rather light, but
there's something to this indifference. A certain kind of indifference is like an armour, a protection. It doesn't mean that you are
not fundamentally concerned, that you're cut off, but you're not
going to be disturbed about things that you—(**Q.** You're not going
to let everything kill you.) and also you—this is more important—you
must realize there are things that are beyond your powers to control.
You can't rectify everything. We can't be gods each and every
one of us; do you know what I mean? (**Q.** Yes.) It's not within our
province. I often say, aa, wouldn't it be wonderful just to demonstrate things to people, let them be God for a day. I would like to
see how they would govern the world. Do you see? (**Q.** Mm.)
Would it be any worse or any better? I think it would be worse than
it is, in its chaotic—seemingly chaotic condition. Do you know?
(**Q.** Well then, really.) And that's what people are doing so often, I
mean, especially (**Q.** Playing God.) in politics. Trying to play God.
Yes.

Q: Yes. We think that we know how other people should live (**A.**
That's right, that's right.) all over the world; our way is the best
way, and therefore we try to impose it—only we don't call it im-
posing.

A: I know, I know. We think we're educating them, let's say.
Yes, I know. We pity them; we feel sorry huh that they do not see
things as we see them.

Q: Well, then, in a sense, one could call you an anarchist.

A: That's exactly what I am. Have been all my life. Without
belonging, you know, subscribing (**Q.** Without labelling with a capital
a.)—yes, yes. Right, right. That's right.

Q: Because the minute that you join a group and say I am an
anarchist, we are anarchists, then you destroy the whole idea—

A: That's right, that's right. That's quite right. That's quite right.
And the only democrats there are, are those who are what,
outside the party (**Q.** Democrats with small d's.)—yes, right, right.
I think a man like Thomas Jefferson was a wonderful one, though

do you know? Even if it was a big D. hah. He was a real—(Q. He was a marvelous man.) yes. One of our great presidents, I think.

Q: And if, if we could only go back to the concepts which Thomas Jefferson had, we we, are spending all of our time now looking for our reason for being. We, we say we've lost something; but most people don't know what it is that we've lost; (**A.** Yes.) they didn't know what it was that we had in the first place. (**A.** Mhm, yes.) And unless we can find our direction, how can we expect to give direction to other people?

A: That's right. Yes. Yes. Yes. And I think that today if there were a Thomas Jefferson, he'd probably be in jail, instead of in the president's chair. (ha)

Q: He probably would.

A: You know, it sounds—some of his things are so explosive and dynamic and vital and real, don't you know, it's a real shock today to hear any—talk—We don't hear such talk any more, do we? (**Q.** No, we don't.) We don't have such open minds either, do you know.

Q: Oh, we have a few, we have Henry Miller. (laughter) Mr. Miller, do you find that writing is more difficult in different places, do you find that then things that you produce vary according to where you write them? For instance are you more at home writing in Big Sur, which I should think would be a very inspiring, marvelous place to write, than you are writing in Europe, for instance, or in New York?

A: No, I don't think the place matters. Let's put it this way—the conditions matter; but let us say the serenity, the beauty of a place, that doesn't have much to do with it, because actually I'll, I'm living in a room when I write, and I'm not even looking at the landscape, though there's a window there; I turn the chair away so that I don't see this. It would interfere with my writing. Do you see? No, all I demand is a certain amount of peace, you might say, and solitude. Of course this is the hardest thing for me to find, always. I'm constantly besieged, intruded upon, you know, through visitors and by correspondence, and my tragedy almost is that I don't get time to write. I'm glad if I can find two or three hours a day for my work. That's all I need, by the way. I don't write five, six, seven hours a day. I feel I can do enough in two or three hours. And I

don't believe in draining the reservoir, do you see? I believe in
getting up from the typewriter, away from it, while I still have things
to say. It's better than to completely exhaust (**Q.** To write your
self out.)—yes yes.

Q: Do you find that you are more inspired by nature or by
people? Do you find that you are more inspired when you're by
yourself or do you find that there's a happy balance between—

A: Well, one never knows—I find I'm inspired by all manner of
things. Nature is very wonder—powerful, yes, but people too
sometimes. The only thing is with people is that it exhausts me, do
you see? It, I burn out in these wonderful relations with people;
you know, where I will get inspired, but all burned out through
the intercourse.

Q: It's an exhausting (**A.** Yes.)—you're defeated afterwards.

A: I think I'm going to write volumes after I see a certain person
or had a marvelous exchange with him—but nothing comes—

Q: No, you pour all of your creative energy into that particular
relationship.

A: Maybe later. That's right. Yes! That's right. Yes. What I find
is a very simple thing that I always think if one leads a normal
life, a happy life, well—this sounds—what is normal?

Q: Yes, what is normal, what is happy.

A: But I mean by that nothing too exciting. You eat your three
meals, you go and walk or play ping pong, or whatever your
hobby is, you lead a natural existence. You don't rely on any
outside things to stimulate you, just from nice easy living it wells
up in you, and if you do this every day, go to your desk, as I
generally do, right after breakfast, and do all the writing I can in the
morning, you see, I'm finished by noon, usually, everything takes
care of itself. It becomes a habit, don't you see, you've cultivated
a certain habit, a way of life—Now that's—I'm always talking about
the way of it, this is my criticism of America, fundamentally, and of
all human individuals, too. Find the way of life and you have the
secret, you have the secret, to happiness and joy, serenity, and
creativeness, do you see? If you can find your rhythm, your rhythm,
don't you know?

Q: But how does each person find this for himself?

A: One can't answer that, because that's for each one to dis-

cover. Each one has a different—(**Q.** That's the joy and the pain
and the challenge.) Yes. Yes. This is one of the reasons, let's say,
we are here on earth, is—don't you know—is to find out such
things. I don't think what we do is so important; it is what we are,
what we learn to be, do you know. Discover our own being, and
and live with it, and act in accordance with our own being. I think
that's the important thing. It doesn't matter that you are not a
Picasso or Rembrandt or Dostoevsky, do you see? One can have as
rich a life without the expression in some medium, I think. I find
people whom just, who are just in themselves a piece of art. Do
you see?

Q: Do you find them all over the world, I imagine.

A: Well, yes, of course, and among humble people, yes, certainly.

Q: Isn't this why you probably enjoy going places, meeting
people, doing things that other people perhaps look askance at,
and say "what does he find in these kind of people."?

A: Yes, yes, yes. You're very right, because listen, I must add
this—you know I never have had inspiration from meeting the
really big people. The big people don't really communicate or give
you anything. They've given it in their works, do you see what I
mean? But with ordinary or eccentrics or strange individuals whom
you don't know, who are anomalous, you know, you suddenly stumble upon something interesting. You want to—you get curious.
When you come to know, meet Picasso, you've already known
him through his work, isn't that right? What more can he add, you
know, in talk or contact? It is so true, by the way, that if there's
only one person who cares, it makes all the difference. He's the
symbol for all, isn't it so?

Q: That's true.

A: Yes. I used to feel that way about the writing, too. If only
one—I have one reader, and he really reads me, and appreciates,
that's enough almost, don't you know? But you need one. Haha.

Q: You need one—well you have many more than one. Henry
Miller, we could talk to you all night. (**A.** We've talked probably
too much, haven't we?) Will you come back sometime?

A: Yes, I expect to, because I like it here, I find, to my surprise.
I enjoy being here. (**Q.** You found that.) I think on my way to
Europe when I come again I'll stop off, yes.

Henry Miller: The Art of Fiction XXVIII

George Wickes / 1962

From *Paris Review*, 28 (Summer/Fall 1962), 129–59. Reprinted by permission of George Wickes.

In 1934, Henry Miller then aged 42 and living in Paris, published his first book. In 1961, the book was finally published in his native land, where it promptly became a best seller and cause célèbre. By now the waters have been so muddied by controversy, censorship, pornography and obscenity that one is likely to talk about anything but the book itself.

But this is nothing new. Like D. H. Lawrence, Henry Miller has long been a byword and a legend. Championed by critics and artists, venerated by pilgrims, emulated by beatniks, he is above everything else a culture hero—or villain, to those who see him as a menace to law and order. He might even be described as a folk hero: hobo, prophet and exile, the Brooklyn boy who went to Paris when everyone else was going home, the starving bohemian enduring the plight of the creative artist in America, and in latter years the sage of Big Sur.

His life is all written out in a series of picaresque narratives in the first person historical present: his early Brooklyn years in *Black Spring*, his struggles to find himself during the twenties in *Tropic of Capricorn* and the three volumes of the *Rosy Crucifixion*, his adventures in Paris during the thirties in *Tropic of Cancer*.

In 1939 he went to Greece to visit Lawrence Durrell; his sojourn there provides the narrative basis of *The Colossus of Maroussi*. Cut off by the war and forced to return to America, he made the year-long odyssey recorded in the *Air-Conditioned Nightmare*. Then in 1944 he settled on a magnificent empty stretch of California coast, leading the life described in *Big Sur and the Oranges of Hieronymus Bosch*. Now that his name has made Big Sur a center for pilgrimage, he has been driven out and is once again on the move.

At 70 Henry Miller looks rather like a Buddhist monk who

has swallowed a canary. He immediately impresses one as a warm and humorous human being. Despite his bald head with its halo of white hair, there is nothing old about him. His figure, surprisingly slight, is that of a young man; all his gestures and movements are young.

His voice is quite magically captivating, a mellow, resonant but quiet bass with great range and variety of modulation; he cannot be as unconscious as he seems of its musical spell. He speaks a modified Brooklynese frequently punctuated by such rhetorical pauses as "Don't you see?" and "You know?" and trailing off with a series of diminishing reflective noises, "Yas, yas . . . hmm . . . hmm . . . yas . . . hm . . . hm." To get the full flavor and honesty of the man, one must hear the recordings of that voice.

The interview was conducted last September in London where Miller was visiting Alfred Perlès, his biographer and crony from Paris days. The setting could not have been more incongruous, a kind of British-air-conditioned nightmare, a big hotel crowded and noisy with American tourists and businessmen.

Interviewer: First of all would you explain how you go about the actual business of writing. Do you sharpen pencils like Hemingway, or anything like that to get the motor started?

Miller: No, not generally, no, nothing of that sort. I generally go to work right after breakfast. I sit right down to the machine. If I find I'm not able to write, I quit. But no, there are no preparatory stages as a rule.

Interviewer: Are there certain times of day, certain days when you work better than others?

Miller: I prefer the morning now, and just for two or three hours. In the beginning I used to work after midnight until dawn, but that was in the very beginning. Even after I got to Paris I found it was much better working in the morning. But then I used to work long hours. I'd work in the morning, take a nap after lunch, get up and write again, sometimes write until midnight. In the last ten or fifteen years, I've found that it isn't necessary to work that much. It's bad, in fact. You drain the reservoir.

Interviewer: Would you say you write rapidly? Perlès said in *My*

Friend Henry Miller that you were one of the fastest typists
he knew.

Miller: Yes, many people say that. I must make a great clatter
when I write. I suppose I do write rapidly. But then that varies. I
can write rapidly for a while, then there comes stages where I'm
stuck, and I might spend an hour on a page. But that's rather
rare, because when I find I'm being bogged down, I will skip a
difficult part and go on, you see, and come back to it fresh
another day.

Interviewer: How long would you say it took you to write one of
your earlier books once you got going?

Miller: I couldn't answer that. I could never predict how long a
book would take: even now when I set out to do something I
couldn't say. And it's somewhat false to take the dates the author
says he began and ended a book. It doesn't mean that he was
writing the book constantly during that time. Take *Sexus,* or take
the whole *Rosy Crucifixion.* I think I began that in 1940, and here
I'm still on it. Well, it would be absurd to say that I've been working
on it all this time. I haven't even thought about it for years at a
time. So how can you talk about it?

Interviewer: Well, I know that you rewrote *Tropic of Cancer*
several times, and that work probably gave you more trouble than
any other, but of course it was the beginning. Then too, I'm
wondering if writing doesn't come easier for you now?

Miller: I think these questions are meaningless. What does it
matter how long it takes to write a book? If you were to ask that
of Simenon, he'd tell you very definitely. I think it takes him from
four to seven weeks. He knows that he can count on it. His books
have a certain length usually. Then too he's one of those rare
exceptions, a man who when he says, "Now I'm going to start
and write this book," gives himself to it completely. He barricades
himself, he has nothing else to think about or do. Well, my life
has never been that way. I've got everything else under the sun to
do while writing.

Interviewer: Do you edit or change much?

Miller: That too varies a great deal. I never do any correcting or
revising while in the process of writing. Let's say I write a thing
out any old way, and then, after it's cooled off—I let it rest for a

while, a month or two maybe—I see it with a fresh eye. Then I
have a wonderful time of it. I just go to work on it with the ax. But
not always. Sometimes it comes out almost like I wanted it.

Interviewer: How do you go about revising?

Miller: When I'm revising, I use a pen and ink to make changes,
cross out, insert. The manuscript looks wonderful afterwards,
like a Balzac. Then I retype, and in the process of retyping I make
more changes. I prefer to retype everything myself, because even
when I think I've made all the changes I want, the mere mechanical
business of touching the keys sharpens my thoughts, and I find
myself revising while doing the finished thing.

Interviewer: You mean there is something going on between you
and the machine?

Miller: Yes, in a way the machine acts as a stimulus; it's a
cooperative thing.

Interviewer: In *The Books in My Life,* you say that most writers
and painters work in an uncomfortable position. Do you think
this helps?

Miller: I do. Somehow, I've come to believe that the last thing a
writer or any artist thinks about is to make himself comfortable while
he's working. Perhaps the *dis*comfort is a bit of an aid or stimulus.
Men who can afford to work under better conditions often choose to
work under miserable conditions.

Interviewer: Aren't these discomforts sometimes psychological?
You take the case of Dostoevsky. . . .

Miller: Well, I don't know. I know Dostoevsky was always in a
miserable state, but you can't say he deliberately chose psychological
discomforts. No, I doubt that strongly. I don't think anyone chooses
these things, unless unconsciously. I do think many writers have
what you might call a demonic nature. They are always in trouble,
you know, and not only while they're writing or because they're
writing, but in every aspect of their lives, with marriage, love,
business, money, everything. It's all tied together, all part and
parcel of the same thing. It's an aspect of the creative personality.
Not all creative personalities are this way, but some are.

Interviewer: You speak in one of your books of "the dictation,"
of being almost possessed, of having this stuff spilling out of you.
How does this process work?

Miller: Well, it happens only at rare intervals, this dictation. Someone takes over and you just copy out what is being said. It occurred most strongly with the work on D. H. Lawrence, a work I never finished—and that was because I had to do too much thinking. You see, I think it's bad to think. A writer shouldn't think much. But this was a work which required thought. I'm not very good at thinking. I work from some deep down place; and when I write, well, I don't know just exactly what's going to happen. I know what I want to write about, but I'm not concerned too mcuh with how to say it. But in that book I was grappling with ideas; it had to have some form and meaning, and what not. I'd been on it, I suppose, a good two years. I was saturated with it, and I got obsessed and couldn't drop it. I couldn't even sleep. Well, as I say, the dictation took over most strongly with that book. It occured with *Capricorn* too, and with parts of other books. I think the passages stand out. I don't know whether others notice or not.

Interviewer: Are these the passages you call cadenzas?

Miller: Yes, I have used that expression. The passages I refer to are tumultuous, the words fall over one another. I could go on indefinitely. Of course I think that is the way one should write all the time. You see here the whole difference, the great difference, between Western and Eastern thinking and behavior and discipline. If, say, a Zen artist is going to do something, he's had a long preparation of discipline and meditation, deep quiet thought about it, and then no thought, silence, emptiness, and so on—it might be for months, it might be for years. Then, when he begins, it's like lightning, just what he wants—it's perfect. Well, this is the way I think all art should be done. But who does it? We lead lives that are contrary to our profession.

Interviewer: Is there a particular conditioning that the writer can go through, like the Zen swordsman?

Miller: Why of course, but who does it? Whether he means to do it or not, however, every artist does discipline himself and condition himself in one way or another. Each man has his own way. After all, most writing is done away from the typewriter, away from the desk. I'd say it occurs in the quiet, silent moments, while you're walking or shaving or playing a game or whatever, or even talking to someone you're not vitally interested in. You're working, your mind is working, on this problem in the back of your head. So, when you get to the machine it's a mere matter of transfer.

Interviewer: You said earlier there's something inside you that takes over.

Miller: Yes, of course. Listen. Who writes the great books? It isn't we who sign our names. What is an artist? He's a man who has antennae, who knows how to hook up to the currents which are in the atmosphere, in the cosmos; he merely has the facility for hooking on, as it were. Who is original? Everything that we are doing, everything that we think, exists already, and we are only intermediaries, that's all, who make use of what is in the air. Why do ideas, why do great scientific discoveries often occur in different parts of the world at the same time? The same is true of the elements that go to make up a poem or a great novel or any work of art. They are already in the air, they have not been given voice, that's all. They need *the* man, *the* interpreter, to bring them forth. Well, and it's true too, of course, that some men are ahead of their time. But today, I don't think it's the artist who is so much ahead of his time as the man of science. The artist is lagging behind, his imagination is not keeping pace with the men of science.

Interviewer: How do you account for the fact that certain men are creative? Angus Wilson says that the artist writes because of a kind of trauma, that he uses his art as a kind of therapy to overcome his neurosis. Aldous Huxley, on the other hand, takes quite the opposite view, and says that the writer is preeminently sane, that if he has a neurosis this only adds to his handicap as a writer. Do you have any views on this subject?

Miller: I think this varies with the individual writer. I don't think you can make such statements about writers as a whole. A writer after all is a *man*, a man like other men; he may be neurotic or he may not. I mean his neurosis, or whatever it is that they say makes his personality, doesn't account for his writing. I think it's a much more mysterious thing than that and I wouldn't even try to put my finger on it. I said that a writer was a man who had antennae; if he really knew what he was, he would be very humble. He would recognize himself as a man who was possessed of a certain faculty which he was destined to use for the service of others. He has nothing to be proud of, his name means nothing, his ego is nil, he's only an instrument in a long procession.

Interviewer: When did you find that you had this faculty? When did you first start writing?

Miller: I must have begun while I was working for the Western Union. That's certainly when I wrote the first book, at any rate. I wrote other little things at that time too, but the real thing happened after I quit the Western Union—in 1924—when I decided I would be a writer and give myself to it completely.

Interviewer: So that means that you went on writing for a period of ten years before *Tropic of Cancer* appeared in print.

Miller: Just about, yes. Among other things I wrote two or three novels during that time. Certainly I wrote two before I wrote the *Tropic of Cancer*.

Interviewer: Could you tell me a little about that period?

Miller: Well, I've told a good deal about it in *The Rosy Crucifixion; Sexus, Plexus* and *Nexus* all deal with that period. There will be still more in the last half of *Nexus*. I've told all about my tribulations during this period—my physical life, my difficulties. I worked like a dog and at the same time—what shall I say?—I was in a fog. I didn't know what I was doing. I couldn't see what I was getting at. I was supposed to be working on a novel, writing this great novel, but actually I wasn't getting anywhere. Sometimes I'd not write more than three or four lines a day. My wife would come home late at night and ask, "Well, how is it going?" (I never let her see what was in the machine.) I'd say, "Oh, it's going along marvelously." "Well, where are you right now?" Now, mind you, maybe of all the pages I was supposed to have written maybe I had written only three or four, but I would talk as though I'd written a hundred or a hundred and fifty pages. I would go on talking about what I had done, composing the novel as I talked to her. And she would listen and encourage me, knowing damned well that I was lying. Next day she'd come back and say, "What about that part you spoke of the other day, how is that going?" And it was all a lie, you see, a fabrication between the two of us. Wonderful, wonderful. . . .

Interviewer: When did you begin to conceive of all of those autobiographical volumes as a whole?

Miller: In the year 1927 when my wife went to Europe and I was left alone; I had a job for a while in the Park Department in Queens. One day, at the end of the day, instead of going home I was seized with this idea of planning the book of my life, and I stayed up all night doing it. I planned everything that I've written to date in about forty or fifty typewritten pages. I wrote it in notes, in telegraphic style. But the whole thing is there. My whole work from *Capricorn* on through *The Rosy Crucifixion*—except *Cancer,* which was a thing of the immediate present—is about the seven years that I had lived with this woman, from the time I met her until I left for Europe. I didn't know then when I was leaving, but I knew I was going sooner or later. That was the crucial period of my life as a writer, the period just before leaving America.

Interviewer: Durrell speaks of the writer's need to make the breakthrough in his writing, to hear the sound of his own voice. Isn't that your own expression as a matter of fact?

Miller: Yes, I think so. Anyway, it happened for me with *Tropic of Cancer.* Up until that point you might say I was a wholly derivative writer, influenced by everyone, taking on all the tones and shades of every other writer that I had ever loved. I was a *literary* man, you might say. And I became a *non*-literary man: I cut the cord. I said I will do only what I can do, express what I am—that's why I used the first person, why I wrote about myself. I decided to write from the standpoint of my own experience, what I knew and felt. And that was my salvation.

Interviewer: What were those earlier novels like?

Miller: I imagine you would find, naturally, you *must* find, some traces of my self in them. But I felt very keenly then that one should have some sort of story, a plot to unroll; I was more concerned then with the form and the manner of doing it than with the vital thing.

Interviewer: That is what you mean by the "literary" approach?

Miller: Yes, something that's outworn and useless, that you have to slough off. The literary had to be killed off. Naturally you don't kill that man, he's a very vital element of your self as a writer, and certainly every artist is fascinated with technique. But the other thing in writing is *you.* The point I discovered is that the best technique is none at all. I never feel that I must adhere to any particular manner of approach. I try to remain open and flexible,

ready to turn with the wind or with the current of thought. That's
my stance, my technique, if you will, to be flexible and alert, to use
whatever I think good at the moment.

Interviewer: In "An Open Letter to Surrealists Everywhere" you
say, "I was writing surrealistically in America before I ever heard
the word." Now what do you mean by surrealism?

Miller: When I was living in Paris, we had an expression, a very
American one, which in a way explains it better than anything
else. We used to say, "Let's take the lead." That meant going off
the deep end, diving into the unconscious, just obeying your
instincts, following your impulses, of the heart, or the guts, or
whatever you want to call it. But that's my way of putting it, that
isn't really surrealist doctrine; that wouldn't hold water, I'm afraid,
with an André Breton. However, the French standpoint, the
doctrinaire standpoint, didn't mean too much to me. All I cared
about was that I found in it another means of expression, an
added one, a heightened one, but one to be used very judiciously.
When the well-known surrealists employed this technique, they
did it too deliberately, it seemed to me. It became unintelligible, it
served no purpose. Once one loses all intelligibility, one is lost,
I think.

Interviewer: Is surrealism what you mean by the phrase, "into
the night life"?

Miller: Yes, there it was primarily the dream. The surrealists
make use of the dream, and of course that's always a marvelous
fecund aspect of experience. Consciously or unconsciously, all
writers employ the dream, even when they're not surrealists. The
waking mind, you see, is the least serviceable in the arts. In the
process of writing one is struggling to bring out what is unknown
to himself. To put down merely what one is conscious of means
nothing really, gets one nowhere. Anybody can do that with a little
practice, anybody can become that kind of writer.

Interviewer: You have called Lewis Carroll a surrealist, and his
name suggests the kind of jabberwocky which you use occasionally . . .

Miller: Yes, yes, of course Lewis Carroll is a writer I love. I
would give my right arm to have written his books, or to be able to

come anywhere near doing what he did. When I finish my project, if I continue writing, I would love to write sheer nonsense.

Interviewer: What about dadaism? Did you ever get into that?

Miller: Yes, dadaism was even more important to me than surrealism. The dadaist movement was something truly revolutionary. It was a deliberate conscious effort to turn the tables upside down, to show the absolute insanity of our present-day life, the worthlessness of all our values. There were wonderful men in the dadaist movement, and they all had a sense of humor. It was something to make you laugh, but also to make you think.

Interviewer: It seems to me that in *Black Spring* you came pretty close to dadaism.

Miller: No doubt. I was most impressionable then. I was open to everything that was going on when I reached Europe. Some things I already knew about in America, it's true. *Transition* came to us in America; Jolas was marvelous in selecting those strange bizarre writers and artists we had never heard of. Then I remember, for example, going to the Armory Show to see Marcel Duchamp's "Nude Descending a Staircase," and many other marvelous things. I was infatuated, intoxicated. All this was what I was looking for, it seemed so familiar to me.

Interviewer: You've always been better understood and appreciated in Europe than in America or England. How do you account for this?

Miller: Well, in the first place I didn't have much chance to be understood in America because my books weren't in print there. But aside from that, though I am 100 per cent American (and I know it more and more every day), still I had better contact with Europeans. I was able to talk to them, express my thoughts more easily, be more quickly understood. I had a greater rapport with them than with Americans.

Interviewer: In your book on Patchen you say that in America the artist will never be accepted unless he compromises himself. Do you still feel that way?

Miller: Yes, more strongly than ever. I feel that America is essentially against the artist, that the enemy of America is the artist, because he stands for individuality and creativeness, and that's *un*American somehow. I think that of all countries—we

have to overlook the communist countries of course—America is
the most mechanized, robotized, of all.

Interviewer: What did you find in Paris in the thirties that you
couldn't find in America?

Miller: For one thing, I suppose I found a freedom such as I
never knew in America. I found contact with people so much
easier—that is, the people that I enjoyed talking to. I met more of
my own kind there. Above all I felt that I was tolerated. I didn't ask
to be understood or accepted. To be tolerated was enough. In
America I never felt that. But then, Europe was a new world to
me. I suppose it might have been good almost anywhere—just to be
in some other, different world, an alien. Because all my life,
really, and this is part of my psychological—what shall I say?—
strangeness: I've liked only what is alien.

Interviewer: In other words, if you'd gone to Greece in 1930
instead of 1940 you might have found the same thing?

Miller: I might not have found the same thing, but I would have
found the means of self-expression, of self-liberation there. I may
not have become the kind of writer that I am now, but I feel I would
have found myself. In America I was in danger of going mad, or
committing suicide. I felt completely isolated.

Interviewer: How about Big Sur? Did you find a congenial environment there?

Miller: Oh, no, there was nothing there, except nature, I was
alone, which was what I wanted. I stayed there because it was an
isolated spot. I had already learned to write no matter where I lived.
It was a wonderful change, Big Sur. I then definitely put the cities
behind me. I'd had my fill of city life. Of course I never chose Big
Sur, you understand. I was dumped on the road there one day by
a friend. As he left me he said, "You go and see such and such a
person, and she'll put you up for the night or a week. It's a
wonderful country, I think you'll like it." And that's how I fell into
it. I never had heard of Big Sur before. I knew of Point Sur
because I'd read Robinson Jeffers. I read his *Women at Point Sur* in
the Café Rotonde in Paris—I'll never forget it.

Interviewer: Isn't it surprising that you should have gone out to
nature that way, since you'd always been a city man?

Miller: Well, you see, I have a Chinese nature. You know, in

ancient China, when the artist or the philosopher began to get
old, he retired to the country. To live and meditate in peace.

Interviewer: But in your case it was something of a coincidence?

Miller: Entirely. But, you see, everything of significance in my
life has happened that way—by pure hazard. Of course I don't
believe that either. I believe there always was a purpose, that it was
destined to be that way. The explanation lies in my horoscope—that
would be my frank answer. To me it's all quite clear.

Interviewer: Why did you never go back to Paris to live?

Miller: For several reasons. In the first place, I got married soon
after I reached Big Sur, and then I had children, and then I had no
money, and then too I fell in love with Big Sur. I had no desire to
resume my Paris life, it was finished. Most of my friends were
gone, the war had broken up everything.

Interviewer: Gertrude Stein says that living in France purified her
English because she didn't use the language in daily life, and this
made her the stylist that she is. Did living in Paris have the same
effect on you?

Miller: Not exactly, but I understand what she meant. Of course
I spoke much more English while there than Gertrude Stein did. Less
French, in other words. Still, I was saturated with French all the
time. Hearing another language daily sharpens your own language
for you, makes you aware of shades and nuances you never sus-
pected. Also, there comes a slight forgetting which makes you hunger
to be able to recapture certain phrases and expressions. You become
more conscious of your own language.

Interviewer: Did you ever have anything to do with Gertrude
Stein or her set?

Miller: No, nothing whatever. Never met her, no, knew nobody
belonging to her set. But then I didn't know much of any set, you
might say. I was always a lone wolf, always against groups and sets
and sects and cults and isms and so on. I knew a number of
surrealists, but I never was a member of the surrealist group or
any group.

Interviewer: Didn't you know any American writers in Paris?

Miller: I knew Walter Lowenfels, Samuel Putnam, Michael
Fraenkel. Sherwood Anderson, Dos Passos, Steinbeck, and Saroyan
I met later, in America. I met them only a few times, no more. I

never had any real connection with them. Of all the American
writers that I have met Sherwood Anderson stands out as the one I
liked most. Dos Passos was a warm, wonderful chap, but Sherwood Anderson, well I had been in love with his work, his style, his
language, from the beginning. And I liked him as a man—although
we were completely at loggerheads about most things, especially
America. He loved America, he knew it intimately, he loved the
people and everything about America. I was the contrary. But I
loved to hear what he had to say about America.

Interviewer: Have you known many English writers? You've had
a long-standing friendship, haven't you, with Durrell and Powys?

Miller: Durrell, sure, but then I hardly think of him as an English
writer. I think of him as *un*British, completely. John Cowper
Powys, of course, had the most tremendous influence on me; but
then, I never knew him, never cultivated him. I didn't dare! I was
a midget and he was a giant, you see. He was my god, my mentor,
my idol. I had run across him when I was in my early twenties.
He used to lecture then in Labor temples in New York, Cooper
Union and such places. It cost only ten cents to hear him speak.
Some thirty years later I went to see him in Wales, and found to my
surprise that he knew my work. He seemed to have great respect
for my work—which surprised me even more.

Interviewer: You knew Orwell in those days too?

Miller: Orwell I met maybe two or three times, on his visits to
Paris. I wouldn't call him a friend, just a passing acquaintance. But I
was crazy about his book *Down and Out in Paris and London;* I
think it's a classic. For me it's still his best book. Though he was
a wonderful chap in his way, Orwell, in the end I thought him
stupid. He was like so many English people, an idealist, and, it
seemed to me, a foolish idealist. A man of principle, as we say. Men
of principle bore me.

Interviewer: You don't have much use for politics?

Miller: None whatever. I regard politics as a thoroughly foul,
rotten world. We get nowhere through politics. It debases everything.

Interviewer: Even political idealism of Orwell's sort?

Miller: Especially that! The idealists in politics lack a sense of
reality. And a politician must be a realist above all. These people

with ideals and principles, they're all at sea, in my opinion. One has to be a lowbrow, a bit of a murderer, to be a politician, ready and willing to see people sacrificed, slaughtered, for the sake of an idea, whether a good one or a bad one. I mean, those are the ones who flourish.

Interviewer: What about some of the great writers of the past that have particularly attracted you? You've done studies of Balzac and Rimbaud and Lawrence. Would you say there's a particular type of writer that draws you?

Miller: That's hard to say, the writers I love are so diverse. They are the writers who are more than writers. They have this mysterious X quality which is metaphysical, occult, or what not—I don't know what term to use—this little extra something beyond the confines of literature. You see, people read to be amused, to pass the time, or to be instructed. Now I never read to pass the time, I never read to be instructed; I read to be taken out of myself, to become ecstatic. I'm always looking for the author who can lift me out of myself.

Interviewer: Can you say why you never finished your book on D. H. Lawrence?

Miller: Yes, it's very simple. The further I got into the book, the less I understood what I was doing. I found myself in a mass of contradictions. I found that I didn't really know who Lawrence was, I couldn't place him, I couldn't put my finger on him, I just couldn't cope with him after a while. I got completely bewildered. I'd got myself into a jungle, and I couldn't get out. So I abandoned the work.

Interviewer: You didn't have this trouble with Rimbaud, though?

Miller: No, oddly enough. He's more of an enigma as a personality, true. But then, I didn't do so much grappling with ideas in the Rimbaud book. Lawrence was entirely a man of ideas, and he hung his literature on the rack of these ideas.

Interviewer: You don't necessarily subscribe to Lawrence's ideas, do you?

Miller: No, not altogether, but I do admire his quest, his search, his struggle. And there are many things in Lawrence I agree with. On the other hand, there are many things I laugh about in Lawrence, things which seem absurd and stupid, foolish. I have a better perspective of him today, but I no longer find it important to say anything about him. Then he meant something to me, I was completely in his grip.

Interviewer: Well now, I suppose we have to go into this question of pornography and obscenity. I hope you don't mind. After all, you're considered an authority on the subject. Didn't you say somewhere, "I am for obscenity and against pornography"?

Miller: Well, it's very simple. The obscene would be the forthright, and pornography would be the roundabout. I believe in saying the truth, coming out with it cold, shocking if necessary, not disguising it. In other words, obscenity is a cleansing process, whereas pornography only adds to the murk.

Interviewer: Cleansing in what sense?

Miller: Whenever a taboo is broken, something good happens, something vitalizing.

Interviewer: All taboos are bad?

Miller: Not among primitive peoples. There is reason for the taboo in primitive life, but not in our life, not in civilized communities. The taboo then is dangerous and unhealthy. You see, civilized peoples don't live according to moral codes or principles of any kind. We speak about them, we pay lipservice to them, but nobody believes in them. Nobody practices these rules, they have no place in our lives. Taboos after all are only hangovers, the product of diseased minds, you might say, of fearsome people who hadn't the courage to live and who under the guise of morality and religion have imposed these things upon us. I see the world, the civilized world, as largely irreligious. The religion in force among civilized people is always false and hypocritical, the very opposite of what the initiators of any religion really meant.

Interviewer: Still, you yourself have been called a very religious man.

Miller: Yes, but without espousing any religion. What does that mean? That means simply having a reverence for life, being on the side of life instead of death. Again, the word "civilization" to my mind is coupled with death. When I use the word, I see civilization as a crippling, thwarting thing, a stultifying thing. For me it was always so. I don't believe in the golden ages, you see. What I mean is that it was a golden age for a very few people, for a select few, but the masses were always in misery, they were supersti-

tious, they were ignorant, they were downtrodden, they were stran-
gled by Church and State. I'm still a great believer in Spengler,
and there you have it all. He makes the antithesis between culture
and civilization. Civilization is the arteriosclerosis of culture.

Interviewer: Now Durrell in that article he wrote about you for
Horizon about ten years ago speaks of obscenity as technique.
Do you regard obscenity as a technique?

Miller: I think I know what he meant. I think he meant a shock
technique. Well, I may have used it thus unconsciously, but I
never deliberately used it that way. I employed obscenity as naturally as I would any other way of speaking. It was like breathing,
it was part of my whole rhythm. There were moments when you
were obscene, and then there were other moments. I don't think
obscenity is the most important element by any means. But it's a
very important one, and it must not be denied, overlooked,
or suppressed.

Interviewer: It might also be exaggerated . . .

Miller: It could be, but what harm if it were? What are we so
worried about, what is there to fear? Words, words—what is there
to fear in them? Or in ideas? Supposing they are revolting, are we
cowards? Haven't we faced all manner of things, haven't we been
on the edge of destruction time and again through war, disease,
pestilence, famine? What are we threatened with by the exaggerated
use of obscenity? Where's the danger?

Interviewer: You have commented that obscenity is mild by comparison to the sort of violence that is very common in American paper-
backs.

Miller: Yes, all this perverse sadistic writing is abhorrent to me.
I've always said mine is healthy because it's joyous and natural. I
never express anything that people are not saying and doing all the
time. Where did I get it from? I didn't pick it out of a hat. It's all
around us, we breathe it every day. People simply refuse to acknowledge it. Between the printed word and the spoken word—what
difference? You know, we didn't always have this taboo. There was
a time in English literature when most anything was permitted.
It's only in the last two or three hundred years that we've had this
queasy attitude.

Interviewer: Well, even in Chaucer you won't find all the words you find in Henry Miller.

Miller: But you do find plenty of joyous, healthy naturalism, plenty of freedom of speech.

Interviewer: What do you think of the comment Durrell made in the interview he did for the *Paris Review?* He said that in retrospect he found parts of the *Black Book* too obscene now.

Miller: Did he? Well, let me say that those are the parts I relish most. I thought they were marvelous when I first read them, and I still think so today. Maybe he was only spoofing, Durrell.

Interviewer: Why have you written so much about sex? What does sex mean for you? Does it mean something special?

Miller: That's hard to answer. You know, I think I have written as much of what my hostile critics call "flapdoodle"—that is, metaphysical nonsense—as I have about sex. Only they choose to look at the sex. No, I can't answer that question, except to say that it's played a great part in my life. I've led a good rich sexual life, and I don't see why it should be left out.

Interviewer: Did it have anything to do with your break with the life you were leading in New York?

Miller: No, I don't think so. But one becomes aware in France, after having lived in America, that sex pervades the air. It's there all around you, like a fluid. Now I don't doubt that Americans enter into sexual relations as strongly, deeply, and multifariously as any other people, but it's not in the atmosphere around you, somehow. Then too, in France woman plays a bigger role in man's life. She has a better standing there, she's taken into consideration, she's talked to like a person, not just as a wife or a mistress or what-not. Besides the Frenchman prefers to be in the company of women. In England and America, men seem to enjoy being among themselves.

Interviewer: Still, your life in the Villa Seurat was a very masculine kind of life.

Miller: To be sure, there were always women about. I had many friends, it's true, but I've had great friendships all through my life. That's another thing in my horoscope: I'm a man who is destined to make friends. That is probably the biggest factor in my life, and perhaps I ought to say something about it. When I

started writing I began to realize how much I was indebted to
others. I have been helped all my life, by friends and strangers too.
What did I need money for, when I had friends? What does
anyone want, if he has friends? I've had many friends, great friends,
lifelong friends. I'm only now losing them through death.

Interviewer: Let's leave sex and talk a little about painting. Now,
you sensed this urge to write about the middle of the twenties;
did you start painting about the same time?

Miller: Very shortly after. I think it was 1927 or 8 that I began.
But not with the same seriousness, naturally. The desire to write
was a big thing in my life, a very big thing. If I didn't begin writing
till quite late—I was 33 when I definitely began—it wasn't that I
had never thought about it. I had put it too far above me, I didn't
think I had the ability, I didn't believe in myself as a writer, as an
artist. I didn't dare to think I could be such a person, you see. Well,
I didn't take to painting in that way. I discovered that there was
another side of me that I could use. It gave me pleasure to paint, it
was recreation, it was a rest from other things.

Interviewer: Is it still a kind of game with you?

Miller: Oh, yes, nothing more.

Interviewer: Don't you find some kind of fundamental connection, though, between the arts?

Miller: Absolutely. If you're creative in one way, you're creative
in another. Originally, you know, music was the biggest thing with
me. I played the piano, I hoped to be a good pianist, but I didn't
have the talent for it. Still, I was saturated with music. I might
even say that music means more to me than writing or painting. It's
there in the back of my head all the time.

Interviewer: You were very keen on jazz at one time.

Miller: So I was. I'm not so keen today. I think jazz quite empty
now. It's too limited. Just as I deplore what happened to the movies,
so I deplore the fate of jazz. It becomes more and more automatic,
it doesn't evolve enough, it's not enriching. It's like having a
cocktail. I need wine and beer, champagne and brandy too.

Interviewer: You wrote several essays in the thirties on the art of
the film. Did you ever get a chance to practice that art?

Miller: No, but I still hope to meet the man who will give me a
chance. What I deplore most is that the medium of the film has

never been properly exploited. It's a poetic medium with all sorts of possibilities. Just think of the element of dream and fantasy. But how often do we get it? Now and then a little touch of it, and we're agape. And think of all the technical devices at our command. But my God, we haven't even begun to use them. We could have incredible marvels, wonders, limitless joy and beauty. And what do we get? Sheer crap. The film is the freest of all media, you can do marvels with it. In fact I would welcome the day when the film would displace literature, when there'd be no more need to read. You remember faces in films, and gestures, as you never do when you read a book. If the film can hold you at all, you give yourself to it completely. Even when you listen to music, it's not like that. You go to the concert hall and the atmosphere is bad, the people are yawning, or falling asleep, the program is too long, it hasn't got the things you like, and so on. You know what I mean. But in the cinema, sitting there in the dark, the images coming and going, it's like a rain of meteorites hitting you.

Interviewer: What's this about a film version of *Tropic of Cancer?*

Miller: Well, there are rumors of it. There have been offers made, but I can't see how anyone could possibly make a film of that book.

Interviewer: Would you like to do it yourself?

Miller: No, I wouldn't because I think it's almost impossible to make a film of that book. I don't see the story there, for one thing. And then, so much depends on the language. Maybe one could get away with this tropical language in Japanese or Turkish. I can't see it being rendered in English, can you? The film is so definitely a dramatic, plastic medium, anyhow, a thing of images.

Interviewer: You were a judge at the Cannes Film Festival, weren't you, last year?

Miller: Yes, though I was rather a dubious choice. The French probably did it to show their appreciation of my work. Of course they knew I was a cineast, but when a reporter asked me if I still liked films, I had to say I hardly ever see them any more. For fifteen years now I've seen very few good movies. But sure, I'm still a cineast at heart.

Interviewer: Well, now you've written a play. How do you feel about this medium?

Miller: It's a medium I always wished to tackle, but I never had the courage. In *Nexus,* when I'm living that underground life and struggling to write, there's a description, a very vivid one, of how I tried to write a play about the life we were then living. I never finished it. I think I got as far as the first act. I had tacked an elaborate plan of it on the wall, and I could talk about it marvelously, but I couldn't bring it off. The play I've just written fell out of the hat, so to speak. I was in a peculiar state of mind: I had nothing to do, nowhere to go, nothing much to eat, everybody was away, and so I said why not sit down and try it? I had no idea what I was doing when I began, the words just came to me, I didn't struggle with it. There was hardly any effort involved.

Interviewer: What's it all about?

Miller: About everything and nothing. I don't think it matters much what it's about, really. It's a kind of farce or burlesque, with surrealistic elements. And there's music, incidental music, which comes from the jukebox and over the air. I don't think it has much importance. The most I can say about it is that you won't go to sleep if you see it.

Interviewer: Do you think you'll go on and write more plays?

Miller: I hope so, yes. The next one will be a tragedy, or a comedy to make one weep.

Interviewer: What else are you writing now?

Miller: I'm not writing anything else.

Interviewer: Aren't you going on with *Nexus?*

Miller: Yes, sure, that's what I *have* to do. But I haven't begun it yet. I made several attempts but gave up.

Interviewer: You *have* to do it, you say?

Miller: Well, yes, in a sense I must finish my project, the project I laid out in 1927. This is the end of it, you see. I think part of my delay in finishing it is that I don't want to bring the work to an end. It means that I will have to turn over, take a new tack, discover a new field, as it were. Because I no longer want to write about my personal experiences. I wrote all these autobiographical books not because I think myself such an important person but—this will make you laugh—because I thought when I began that I was telling the story of the most tragic suffering any man had endured. As I got on with it I realized that I was only an amateur at suffering.

Certainly I had my full share of it, but I no longer think it was so terrible. That's why I called the trilogy *The Rosy Crucifixion*. I discovered that this suffering was good for me, that it opened the way to a joyous life, through acceptance of the suffering. When a man is crucified, when he dies to himself, the heart opens up like a flower. Of course you don't die, nobody dies, death doesn't exist, you only reach a new level of vision, a new realm of consciousness, a new unknown world. Just as you don't know where you came from, so you don't know where you're going. But that there is something there, before and after, I firmly believe.

Interviewer: How does it feel to be a best seller after enduring the plight of the creative artist all these years?

Miller: I really have no feelings about it. It's unreal to me, the whole thing. I don't find myself involved. In fact I rather dislike it. It gives me no pleasure. All I see is more disruption in my life, more intrusions, more nonsense. People are concerned about something which no longer concerns me. That book doesn't mean anything to me any more. People think because they're all worked up about it that I am too. They think it's a great thing for me that I'm accepted at last. Well, I feel that I'd been accepted long before, at least by those I cared to be accepted by. To be accepted by the mob doesn't mean a thing to me. In fact it's rather painful. Because I'm being accepted for the wrong reasons. It's a sensational affair, it doesn't mean that I am appreciated for my true worth.

Interviewer: But this is part of the recognition that you've always known would come to you.

Miller: Yes, of course. But then, don't you see, the only real recognition comes from those who are on the same level with you, from your peers. That's the only kind that matters, and I've had that. I've had it for years now.

Interviewer: Which of your books do you think came off best?

Miller: I always say *The Colossus of Maroussi*.

Interviewer: The critics, most of them, say *Cancer* is your great book.

Miller: Well, on rereading *Cancer* I found that it was a much better book than I had thought. I liked it. I was amazed, in fact, I hadn't looked at it for many years, you know. I think it's a very good book, that it has lasting qualities. But the *Colossus* was written from some other level of my being. What I like about it is that it's a joyous book, it expresses joy, it gives joy.

Interviewer: What ever happened to *Draco and the Ecliptic* which you announced many years ago?

Miller: Nothing. That's been forgotten, though it is always possible that I may one day write that book. My thought was to write a very slim work, explaining what I had been trying to do in writing all these books about my life. In other words, to forget what I had written and try once again to explain what I had hoped to do. In that way perhaps to give the significance of the work from the author's standpoint. You see, the author's standpoint is only one of many, and his idea of the significance of his own work is lost in the welter of other voices. Does he know his own work as well as he imagines? I rather think not. I rather think he's like a medium who, when he comes out of his trance, is amazed at what he's said and done.

Meeting with Henry
Lionel Olay / 1963

From *Cavalier*, 13:121 (July 1963), 6–9, 84–87.

Henry Miller, benign and chipper as an old pippin, is seventy-one. The old rascal, who thirty years ago was conniving and scheming his way through the underbelly of Paris, now lives in a very elegant, two-story, Georgian house in exclusive Pacific Palisades, California, for which he plunked down 77,000 unheard of dollars. Let it be said, lest the scoffers get the impression that the sweet singer of whatthehell has turned into a flabby bourgeois, the house is primarily a place for his two attractive teen-age children, Val and Tony, and their mother, Lepska, who was the third of Miller's four wives. His end consists of a quiet nook, use of the pool, a little peace for this final lap on what has been a most unusual journey. Miller still owns but one suit, and that of corduroy, has only a bicycle to take him where he has to go, and, aside from a gourmet palate and a fine nose for expensive wines, is still as disdainful of cash as ever.

Slim as a boy, spry and alert as a fox, with nervous, graceful movements, he still insists on playing the naïf, the "kid from Brooklyn," as he likes to refer to himself. But he's as sharp and alert to the foibles and absurdities of his fellow creatures as he ever was.

For, make no mistake, those of you who are his fans or those who think him a foulmouthed boor, the Henry Miller he writes about is not he, never was and never will be. "No man ever wrote a satisfactory biography of a writer," observed Scott Fitzgerald. "How could he, when a writer is so many different people?" Well, if that be true, then "Henry Miller," the "I" of his *Tropics* and all his other supposed autobiographies, is his finest creation. If the man in the Palisades is "Henry Miller," then Saul Bellow is *Henderson the Rain King,* for this one is a conscious artist, an astute student of world literature, a man dedicated to writing as few writers have ever been. To equate him with the free-swinging rebel, the oath-spitting, old, shameless rascal that he claims to have been in his stories is to misread the man and make light of his achievement.

But that is the final irony, and is perhaps not lost on the old fox: That in this day when we try to fit our actuality into fiction—vide *Fail-Safe, Advise and Consent, The Prize,* et al.—we become incensed at the *Tropics,* not because of the language, since lots rougher goes out unremarked, but because, presumably, it's all true. That, however, is a minor thorn in the leather-tough side of Miller, who has held his position like a bulldog from that day thirty years ago when he upchucked the whole mess he'd made of his life in America and set off for Paris at age forty to do or die, sink or swim as an artist, a writer. Neither acclaim, slander, hardship, windfalls, three busted marriages, nothing could turn him away again; he had become the Happy Maniac, a writing fool for whom everything else had to take a back seat. Purity of heart is to will one thing, said Kierkegaard, and, if the gloomy old Dane was wired in when he got that one, then Henry is among the purest men of our time.

"But what made you do it, Henry?" I asked him. "What possessed you to take that jump at the age of forty, a bald-headed man with a wife and kid behind, to take off for Paris like some 22-year-old innocent?"

"It was desperation," he said, simply. "You see, in 1927, when I was working for the Parks Department, I made an outline of everything I was going to write. I projected into a notebook everything I hadn't the ability yet to set down. It came to about thirty typewritten pages, telegraphically written. Only I could understand those notes. And this is the substance of everything I've written that concerns my life. . . .

"Then, afterwards, in Paris, you might say that *Cancer* came about accidentally. In a way that makes it different from everything else I've ever done, different perhaps from all but a handful of books ever written. You see, *Cancer* was written in the living moment, on the spot, while I was living it . . . it was the story of how I'm writing *that book,* you see . . . it's a book about how I'm writing a book. And when it was finished it broke the ice for me, enabled me to find my own way."

"Which makes it different then," I suggested, "from the other *Tropic, Capricorn,* and from all the rest."

"Yes, completely" Henry agreed. "*Cancer* was the one which gave me the courage to go on, to *be* the writer I said I was. Then the books go backward, counterclockwise, so that right now I am finishing the last volume of the whole series, and I'm reaching the point where I finally decide to go to Paris. And here I am, it's been thirty years, and when I started I'd thought of only writing one book, one thick book. That would be the story of my life, of my misfortune. And then, you see, all the books I wrote on the side. . . ."

I fell silent, trying to extract whatever kernel of truth there was for the chewing.

"And it all started with . . . what would you call it? An act of desperation," he said. "I had arrived at the last ditch already in New York, and the desperate step was going over to Paris to get on a new footing. It was as much to re-establish my personal life as it was my life as a writer."

"They were, even then, inseparable, weren't they?"

"True. So when you ask for a philosophy in *Cancer,* the philosophy would simply be . . . I was telling Bernie (Bernard Wolfe, who is doing the screenplay of *Tropic of Cancer* for Joseph Levine and working closely with his old buddy Henry, whom he knew in New York when both were living catch-as-catch-can existences) that the philosophy is simply to stay alive as best you can, don't go down, don't be defeated, do anything and everything—like a criminal almost—to keep alive, to keep going; don't get morally defeated. Live like a bedbug or a cockroach if necessary.

"But at the same time, in the book, I tried to emphasize that in doing this, I never got cynical or bitter. And I ceased to blame society or my parents or this or that. In this process I discovered only I am to blame for my condition. I gave up saying it's the fault of the community, or bad times, or mistreatment of artists, and so forth. I took it all on my own. The moment then that you assume responsibility for everything, whether it be true or not, you're moving. The other way you're only sliding back, like a Sisyphus, you know. . . . And then I must say another thing here which is true about all writers who are serious. You write to find out about

yourself, who you are, what you are, where you're going. You don't
know that when you start.

"When I started to write the story of my misfortunes, I didn't
know what would be opened up inside me. I might have thought:
That's a bare physical account; but then you begin to relate them,
you understand all the inner psychological workings and everything. You discover something about it, and that's the whole enjoyment of writing, finding out about yourself and getting reconciled
to yourself, if it's possible; getting ready to be something with all
your defects. I think most writers, most artists in general, do not
learn this lesson; the ego has to be annihilated just as in a religious
experience, it's the same thing, and that art is only a vestibule to
a larger life."

At this point we were interrupted when Lepska, the handsome
mother of his two handsome children, came in to inquire about
instructions as to what to say to someone on the phone about a later
visit. Henry winced. He truly does not enjoy the vicissitudes of
fame, and much less of notoriety. After Lepska had gone, I wanted
to get his view on the two Henry Millers and asked him about the
relationship between him as the Germanic, courtly and rather shy
artist and the lecherous old rake of his novels.

"I call myself 'I' throughout the whole book," he said. "Sure,
it's I, but from many angles. The thing I discovered in going along
is that this I, your identity and all, that's not the thing that's doing
the work. All you are, I feel, is a medium. And here's the biggest
thing I found out. Again, as with religious people, if you lead the
good life, if you're honest and faithful to yourself, your antennae
will connect up with those forces which are ready to pour in on any
man who will open up. He doesn't have to be a genius or even gifted,
in my opinion. I think we're just drawing all the time. Whatever we
get is out there, it surrounds us, it's inside and outside us, it's all
one, it's an effluvium. Most of us don't connect because we're not
living right. We don't attune ourselves. We don't refine our
sensibilities."

I asked him about the hallucinogens; mescaline, lysergic acid, the
mind-changing drugs that Aldous Huxley and others have become so
interested in.

"I've heard of them," Henry said, "and talked to people, but,

no, I've never taken any. I know that to sustain these true
moments of insight one has to be highly disciplined, lead a disciplined life. Of course, I don't believe in that too much; for me it's just
good enough to do what I want to do. You know, I haven't any
point to make, there's nothing to demonstrate, no message. . . ."

"You know," I said, "in one of your exchanges with Lawrence
Durrell, which I have just been reading [*The Miller-Durrell Correspondence* is a Dutton book on the stands now], he expresses bitter
disappointment with *Sexus,* feeling it to be unworthy of you. And
you answer him, saying that if you like a writer you enjoy even
his faults."

"That's right. You like writers as you like a friend. You don't like
a friend because he's perfect, but *with* his imperfections, and they
add to his quality, don't they?"

"And yet," I reminded him, "the public and the critics jumped
all over Hemingway for his one mistake, *Across the River and
Into the Trees.*"

"I didn't read it. But, you know, I've always felt this about the
hard-boiled writer, those men who go out and lead adventurous
lives: Underneath they are tender as babies, they're all lambs; this
is all compensation for their extra-tender qualities. All the tough
men I know are this way."

There was something else I wanted to know, and had hesitated,
realizing that Henry is reluctant to talk about personal things,
which is a strange thing to understand unless you can hear how
curiously impersonal he is when talking about the "other Henry
Miller." But I decided I'd try. "Are you any happier now, Henry,"
I asked him, "than you were before? Now that fame and wealth
and recognition have come, perhaps even an assurance of immortal-
ity, has it all made you happier than when you were struggling
and uncertain?"

Henry smiled that mandarin smile of his, which made him resem-
ble more than ever a strange, skinny Buddha. "I used to have
great ups and downs," he said, "euphorias and depressions. That's
left me. Every once in a while, sure, I go into a deep depression.
There's no reason for it; suddenly I'm at the bottom and I'm really
suicidal. This happened to me traveling through Europe when I was
at, you might say, the height of my fame. I had money, I could go

anywhere and do anything, and that was the most miserable time
of my life. That was worse than, in *Tropic of Cancer,* being hungry
and walking.

"There are two kinds of those depressions. One is like a metaphysical depression where suddenly, for no good reason, there's
a hole in everything: You peer down into a bottomless pit; life takes
on a senseless quality; all the veils that you've bolstered yourself
up with fall away, ideas, philosophies, etc. And suddenly there's a
rent in it all, and you see that chasm, and that's what they talk of
in the Old Testament. All the early Christian saints had a great
dread of that mark. It's the furthest doubt that you can reach,
you doubt everything. It's the dark night of the soul, you don't
know why. I think they're inexplicable, these seizures. Whereas
other people are fortunate and can say, 'I lost my wife' or 'I lost
my money,' you can't say what you lost. You lost your vision,
you lost your faith momentarily. It comes back.

"You know, people often ride me because I speak of astrology.
The only reason that I'm so interested in astrology is that it
provides an explanation that no other single point of view does. It's
looking all around, you might say, through all the twelve houses and
all the planets, every aspect of life, and it has a cyclical element,
and I find in life there is this rhythm. You can never say, 'Now I
am there,' because tomorrow you begin to go down again. There's
nothing but that rhythmic line, it seems to me, that wave, and it exists
through all of nature, everything we read about, the wave is there."

"We can't sustain moments, we just have to wait for them to
recur," I ventured.

"Yes," he said, "and we should be thankful that they come,
instead of wanting to clutch them and hold them. If we open our
hands and let things flow always, we'll get it back again. But the
moment you want to seize something and hold it forever, that's
annihilation. Isn't that so?"

"It's so, but it's hard to accept."

"That's what Whitman meant by acceptance. That's why I love
Whitman. 'It's good to be born, it's also good to die.' He accepted
everything, every situation. That's why he could never distinguish
between a criminal and a saint, they're all one. . . . No man could
be a saint unless he had first been an arch sinner. You can't make a

saint out of a nice, gentle, neutral character. A saint has to be a rebel and a violent character and everything that's derogatory. There has to be antagonism. Another thing . . . in astrology, if they draw up a horoscope of a man who's got nothing but good aspects, he's a very uninteresting person. The best and most interesting horoscopes, like scores of music, are those where there is violent antagonism in the character. He's got to fight all the time, struggle with himself.''

"Who draws up these horoscopes, and what is his source of information?"

"The information anybody can obtain. It's a mechanical thing because you know when a man was born. Therefore, you know the position of the planets at the time of his birth, the angles at which they shine into his various houses. It's a pure mathematical formula, as it were. But the difference of interpretation between an ordinary astrologer and a poet is a vast one. That obtains to criticism, to interpretation in music. It's the difference between an ordinary violinist and a virtuoso playing the same piece.

"Everything, to my mind, finally relates back to interpretation, the gift of interpretation. We are all in the world every day reading the same newspaper, and we all draw different conclusions. Some of us put a bullet through our head when we see certain things, and others are unaffected or say, 'Oh, well, that will pass' or 'Maybe it's a good thing' . . . not change the world, change worlds. . . . Nowadays you encounter in criticism . . . I was reading about Paul Klee the other day, who's one of my favorites, and the emphasis that they're trying to put now on reality versus realism. This is something I've been trying to talk about all my life. Then people say, 'What the hell do you mean by reality?' Well, you can't define it. It's a totality that goes all through you, but is utterly different from this thing called realism, which is always a peripheral thing. What does the skin feel? And the other is something that penetrates through and through.''

"Would you say Zola was dealing with reality or realism?"

"Zola is on the realistic side, but with a different tinge than ours. . . . Where Zola had wonderful ideas, sociological, metaphysical and so on, you can't call him an ordinary realist. He was more than that or he wouldn't have lasted. The others are ephemeral. And that's why I think all the writers who have a metaphysical cast are always exciting. They introduce this element which is disturbing and to which there is no answer. The realist is always giving you an answer, everything is always clarified and explained. But a real writer leaves you with a question mark, I feel, for you to find out for yourself. He just poses a great problem to you.

"Another thing, I think that art is always *about* and *around* whereas metaphysics tries to answer, science tries to answer. But art is a skirting of everything, picking everything up and looking at it from every angle. And that's why it's endless, why art will always go on, because you can do this infinitely. The moment you go direct to the bull's eye and say, 'That's it!' then it's finished, then there's nothing more to say. . . ."

"Artists play, then."

"Yes, in the high sense of the word. That was the Chinese conception about the universe itself and life itself; that it's a great game, but it's the highest game. It has no goal except to do this; that's enough, that *is* it. . . . You've put your finger on the real sore point. In this whole world, where we have many beliefs and isms, nobody, virtually, is practicing these things that they talk about. And this is where the real cancer is in society, that they're two-faced. Everything is a fraud, everything is a lie. Just like I always say, if I have a tombstone I want to put Rimbaud's words on it: 'Everything we are taught is false.' Every day I feel that stronger and stronger. There is no justification for all the assertions that are made. And the only men you might say who lived up to these truths were crucified. They were the only ones. After them came their followers, who are the caricatures, who reverse everything. . . .

"I always feel that as a member of a community, and I don't care what the community or where it is, one is almost doomed to lead a double life. A community, by definition almost, is a group that has certain ideas and a way of living that it has to go by, otherwise it falls apart. And this thing is not flexible, it is not changing enough. If it were changing every day, with the consent and approval of everybody, it would be marvelous. You're allowed as an individual to change your thoughts, but·the community can't change its basic notions. . . .

"The other day I saw a clipping in the New York *Times* from
London, and it says that there is a group in the Quaker movement
in England that has come out begging the Quakers to take another
view of the whole sexual process; that it's not broad enough, not
flexible enough, it isn't reality. It says you can't talk about extra-
marital relations, adultery, childbirth without marriage. This is all
nonsense. It has no part of reality. This is reality, what's going on.
. . . Another funny thing is that so much has to do with the family
as a strong element in our society. Yet the family is being attacked
from every angle, being disintegrated. It isn't just in China, where
they're trying to make a big thing of it, it's right here. Here is where
divorce occurs, and disruption and whatnot. . . . By the way, I
want to ask you something. Do you feel that writers are not keeping
pace imaginatively with the scientists and their searchings and
gropings?"

"It's becoming harder and harder for the writer to stay well
versed in what's happening," I replied. "All the science-fiction
imagination of ten years ago is outdated because it's actually in
practice. Is that what you mean?"

"Yes. I don't think that they can vie with one another on the
same grounds. That is to say, if I'm going to write imaginatively
about outer space, I mustn't first find out everything that science
knows about it. I must reach out with *my* conception and equipment, take an artist's standpoint regardless of truth or fact. Every
day I am impressed with the fact that we are in a totally different
world today than we were ten or fifteen years ago, that we really
crossed the line and that this world of tomorrow will be unrecog-
nizable to the man like myself.

"When I grew up at the end of the century . . . Holy God, is
there going to be any comparison whatever? There isn't anything
I can see that's going to remain of this old epic. We've gone through
the iron age, steel, stone, electronic, guns, and it's atomic now. Why,
we don't know what they'll call it five years from now. . . . The
whole framework of civilization is completely threatened by the
sense of a great change, and this, to my mind, is somewhat the
explanation of all the other upheavals in domestic life, economics,
etc. It's because something much bigger is going on. Life is going
faster than we are, our rhythm isn't adapted to the other rhythm.

"Do you think, in that connection, there's something intriguing there? Man, they say, has now grown used to the idea of devastating his planet, wiping himself out. Do you think that if he really reconciled himself to this idea, had the courage to face it . . . because now he's really like that, isn't he? He says it but he doesn't mean it. . . . But, if he meant it, once got on that level, might he not then change his thinking entirely, arrive at some new state of consciousness, so to speak?"

"But what a risk to take, what if he went the other way?"

"That's right, but I think all advances have to be made with a great risk, or based on a great risk. It's life or death always, a real advance. What we are suffering from today is the two-faced, the indecision. It's so strange. Here we've based our thoughts about civilization on the idea that man gets more refined, more ethical, moral and so on, and we have arrived at the very opposite of that. We are worse than any age that has ever lived, worse than the stone man; more barbarous, more cruel, more ruthless, more heartless, conscienceless. This is the end of all our ethical upbuilding. We've come out through a tunnel, and here's the other end.

"It is frightening, but it might also be the means to a great new inspiration. Knowing that we have this power and that we could annihilate, but we won't. We will abandon the thought, but we know we *can* do it. This goes on all the time in daily life; we're caught in law. You always see some respectable man hailed to court for killing somebody. Maybe he even did worse and chopped the body up. Who could have thought that man, so eminent, so respectable, could do that? But this is what we have to learn, that we *can* do those things, that we are all capable of this. . . . And this brings you back to all the religious discussions about good and evil, and is God both good and evil? Since He's omnipotent, all, He contains everything. Therefore He must contain the evil too . . . that's why they invented the devil, he's a shadow, a name, just like death is a word."

"What about the phenomenon of guilt?"

"Guilt, it's a big question. But it's true that in the West we seem to be more ridden with guilt than in the East, and the Protestant more than the Catholic. The Catholic is able to relieve himself through confession, and the Protestant who goes to an analyst doesn't

get the same results. An analyst turns you back and says now
you're adapted to the world. A real man doesn't want to be. This
is just what you don't want. You want the world to be adapted to
your advanced thinking. You don't want to be readapted to bad
conditions that made you this way. . . .

"We were talking about the grand project that I mapped out, and
now I've come to the end, and I did write a lot of things on the
side. The last thing I wrote was a play. I would like to try more
plays. That was just a break, an attempt. I don't attach any value
to it, but I found it great fun to do and I think I would rather write
fantastic, humorous and surrealist things than serious things. I
hate all these current plays dealing with sociological problems that
are paralyzing. They bore the sh— tears out of me. Whereas the
theater with Ionesco has found a wonderful outlet."

"Did you see *The Connection*?"

"No, and I have a feeling I wouldn't care to see it. I don't like
the needle and all that."

It was getting late, a little chilly. Together we had smoked through
two packs of cigarettes, and my mouth felt like a warm, wet
galosh. Yet I didn't want to end it. I wanted more.

"What about the relationship of art to identity?" I asked him,
not at all happy with the question, but certain it would trigger off
some more Miller.

"You almost know this with art," he said, "from the beginning,
where you set up a melody which is your rhythm, your wave length.
That's why, too, I don't think Ernest Hemingway's type of meticu-
lous writing is the important thing in writing. The important thing
is to sound your basic note, identity. Get your identity across
because everyone is an interesting person and unique, but only a
few people know how to convey this. And once you have found this
inner man, this true identity, I don't care what tune he sings or how
bad he plays even, it's him. I've read books that are poor writing,
but they had something, and I prefer them to the well-written
books by Mr. Anybody.

"I was fascinated with Errol Flynn's book. It was a very amazing
revelation. You'd think, now there's a book you don't go shouting
about. But he wrote the book almost as he lived, it had a great
honesty. There was one touch in it that I liked very much. In Australia

when he's desperate and wants money, he falls into a relationship with some married woman. She had money and was keeping him. Then, one night in bed, he gets up and takes all her jewels. And then he has a job to hide them when he takes the boat, and I think he lost the great part. Finally, when he makes the gravy here in America, he hires detectives to try to find her to give the jewels back, and he can't find her. That's a classic.

"You know, in my life there was a man like that called Ronald Millar, and he was the editor of *Liberty Magazine,* a five-cent magazine. In the very beginning I had gone to him with my manuscripts, hoping he'd take something and give me a job also as a sub-editor. I brought my wife along, who was very attractive, and he seemed to take a fancy. . . . I could see him, leafing through, reading a line here and there, and finally he said, 'I see that you know how to use the language. You love words, don't you?' I said, 'Yes.' He said, 'Well, I don't want to take any of these now, maybe later. But you go home; here's a commission. Give us an article on words.' This was a job for me! So I did this: I gave him the article, and he gave me $250, which was an enormous sum in 1925 or 1927 for me. And they never published it. But the thing I remember is that day when he was saying goodbye to me. He escorts us to the elevator and presses the button. I shake his hand and I feel something in it. Going down in the elevator I find that it's a twenty-dollar bill. Now I've looked for that man all over. He was a friend of Ben Hecht and Charles MacArthur and that actress who was the mistress of Belasco—Lenore Uhlric. I've written to people: Where is this man? I started this already in Paris. Ronald Millar. . . .

"I still have a list in my notebook of my debts. As I paid them I crossed each one out. They were $2, $5, $6 kind of debts. But all through life I find that, when I'm finally getting on my feet and have a little money, every time I start to look for these old fellows who gave me more than that, $100, $200, they're dead. So, you give it to the next guy. . . .

"Now there's another thing. I constantly get criticism that in Henry Miller's books, he never really shows any love for a woman. There are two answers to that. First, I don't think it's altogether true. If you would study the character Mona, who goes

throughout, I think it shows there is a real love. But, secondly, I
haven't wanted to talk about the real ideal (I did have it), but that I
think is not for the public. That, I'm not revealing. Do you see what
I mean? It isn't that I made a deliberate choice, but maybe some
inner thing in me withheld that. It always makes me laugh because
I feel that I have the unfortunate quality of being able to fall over-
whelmingly in love."

"One man," I said, "who spoke feelingly of love was Hermann
Hesse, a great favorite of yours.

"I love him," Henry said, "I can pick him up and reread him. I
do that with very few authors. When I was traveling a year or so ago,
I made a big trip through France, Switzerland, Italy and whatnot.
In Southern Switzerland there's this Italian part, and Hesse had two
homes there [Hesse has since died, age 86], one on the lake and one
on top of a mountain. And I went to both of them, but I didn't
knock on the door. I couldn't do it because I remembered having
read in some magazine that he had put a plaque up outside one of
those doors, and it said: 'I am a man who's in his old age now, I've
done my work, I don't need communication with visitors. If you
like me, spare me, go home and don't knock on my door.' Something like that . . . he said it was from a Chinese author, but I
suspect he wrote it himself. . . ."

Now there was a silence and I felt that surely, if Hesse had
invoked a fake Chinese, then Henry had used the both of them to
drive home a point that he himself was too polite to make in his
own voice. It was time to go, he was tired, and there is much he
has yet to do. When I was driving back I recalled the words of a
poet friend regarding Henry:

"He is one of those who are blessed," the poet said, "and I am
one of those who bless him."

Playboy Interview:
Henry Miller
Bernard Wolfe / 1964

From the *Playboy* Interview: Henry Miller. *Playboy* Magazine
(September 1964). Copyright © 1964 by *Playboy*. Reprinted
with permission. All rights reserved. Interview conducted by
Bernard Wolfe.

Novelist Bernard Wolfe, who conducted this exclusive interview for
Playboy, has been a close friend, colleague, drinking companion
and brother iconoclast of this month's interviewee for almost 25
years. Fellow literary lights in New York during the Forties, they
are now neighbors in the fashionable suburbs of West Los Angeles—
where, beside the pool and in the rustic living room of Miller's
roomy split-level home, the following conversation was recorded.
A long-time *Playboy* contributor, the 49-year-old Wolfe debuts
herein, with hard-hitting authority and familiar expertise, as a
Playboy interviewer. Of his subject he writes:

"When the first copies of the first Paris edition of *Tropic of
Cancer* reached our shores in 1934, appetizingly camouflaged in
the dust jackets of Escoffier and Brillat-Savorin cookbooks, mine
were among the damp hands that reached for them. It was our
good luck that the desultory hawkshaws of U.S. Customs never
stopped to wonder at this surge of undergraduate passion for l'haute
cuisine: for more than a few of us cut our literary eyeteeth on that
contraband book. To us it was, as its author fistily proclaimed, a
badly needed 'gob of spit in the face of Art,' as well as an incendiary
demonstration of the napalm still latent in the English language.

"We campus malcontents worked up a lively image of the ber-
serker who concocted that paper-backed bombshell—and the
equally explosive volumes that followed. Such a prancing bull of
the prose pampas had to be out-dimensional in every aspect: a
brawler in rude denim jeans, defiant locks snapping in the Seine
breezes: a debauchery on the grand scale who consumed Gargan-
tuan daily rations of wine, women and songs; an expatriate Johnny

Appleseed standing, at a conservative estimate, 12 feet tall. We knew
a giant when we read one; the deeper underground a book was
driven, the taller grew its author.

"Years passed. World War II drove the wild man out of Europe,
and when he showed up one day on the streets of New York,
where some of us had settled with our typewriters and our distem-
pers, we gaped. The Rimbaud of Myrtle Avenue, the Villon of the
14th Ward, was nowhere near as big or as loud or as rambunctious
as we'd imagined him. He was slight and bone-thin. His voice was
soft, mellifluous. The gray hair that fringed his bold bald pate was
neatly crew-cut. His jowls were as clean-shaven as his nails were
clean and manicured. He wore impeccably tailored Bond Street
tweeds and a natty plaid ulster. He was kind, courteous, consider-
ate, mild, modest, gentle, and all but old-worldly in his gallant
manners with the womenfolk—the very antithesis of the capering,
carousing cutup called Henry Miller in the books of Henry Miller.
The rapacious desperado of *Cancer* had turned out to be everybody's Dutch uncle . . .

"But with something added—something not exactly avuncular,
some special clear unblinking light in the deceptively mild blue
eyes half draped by slanty mandarin lids, some special husky
vibrant sound in the misleadingly gentle voice that has never
deviated from the flat Brooklyn tones of his birth. You couldn't pin
a name on this laxed electricity in him, but you knew when it was
turned on. You would stand with the unstagy man at a Third Avenue
bar, talking easy about nothing in particular. The barflies would
stop mumbling into their boilermakers and perk their ears to Henry's homey sound. They would raise their eyes from the sawdust
to study his good-neighborly, ostensibly bland face. They would
gather up their beers and drift toward the source of that ingratiat-
ing sound and stand in a circle around that good-guy face, asking
mutely for something—benediction, warming, the gift of such energy
as tightens no muscles, a shot of some unnamable balm. It was
impossible to carry on a conversation with Henry in a public place.
Too many winos made their mothlike way into the glow that
emanated from any bar stool he graced.

"Henry went West. He holed up for a time in the Santa Monica
hills. Later he settled in his aerie on the highest rise of the Big Sur

mountains in northern California, to stay put for 20 years. Now
bestsellingly U.S.-published, duly stamped with the Supreme
Court seal of approval, and socially acceptable among all but ladies'
auxiliary literary tea societies, he's back in the Los Angeles area,
living in Pacific Palisades to be near his two teenage children by his
third wife. Our paths cross often, and I am forever amazed at how
little he's changed. At 72 he's still lean as an ax handle, with eye
undimmed and Brooklyn drawl intact. About the only sign of
wear in him is that his appetite for walking is somewhat diminished
by a thinning of the cartilage in the socket of his left hip, a
memento of all the decades exuberantly spent on foot. But if he
doesn't walk up and down the Cathay he makes of Pacific Palisades
quite as much as he once walked the Cathay he made of Paris, he
certainly rides—on his English racing bike, dressed, of course, in
faultlessly tailored Ivy League corduroys. The astonishing low-
keyed grace is still there, and the unproving, unpushing energy.
And the disciples—barflies and children, aesthetes and novice writers—still flock to that benevolent voice and benign face, begging
for the grace without a name."

Playboy: One critic has described your work as "toilet-wall scrib-
bling." Just to set the record straight: Are you now, or have you
ever been, a toilet-wall scribbler?
    Miller: No, never. But that reminds me of a story about the
French *pissoirs* which might apply to me. A university professor was
just coming out of the *pissoir* while another professor was entering.
As they passed each other, the one entering noticed that the one
leaving had a pencil in his hand. "Aha," he snickered. "So you're
one of those who writes on toilet walls?" "Oh, no," said the departing
gentleman, "I was just correcting grammar."
    Playboy: Your books have been widely branded—and banned—as
pornography. What's your reaction to the charge?
    Miller: Well, I *can* be said to have written obscene things, but I
don't think of myself as a pornographer. There's a big difference
between obscenity and pornography. Pornography is a titillating
thing, and the other is cleansing; it gives you a catharsis. It's not
done just to tickle your nerve ends—though I would add parentheti-
cally that I don't go along with those judicious-minded critics and

intellectuals who try to pretend that when you write erotically, with
obscene language and all that, the reader should be impeccably
immune, never have a lustful thought. Why the hell *shouldn't* a
reader have lustful thoughts? They're as legitimate as any other
kind. I might also add that apparently I'm even capable of arousing
other kinds of thoughts. I get many letters from readers who say,
"We're not at all interested in your sexual writing; it's your philosophy we find stimulating."

Playboy: Still, as far as stimulation is concerned, wouldn't you
say that most readers prefer your erotica to your philosophy?

Miller: Perhaps so, but the importance of my work lies in my
vision of life and of the world, not in the free use of four-letter
words. These banned books of mine fit in with the tradition of
literature widely known and accepted in Europe for the last
thousand years. Unfortunately, for the last three hundred years,
English-language literature has been castrated, stifled; it's pallid,
lacking integration and totality. Preceding this period, sex communication never had contained this shocking quality. There was a
freedom of expression. There was no emphasis put upon sex. It
fitted in naturally because it was and is a part of life. But the Anglo-
Saxon people, in the past three centuries, have been terribly deprived—starved, literally speaking, for the natural and normal
expression of sex which can counteract unnatural feelings of guilt.
So now they leap on the sensational, and because they have found in
me this missing element, they overemphasize it.

Playboy: Hasn't it been said that *you* are the one who overempha-
sizes it?

Miller: It might just as well be said that I overemphasize the
subject of the freedom of the individual. I feel I have simply
restored sex to its rightful place in literature, rescued the basic life
factor from literary oblivion, as it were. Obscenity, like sex, has
its natural, rightful place in literature as it does in life, and it will
never be obliterated, no matter what laws are passed to smother
it. Let me tell you about an incident that may give an indication of
my point of view. My little son and I were walking in one of the
great forests of northern California. All alone, not a sound, not a
person around for miles. Suddenly he started looking frantically
about, holding himself, you know. "What's wrong?" I asked him.

"I have to go to the bathroom," he said. "Well, you can't," I replied. "There's no bathroom here. Do you mean you have to take a leak? Come on, do it right here near this big tree. Come on, I'll show you. You can't 'go to the bathroom' on a tree." And so there we stood, father and son in the beautiful forest, pissing on a tree. So you see, in life as in writing, I use common words to express myself because it is the only way for me. I haven't considered, chosen or selected. One might just as well ask why I've written the way I have about people, countries, streets, religion, and so on. I haven't singled out sex for special treatment, but I've given it the *full* treatment. I had been writing for fifteen years and getting nowhere. Everything I had written was derivative, influenced by others. Then finally I decided to please *myself*. It was a great gamble, but finally I cut the umbilical cord, and in severing it I became an entity. I became *myself*, you see? When they speak of tradition in the literary world, they are speaking of men who are individualists, who are entities, who, in becoming themselves, become part of tradition. As for being obsessed with sex, *they* are the ones who are obsessed: they who make so much over the sexual content of what I have written. When people have been deprived, they make up for lost ground the moment the barriers are down. This is what is happening with the banned books. Other countries accepted them as a basic part of life. All over the world they think of us Americans as a people obsessed with the *idea* of sex but lacking a full and natural experience of sex. The English-speaking peoples are precisely the ones who understand the least what I've written and why.

Playboy: Would you care to enlighten them now?

Miller: I can try. I was sick to death of the lack of substance in English literature, with its portrayal of a truncated, partial man. I wanted a more substantial diet, the whole being, the round view you get in the paintings of Picasso, the works of Montaigne and Rabelais and others. So I rebelled, and perhaps overgenerously made up for this lack and weakness in the literature of my time.

Playboy: One critic has alleged that your "overgenerous" depiction of sex—far from fascinating readers—has actually rendered the subject uninteresting as a literary topic. Do you think he may have a point?

Miller: Naturally, anything done to excess becomes uninteresting. But I don't think we need worry about making sex uninteresting. All that was taken care of by the Creator when He created male and female. What is important is whether we have a healthy or a sick attitude toward sex or anything else.

Playboy: Though willing to concede that you personally may not be obsessed with sex, another detractor has accused you of "using freedom of expression as the high-sounding cover-up for a cynically commercial effort to cash in on the sure-fire sales appeal of sex." Have you?

Miller: I have never knowingly been cynical or insincere. And as for the commercial aspect, that was farthest from my mind. I was merely determined to write as I pleased, as I viewed life, do or die, without thought for the consequences.

Playboy: Did you anticipate the worldwide storm of public protest, censorship and suppression that followed the publication of *Tropic of Cancer*?

Miller: I was not concerned with this problem. I had had fifteen years of punishment and rejection before *Cancer* was published. It was something I had to do, and that was all there was to it.

Playboy: What was the initial reaction of European critics to the *Tropics*?

Miller: A very broad question. Shall I say "varied"? Critics are the same all over the world. They judge by what they are—which we won't go into. On the whole, however, I must say that whether for or against, their approach to my work was on a higher level than that of the Anglo-Saxon critics, who, now that these books are being published here, are saying, after condemning them—and reading them under the counter—for nearly thirty years, "It's about time" or "So America is really growing up at last."

Playboy: Do you agree with them, at least, that popular acceptance of the *Tropics* in the U.S. means that "America is really growing up at last"?

Miller: Times *have* changed—but whether in the direction of more freedom or less is difficult to say. There is still a great gap between the accepted behavior of individuals, as regards sex, and the freedom to express this in words. I don't delude myself that the world suddenly sees eye to eye with me on the subject of sex—or any other subject, for that matter. Only the Scandinavian countries, Sweden and Denmark, seem to me to be truly liberated in this sense.

Playboy: Still, don't you view the American publication of the *Tropics,* and the Supreme Court decision upholding it, as a kind of personal vindication?

Miller: I had my victory, if you wish to call it that, long before this American success, if you wish to call *it* that. In the countries where my books circulated freely, I was, if not a popular writer, certainly an accepted writer. I had my reward in being accepted and acknowledged by many of the foremost writers and thinkers in Europe. One is truly accepted or understood only by one's peers.

Playboy: In addition to literary admirers, you've acquired, along with a controversial reputation, a coterie of disciples so worshipful that it has been called a cult. Are you flattered by this sort of idolatry?

Miller: Of course not! The most devastating thing about achieving any success as a writer is to meet the people who rave about your work. It makes you wonder about yourself.

Playboy: Though many critics share the admiration of your fans for the vitality of your work, others have used the following adjectives to describe you as a writer: "undisciplined," "chaotic," "confused," "self-contradictory" and "over-emotional." What's your reply?

Miller: Isn't it enough to *write* books without being obliged to answer for them? It's the function of the critic to criticize. He's like the fifth wheel on a wagon. Oh, well—by conventional standards, I suppose I *am* an undisciplined, chaotic, disorganized writer. But some of us, fortunately, pay no heed to standards. Undoubtedly I'm as muddled as the next man. But look at the great philosophers—are they so clean and clear? Kant—my God, what murky, cloudy thinking that is! Or take Aristotle—I can't read Aristotle, it's a jungle of nonsense to me. I like Plato much better. But I can get lost with Plato, too. I'll tell you, it may be because of my eclecticism that I'm misunderstood. One time I'm talking this way, another time that way. Naturally, I contradict myself now and then. Who doesn't? One would have to be stagnant not to do so. But I contend that I'm always driving at truth. One has to approach reality from

all directions—there's no one way to go at it. The more avenues
you open up, the clearer the ultimate thing should be. I'm anti-
structure, yes. But that's hardly confusion.

Playboy: It's also been said that you suffer from "verbal diar-
rhea," that your "billowing, undisciplined, rough-hewn prose
urgently requires the attention of a sharp blue pencil." What do you
have to say about this?

Miller: I've never pretended to be a careful, inch-by-inch writer,
like Hemingway was—but neither am I one of those careless,
sprawling writers who feel that the slag belongs with the ore, that
it's all one, part and parcel of the same thing. I must confess there's
a great joy, for me, in cutting a thing down, in taking the ax to my
words and destroying what I thought was so wonderful in the heat
of the first writing. You think when you spew the words out that
they're imperishable, and a year later they seem trivial or flat.
The ax-wielding is as much a part of the creative process as the first
volcanic gush. But this editing, at least for me, is not aimed at
achieving flawlessness. I believe that defects in a writer's work, as
in a person's character, are no less important than his virtues.
You need flaws; that's what I'm trying to say. Otherwise you're
a nonentity.

Playboy: Nevertheless, in recent criticism of your work, novelist
Lawrence Durrell, a long-time friend of yours, has taken you to
task for these very flaws—and for excusing them in yourself. Have
his remarks affected the cordiality of your relationship?

Miller: Not at all—as you'd know if you'd read my answer to his
criticism of my later books. You'd see that I took it all in good
part. He could have said much worse than he did, and it wouldn't
have altered my feelings toward him.

Playboy: Which are?

Miller: As a man, I still like and admire him. As a writer, I could
make the same criticism of him that's made of me: that the big
passages, the panoramic frescoes, really grip you—his wonderfully
descriptive purple passages, majestically done, marvelously elaborate
and intricate, which exist in and of themselves—whereas the philosophical sections, presenting his thoughts on art and aesthetics, seem
drab by comparison—at least to me. Durrell, you see, is first and
foremost a poet. He's in love with language itself. Some people find

him too ornate, but I love his excesses—they reveal the artist in him.

Playboy: Which other contemporary writers do you regard as artists?

Miller: I don't think I really keep up, but let me think. O'Casey and Beckett and Ionesco I admire very much. But some of our better-known American playwrights leave me cold. I don't get any kick, any lift out of them. I can't read Nabokov. He's not for me; he's too literary a man, too engrossed in the art of writing—all that display of virtuosity. I do like Kerouac—I think he has a marvelous natural verbal facility, though it could stand a bit of disciplining. Such a wealth of feeling—and when it comes to nature, superb. Burroughs, whom I recognize as a man of talent, great talent, can turn my stomach. It strikes me, however, that he's faithful to the Emersonian idea of autobiography, that he's concerned with putting down only what he has experienced and felt. He's a literary man whose style is unliterary. As for Saul Bellow, I've read only one of his books, *Henderson, the Rain King,* and I must say, I was infatuated with it. I wish I could write something in that vein. For a while I was interested in Ray Bradbury; he seemed to have opened a new vein. But I think he's shot his bolt. There are still startling ideas in his books now and then, wonderful flashes; one senses an inventive mind at work. But it's all in an area that doesn't excite me too much. Science fiction just isn't rich enough.

Playboy: As one whose writing is strongly sexual in flavor, are you as interested in, and influenced by, Freudian psychology as some of the writers you've mentioned?

Miller: When I first read Freud thirty or thirty-five years ago, I found him extremely stimulating. He influenced everybody, myself included. But today, he doesn't interest me at all. I think it's fine for a writer to roam about wherever he wants; anything that's of deep import to an artist must certainly nourish him. But the whole subject of Freudianism and analysis bores me almost as much as talking to analysts, whom I find deadly dull and single-tracked.

Playboy: What's your objection to analysis itself?

Miller: Let's put it this way—the analyst is sitting there as an intermediary, father-confessor, protector; he's there to awaken his patient and give him greater strength to endure whatever he has to endure. Well, I say that experience itself, whatever it be—brutal, sorrowful or whatever—is the only teacher. We don't need priests and we don't need analysts; we don't need mental crutches of any sort. More than anything, what I criticize is their efforts to restore the maladapted person to a society whose way of life *caused* him to be maladapted in the first place. They want us to accept things as they are. But things as they are are wrong.

Playboy: But you've often insisted that people are really self-determined, that it's really a dodge to blame society for our troubles. Isn't that a contradiction of what you've just said?

Miller: It seems contradictory, but to me it isn't. Look, when you develop the proper strength, you can live in *any* society. You can achieve a certain immunity—not a total one, certainly, but enough not to become sick, not to be paralyzed. I say if there's strength to be gotten, where else would you look for it than inside yourself? Now it may be that some of us are doomed, some won't have the strength, and will go down—but that's an inescapable fact of life. Some can rise up to meet it and others can't. But to say that we can catch those who are sick and sinking, and buoy them up through analysis—I don't believe it.

Playboy: You were quoted recently as saying that the American approach to things sexual, particularly in plays, movies and television, is becoming increasingly "cute." Do you regard this trend as psychologically sick—and how significant do you feel it is?

Miller: Of course it's sick—and it could be significant. Cuteness has its part, like anything else, but playing around with sex on this teasing level, the look-but-don't-touch sort of thing, could make the American male perpetually dissatisfied with his wife or girl. It's another version of this phony misleading drive of Americans to coat everything with glamor—creating a glamorous world of illusion and then trying to live in it. It doesn't work. I think the cute approach to sex is about on a par with a cute approach to the atom bomb. But it *is* nice for men to be fussed over and titillated; they need that. It's a part of their basic nature, regardless of the fact that they may be in love with their own wives or girls. Take the geisha in Japan: She is an important part of man's life. American women should be educated in school, taught as the Japanese are taught how to treat a husband or lover. There wouldn't be so many marriages that fail. In the Western world, a couple gets married in romantic mood, but then there's nothing to show them how to go on increasing and nurturing their love. Instead of waiting until they turn out the lights, why not learn how to make a man happy at the dinner table or just sitting about reading? Why don't they wear something flimsy, keep acting out the love role as they did in the beginning? It might make the difference. But it's like churchgoers who run to church—on Sundays and then forget religion the rest of the week.

Playboy: Who do you feel is responsible for this situation?

Miller: I blame most of this unhappy sexual situation on the men. They don't behave as men, as the boss, the dominant head of the family. They allow the women to jockey with them for equality, to become their rivals. This does not make for the ideal sexual climate. In Europe the man is still the boss. He even slaps his woman around a bit, but the woman is happier in this subordinate role.

Playboy: In view of what you indicate is their more feminine, less competitive role, do you feel that European women are more exciting sexually than American women?

Miller: Any *real* woman, European or otherwise, is exciting. Frankly, I know of only one sexual type: Either she has *it* or she doesn't.

Playboy: Will you describe "it"?

Miller: Everyone of any sensitivity knows when he is in the presence of a great person or a saint. The same applies to a woman with *it*. She exudes *it*. She neither shrinks from sex nor juts forward unnaturally when the subject arises. American women seem to have to prove themselves. They wear sex on the surface of their beings like a patina. But the natural ones *feel* it, as a part of their very being. Sophia Loren is an example. She is *living* it. She is all woman. Most of your American sex symbols of the cinema, on the other hand, are just wearing it. It's all on the outside. They feel nothing, really—so neither do you.

Playboy: Would you be willing to tell us what kind of sexual relationship you've found most gratifying—with whatever nationality of woman?

Miller: I prefer to keep that information to myself. It's nobody's business but my own. Even an author has *some* rights! But I will

say that the atmosphere of hazard, peril or danger of embarrassment
is most exciting—the encounter with someone, even a stranger, in an
alleyway, a dark hall or doorway, maybe even a telephone booth.

Playboy: Why?

Miller: Well, I suppose it's because it's the opposite of our
everyday experience. The element of surprise is what makes it so
intriguing—you aren't set, you have no stand one way or the other.
I must amplify: I feel that I'm a man to whom things happen. I seldom
deliberately set out to bring things about. I'm always sort of open
and vulnerable, waiting for something to come about—which
actually *permits* things to happen much more frequently, don't you
see? If I set out to have an experience, a sexual or love experience, it would have a totally different tonality to it, it seems to
me—probably in a lower key.

Playboy: You've said that the "hero" of *Cancer* is a man who
initiates nothing, who merely accepts things as they come to him.
Isn't that a Buddhist view?

Miller: Perhaps. I make no secret of the fact that I have been
much influenced by Taoistic writing and Oriental philosophy in
general. I think we all take from others. I don't think there's such a
thing as an original artist. We all show influences and derivations.
We can't avoid using or being used. When it comes time to express
yourself, what you put forth should be done unconsciously,
without thought of influences. But all this is in your blood already,
in the very stream of your being. I've come to believe that I'm at
my best, I express myself best, when I'm following the philosophy
of the East, but I wouldn't propose it as the one way. I think each one
has to find his own unique route.

Playboy: Does this imply that you incline toward the role of
observer rather than protagonist?

Miller: No. I think the peculiar quality of an artist is that he's
both participant and observer at the same time. He's playing a
dual role always. I mean, I don't go through life as a writer who's
always making notes in a mental diary, though I *am* aware of
making note of things for future use. I can't help it; it's my nature.
But I don't enter into things in a spirit of detached research.
When I participate, I do so as a human being; I'm simply more
aware than most men of what's actually happening.

Playboy: You just referred autobiographically to the role of the "artist." Yet you've called *Tropic of Cancer* "a gob of spit in the face of Art." Do you see any contradiction between this scorn for "Art" and your self-identification as an artist?

Miller: No. I think that only a man who has been steeped in art, who is truly inoculated, as it were, with culture, can see the defect in it. This is a double-edged thing. One has to be an artist in order to speak against art. Coming from a layman, it has no validity. Only someone immersed in art could renounce it. I mean that one should lop off all that is stupid, nonsensical, unimportant—all that goes with capital letters when one invokes the words "Culture" and "Art." We have an analogy in what happened to the philosophy of Zen when it was brought from India to China. What did the Chinese do? They took Buddhism as the Hindus had known it and they lopped off the superstructure; they brought it down to earth and made it viable, livable, I would say. My purpose, when referring to art in this denigrating way, is to bring it closer to life. Art has a tendency to detach itself from life. One has to bring it back again, like a gardener taking care of a plant—cut away the overgrowth, give the roots a chance to breathe.

Playboy: Do you feel that you've done this in your own writing?

Miller: I hope so, in my own small way. What I've strived to do is to get away from the fictive and down to the reality about oneself, embrace every aspect of one's being, look at it all clearly, boldly. That's the whole purpose of writing, isn't it, to reveal as many sides of yourself as possible? Though I've done all sorts of short-term things, books of the moment, offshoots without any consistent note running through them, there has also been the long-term job, the record I want to make of my life, no matter how long it takes or how many volumes. That is a planned work: *The Rosy Crucifixion* is the master title. Though I haven't thought about it every minute, it has always been in the back of my head.

Playboy: When did you decide to write it?

Miller: I laid it out way back in 1927, in about thirty-five pages of telegraphic notes, and I'm still working from them, from the very last pages. *Sexus* and *Plexus* both came out of these notes, and now the concluding volume of *Nexus,* which I've nearly completed.

Playboy: Would you read us a sample of those notes?

Miller: Well, if you insist. Here are a couple of pages I used as raw material in writing *Plexus* and *Nexus*. They begin like this: "L. decides to make puppets and sell them. Also death masks. At dawn I go out and steal milk bottles and rolls that are left in vestibules. Panhandling along Broadway outside the burlesque shows and movies. Incident at Borough Hall when the guy throws money at me in the gutter. I begin to paint the walls myself and hang up crazy charts. S. arrives and looks on, nodding his approval of the disruption. Reminiscences of childhood. Relations with L. are improving. Sleeping three abed. J. now jealous. Working this to death. More gold digging on a grand scale, only now it's a burlesque. The two of them look like freaks. L. hiring herself out for experiments of all kinds. I get the idea of selling my blood. Begin visiting the hospitals. Must eat better food, drink milk, red wine, and so on. The jujitsu expert at Hubert's Cafeteria bringing the rent to us while we are in bed, slipping it under the door. The German savant—a ticket chopper on the elevated station. The two sailors listening in to scenes from the shed outside of L.'s room and freezing to death. Drunks with B., the Cherokee Indian. The night of S.'s birthday. We go out to celebrate, I in a torn khaki shirt. The night club uptown. Drinking everything in sight. Then the line-up and search by thugs. S., in his crazy way, calmly palming off a bad check on them for $125. The scene in the vestibule of cloakroom when the expugilist beats the piss out of the drunken customers. Returning at dawn to find L. sleeping in my place. Dragging her out of the bed by the scalp. Peeing over her on the floor. Then falling asleep in the bathtub, nearly drowned. Return to Paul & Joe's near 14th Street. Waiting at the Bridge Plaza to see if J. is coming over the bridge in a taxi. Finding her home in bed, paralyzed with drink. Next day vomiting begins. Continues for three or four days, night and morning. The story of rape by jujitsu doctor. J.'s explanation. Go in search of wrestling doctor, murder in heart. Returning silently and listening to their conversation on the stairs. Suddenly the explosion in Jersey City and discovery of L. standing on stairs. Last confrontation. Dragging her along in the snow despite protestations and denials. I leave for the West . . ."

Playboy: You seem to have led a rather violent life in those days.

Miller: I was a pretty turbulent character, all right—and not a very agreeable one, either. Though I never failed to make friends, I was always in hot water, always arguing and disputing. I was an obnoxious sort of chap who had to get his ideas across, who was forever buttonholing people and bludgeoning them with words. I made a pest of myself. I was an idealist and a rebel—but an unpleasant one. As I've grown older, I've become even more rebellious—but also more adapted, at least to myself. Maybe I've become more skillful in the art of dealing with people and circumstances, so that I don't blow my top so easily anymore. But I'm still entirely capable of violence. In fact, one fear I have about myself is that I may lose control one day and do something unthinkable. But of course we're *all* incipient criminals. Most of us simply lack the courage to act out our criminal urges. I've been fortunate enough to find an escape valve in writing. I've been able to act out my antisocial urges, stir up trouble, deal out my shocks and jolts on paper; and thanks to the release of all this steam, I've slowly become—well, more human, let's say.

Playboy: Do you find, with your lengthening emotional distance from the early experiences recorded in your notes, that it has become easier to write about them?

Miller: Technically, yes. But with time, of course, everything tends to grow cold. One has to blow on the embers. It's not easy to warm a thing up again, to put yourself back in the old positions, at the emotional pitches you once attained, to re-create the conversations—talk that lasted all night, ten hours, full of fight and struggle, going the whole gamut from personal trivia to literature and history and every damn thing. Today these things are easier to write about, yes, but they're almost impossible to recapture in their pristine fire and substance. You have to fall back on your imagination, to rely on your artistry.

Playboy: But it's been said that in *Sexus* and *Plexus* you seem to show total recall of both emotions and events.

Miller: I may give that illusion, but if you could compare my reconstructions with tape recordings of the original scenes, you'd find a tremendous disparity. Lately I've been inventing more freely than before, but always in conformity with the remembered feel of the thing. I never invent in the sense of disguising or altering: I always want to recapture, but not in the strict photographic-

phonographic sense. Also, of course, I've left a lot out. One can't
put everything in, even if one lives to be a hundred.

Playboy: You've been working on *The Rosy Crucifixion,* on and
off, for some thirty-seven years now. Why has it taken so long?

Miller: Well, you see, the more one writes about oneself, the less
important it all seems. One writes to forget himself, or better
said, to forget *the* self. When I started writing, especially the
Tropics, I thought: No one has suffered as much as I. I had to get
it out—so many volumes, so many millions and millions of words.
And now that it's almost finished, I don't want to write like that
anymore, understand? But I find that I'm caught in my own web.
Now that the *Tropics* are socially acceptable, I've suddenly
become fashionable, and people are hounding me from every direction to translate these books into plays, films, librettos. I can't do
this! I can't change these books into something else. I thought once
I'd finished writing them that that was the end. I wanted to forget
them. But they're coming back to haunt me.

Playboy: Don't you take some comfort in the very fact of this
social acceptability, however belated, and in the royalties you've
been reaping?

Miller: It's sort of amusing, but also it's absurd and a bit of a
headache. You see, in a way it's too late. The money should have
been there in the beginning. Getting it now doesn't alter my life in
the least. I continue to live on very little for myself. My problem
now isn't how to get money, but how not to get too *much* of it. It
frightens me. *Millions,* these movie people talk about! Can you
believe it? Already I've given away to my friends and family over
half of what I've received from *Cancer.* It's just too *much.* Having
too much of anything worries me—especially money. It makes me
uncomfortable. But I have to think of my children. They have to have
their schooling and their living. Nowadays, at least, if they want to
go someplace or do something special they dream up, I can give
them a hundred dollars and it means nothing. But do you know I'm
contributing to *three* families? Me and my divorces. I think I'll
have an aspirin—maybe three. Would you care to join me?

Playboy: No, thanks. But tell us: With all your extracurricular
commitments, how do you find time for writing?

Miller: Good question! The phone calls, the correspondence to

answer, propositions to consider, contracts to decide on! Do you
know it takes me a good four hours a day at least? I have hardly
any time *left* for writing. I should have a secretary. Well, maybe
not, because if I did, naturally I would fall in love with her, and
then I wouldn't get *any* writing done. You see, I couldn't possibly
have an ugly old girl for a secretary, could I? She must be beautiful,
attractive. And there I'd be—again. I fall in love so easily.

Playboy: Still?

Miller: It seems normal to me to fall in love over and over. Is it a
sign of youth or of wisdom? It seems to me that most of us grow
old long before our time. Being in love is the natural condition of
the heart. I'm talking about loving someone *else,* of course, not
yourself. But I was talking about work. The demands are never-
ending. The moment one starts getting big money, he becomes
involved with tax problems, lawyers, people who want money from
you for a thousand causes—especially themselves. You have to
suffer because of it. It's a challenge to your normal way of life.
Time that should be spent working is taken up with all of these
unvital, unpleasant things. I feel sometimes as if I may throw in the
sponge and quit writing entirely.

Playboy: Are you serious?

Miller: Probably not—but if I decided tomorrow to take up some
other pursuit, I'd certainly have no qualms about it. Sometimes I
think it would be lovely to be a gardener or a nurseryman. That way
nobody would get hurt, cheated, deceived or disillusioned; authors aren't the loveliest people in the world, you know. But if I
don't stop writing, at least I want to start having some fun with
it. I'm tired of doing those long, somber, serious things. Why
shouldn't I have some fun now with writing?

Playboy: No reason at all. What sort of thing would you enjoy
writing?

Miller: It happens that I wrote a play a couple of years ago—a
satirical farce called *Just Wild About Harry*—because for thirty
years I'd been wondering if I could write in that form. It was fun.
Now I'm working on another. If I do more plays, they'll continue
in the vein of the farcical, the satirical and the burlesque. I would
like to write what I call pure nonsense. It wouldn't be unintelligible, but it wouldn't pretend to have any profundity or any relation

with actuality; I wouldn't take up "meaty" subjects, social problems and all that. It would be a pure exercise of the imagination and
of my skill, whatever that may be, and an enjoyment of the medium
itself with no ulterior thought whatsoever—perhaps, finally, with no
thought at all. I know I've been called a thoughtless writer, and it
doesn't offend me at all. Perhaps that's the state in which I'm happiest.

Playboy: Will sex be as big a factor in your future writings as it
has been?

Miller: I doubt it. Not because I have lost interest in sex, but
because I have about come to the end of my autobiographical
writing. As I said earlier, it seems to me that people have focused
too strongly on this element in my work: they think it's—how
shall I say it?—the dominant note of my writing because it has the
quality of shock. At least it had for the early readers. Especially
in America, many were too taken aback by the forthrightness of the
Tropics to see in them, as I do, a quality of lyricism. Though it
may sound immodest, I'm forever amazed at the singing passages
in them. They're not always pleasant, of course, but even when
sordid and nihilistic, they are nevertheless poetic. Critics abroad
have always pointed this out. But I think there's a range of
thought and feeling that goes far beyond either of the *Tropics* in
some of my later work—in *The Books in My Life,* for instance,
and such collected works as *The Wisdom of the Heart* and *Sunday
After the War,* in which essays are mingled with stories.

Playboy: Do you consider these your finest works?

Miller: No, *The Colossus of Maroussi* is my own favorite, and I
find it's coming more and more to be accepted by the public. I'd
rather be known in the future by *The Colossus* than by any other
effort. It shows me at my best—a man who's enjoying himself
and appreciative of everything.

Playboy: Was this change in style and attitude from the nihilism
of the *Tropics* the result of a change in your life?

Miller: I would rather think so. One might say it was due to the
feeling of exultation and exaltation that came over me in Greece.
I wrote *Colossus* just after returning to the U.S. I wrote it hot, as
it were.

Playboy: But then you reverted to a more pessimistic tone in *The*

Air-Conditioned Nightmare, a grim chronicle of your disenchantment with America. Why?

Miller: It was the disparity between the two countries. I set out
on a tour of America with hopes that I might write, maybe not an
exalted report, but a book of appreciation of my country after a
long absence. But everywhere I went, I was let down. And I
would be again, I think, if I took another look today. Perhaps even
more so.

Playboy: Why do you take such a dim view of your homeland?

Miller: I've always felt that I'm *in* this country and not *of* it. I
feel little connection with the things around me here. I'm not
interested in political or social movements. I live my own restricted
life, with my friends. What I read about the American way of life,
about what goes on here, fills me with horror and dismay. It's
become even more of an air-conditioned nightmare than it was
when I wrote the books. I'm being corroborated, I feel, by events.

Playboy: How do you mean?

Miller: Well, it seems to me that in the seventy-two years I've
lived, we've advanced—what, half a millimeter? Or have we gone
back a few yards? This is how I look back on what we call our
"progress." However civilized we seem to be, we're still just as
ignorant, stupid, perverse and sadistic as savages. For seventy-two
years I've been waiting to see some breakdown of the artificial
barriers surrounding our educational system, our national borders,
our homes, our inner being—a shattering of the wretched molds
in which we've lived—but it never happens. We have the dynamite
but we don't set it off. I get sick of waiting. Despite the rosy
dreams of the politicians and the so-called intellectuals of today,
we're not going to bring about a better world peaceably and in an
evolutionary manner, through piecemeal improvements; we progress, as we regress, in catastrophic jumps. And when I talk about
the violent, explosive alteration of things, it's a wish as much as a
prediction of future events. To me it means a new chance, a new
birth. I'm tired of history. I want to see everything swept away to
clear the ground for something new. I want to get beyond civilization to what has been called the posthistoric state and see the new
man who will live without all the restrictive, inhibiting barriers
that hedge us in.

Playboy: Do you think this is a realistic hope?

Miller: How can we tell? If we knew what was coming—good or bad—we'd probably give up struggling to achieve it. It's true enough that the evidence of the past gives us little reason to believe that we ever will, for in the unfolding of history, the advances we have made have seemed to me illusory. We relapse time and time again. It can be argued that we always will, that man will always remain basically the same—that he's spiritually incurable. Well, maybe that's true about the majority of mankind, but there have been enough emancipated individuals throughout the course of history— prophets, religious leaders, innovators—to make me believe that we *can* break the old, suffocating molds, that we *can* somehow end forever the vicious and futile cycle of aspiration and disenchantment, transcend the age-old and recurring dilemmas, rid ourselves of the appurtenances of so-called civilization—jump clear of the clockwork, as someone put it. If we can, it's just barely possible that someday what's buried in us and longs to come out will find expression. I can't imagine what the form of that ideal future may take—but it will mean giving egress, however belatedly, to the human spirit.

Playboy: Do you feel that your own career has made any lasting and meaningful contribution toward that end?

Miller: Who could dare to hope for that much? I'd say, undoubtedly, that I have brought about a tangible revolution which has won for English-language authors a certain degree of freedom from censorship—at least temporarily. I wonder, however, now that you put the question, what sort of effect I would *want* to have, were I capable of having one—I mean, in an *everlasting* way. But of course nothing is everlasting, unless it be the endless cycle of creation and destruction on which you and I and each of us, for good or ill, leaves his own unique but infinitesimal mark. We are just men and women, after all. And the lowest is not so different from the highest. To be human, truly human, that is quite enough for me.

Olle Länsberg at Home with Henry Miller

Marianne Ruuth / 1966

From *Idun-Vecko Jorunalen*, 20-3:5 (May 3, 1966), 20–26. Translated by Ulf Kirchdorfer.

Olle Länsberg flew into Los Angeles on a Sunday night, and early Tuesday morning he continued on. Wary, he had refused to be blinded by that Hollywood which is not so much a geographical concept as it is a sea of lights harboring illusions. He had let himself come awash in spotlights, flashes and the glowing compliments of celebrities; he had been swayed by sweet-smelling promises and the one or other dollar-shimmering movie offer; he had brushed up to an Oscar statuette. But all this he had willingly given up for one thing: the opportunity to meet Henry Miller.

This might sound a bit simpler than it was. The veteran of the genre, which without reconsideration is referred to as the sex-novel, has withdrawn into seclusion to his eagle's nest high above the motion picture city, shying away from strangers, interviewers and photographers. "I'm tired of the questions—they are always the same."

He made an unexpected exception with Olle Länsberg when *Idun VJ* called and asked. He promised a short half-hour that turned into two long hours; only a promise of honor to attend the Oscar gala caused Olle Länsberg regretfully to break up their meeting. Because here two friends met, instantly getting along, understanding and liking each other.

It was one of those afternoons in April not even the California tourist brochures can do justice. A salty breeze from the Pacific Ocean down below the hill swept around us as we neared the roomy white house with black shutters in the peaceful-elegant Pacific Palisades. And there stood Henry Miller, the banished, the praised, the damned, the beloved legend. The years (seventy and then some) have sprinkled silver in the rapidly thinning hair, but there is fire in the friendly, sharply intelligent eyes (violets in a rifle muzzle?). An energetic, rail-thin figure in light clothing, a man with an electric mildness surrounding his person.

The miracle happened—as it does sometimes when people meet. Olle Länsberg said afterwards: "There were no barriers to cross. You just stepped right inside the heart."

So came about a special encounter between a pupil and his master. From the beginning, there was warmth, the heart, sympathy, two souls finding each other. It would be injustice not to attempt to render verbatim what they spoke about, in a heated, passionate conversation—an exchange of dialogue in a sort of drama.

Länsberg: There is little need for us two to talk about sex. Because we've accepted it, and like it as one part of everything else.

Miller: I always wanted to write the whole truth about life the way I saw it. About life and death and hunger and hate and sacrifices and the sun and the smut and compassion and flowers and friendship and erotica and love. The *whole* truth about a person—me—of which sex is one part.

Länsberg: I recently read something you said. It had to do with the so-called renaissance of sexuality in modern literature. You said something in the way of "Can't they come up with something new, these young authors?" You've already written about the subject—you've finished the job.

Miller (laughing): Yes, I recall saying something like that. And I meant half of it. Mostly I was dead-tired of being asked the same questions year in and year out . . . But of course I'm also tired of the imitators, those that do what's in. In all areas I'm interested in the person who seeks to do the original, what isn't copied, "his personal truth." . . . Sex is popular today—just look how Miller's books sell, they say. And so they write about sex—but it's a cold, joyless kind of sex. Sex for money, sex without love. They combine the perverse and the sadistic; they make the orgasms bigger and more mechanical. Have they forgotten that sex is joy?

Länsberg: Your accounts of the time you worked in America for the telegraph company—midst people who were bleeding and starving—that's what first appealed to me in your books. One day I was standing in a bookstore. All of a sudden someone was squeezing my hand. It was a woman, maybe 55 years old. "Just keep up the writing, Länsberg," she said. "Because it is the way things are." That kind of recognition, knowing exactly what is meant—that's what your books have given me.

Miller: Many authors today—the French for example—start off somewhere on the Classical heights. They've lost touch with the earth, with the people. If they ever were in touch. You've been poor, you've been down and out, haven't you? Yes, that's what makes you feel. We've lived among people of flesh and blood, who knew they were made of flesh and blood, with a skeleton inside that grew cold, let out piercing screams, drank, made a pig of itself, struggled, hoped, loved and hated.

Länsberg: I've seen the same happen in Sweden. There are many who want to start off as Nobel laureates. I'm glad I wasn't born with a silver spoon in my mouth. That I started out as a laborer—without any schooling.

Miller: How did you get started writing, Olle?

Länsberg: I read. Everything I could get my hands on. Mostly the cheap weeklies. I read them until I was fed up to here with them; then I started to look somewhere else. I was reading and happened to come across a book by Knut Hamsun. He's the one who has taught me the most—some pages I've read several times over.

Miller: Knut Hamsun! He's the one who got me started. I've sat with his books and tried to squeeze the magic out of the pages! Because magic is what it is.

Länsberg: How did you come across him here in the U.S.?

Miller: One of my marriages had just broken up. She was a concert pianist—she gave me lessons until we got married, then they stopped. Finally everything came to a halt. I was also finished—almost. Depressed and tired I got on a train. Alone. Unbearably alone. With nowhere to go. That's when I felt something in my coat pocket. She'd put a little book there. It was Knut Hamsun's *The Hunger*. I started reading and mountains moved. And I who had thought she couldn't read! He made me realize that what I wanted to do was to tell what I was seeing.

Länsberg: Extraordinary—I also discovered Hamsun through *The Hunger*.

Miller: We *do* have some things in common, don't we? Have they also called you all sorts of things—disgusting pornographer or worse? Or are things different in Sweden? Sweden was, after all, one of the first countries to publish me without cutting large chunks of my books.

Länsberg: They've called me all sorts of things—what does it matter? Critics get so upset when *they* don't get to decide whether or not a book becomes a success. They just hate it when the readers themselves get to decide what they think.

Miller: A critic is the author's worst enemy—followed closely by the publisher.

They continued to joke about the problems of the writing profession, every now and then touching on serious issues. Neither tried to impress the other with quoted passages, deep meanings, or difficult vocabulary. About writing and life they had this to say, for example:

Miller: It's important to love what you do, whether it causes notoriety or not.

Länsberg: Your love of humanity always shines through. An author has to like people, has to love even when he undresses and reveals . . . If he doesn't like people, I don't think he is a good author.

Miller: The most important thing for an artist is to fight and overcome his ego and embrace humanity.

Länsberg: What is so exciting to me in *your* writing is that you've had the courage to open up and just let it all flow. Perhaps a passage here and there has overflowed all rules and boundaries—but how beautiful that is! Somebody was needed who had the guts to open up *all the way* so that others after him could at least try . . . Sometimes I think you have an impossible dream—to write a book that won't stay between the covers.

Miller: That's my life. It sometimes runs over.

Länsberg: Just think, if all the passages we cut were the ones we should have allowed to stand!

Miller: I've often neglected to cut, when maybe I should have. But my life hasn't had any passages cut out—I've always lived with the contrasts, contradictions, the illogical. What is important for all of us is to stop fighting so frenetically against everything surrounding us, to stop writhing in hysteria, to start to relax and feel how the shackles fall off, to allow ourselves to be soft-skinned, open for attacks . . . Become skinless, defenseless, allowing it to hurt . . . Nothing is bad—what we think of as misfortune often makes us presentable to the good we otherwise would never have encountered.

Länsberg: We're so afraid. We all want something from others, and have a hard time understanding the simpler truth, which is that we only receive if we give.

Miller: It's fashionable to observe from a distance, not to engage yourself.—Whatever happened to . . . yes, why not, the *worship* of a person you love? A mutual admiration and respect, in which no one dominates the other. Master and slave doesn't hold up between people—or between nations. Who draws the shortest straw—the master or the slave?

Länsberg: Certainly man and woman are different at the bottom of their being; they react differently. . . . A miracle, a wonderfully blinding miracle that we sometimes reach each other.

On the wall over the sofa in the room where he works, Henry Miller has mounted a sort of scribble-board. On it he has written in a firm hand his motto:

"Quando merda tiver valor pobre nasce sem cu," a juicy Portuguese expression, which, much toned down, can be translated as:

"When it rains porridge, the poor have no spoons."

There is much else on this board also, done with a paintbrush or in regular pen, in a moment of insight or inspiration. It is possible to follow a rapid exchange of dialogue taking place here: "Is God a man or a woman? Neither? Both? And what color?" And below, all of a sudden, "Ask him yourself!"

Miller: Life has so many nuances. You're sitting on the toilet and you see a spot on the floor that takes on different shapes. Nature or a face is even more fascinating than a spot of dirt. I started painting in 1928; I didn't think I could paint, but I wanted to try to render what I saw, what one ear was whispering to me.

Länsberg: This is personal, and it's none of my business—but are you working on anything right now?

Miller: In 1927 I used to stay up for 36 or 48 hours at a time and write till my fingers ached, in telegram form, notes about what was happening. Reams of notes, as in seven years of my life—it was

my life. It was a woman. We loved each other and we tortured each
other. She became my wife. We lived on poetic heights, where the
skin burned and became transparent . . . and we lived in the
stench of scum. Sometimes we lived like . . . well, call it a pimp and
his prostitute, if you want. . . . These notes I haven't made use of
yet. Three years ago I began what will be the last book written from
them—work on the book has been interrupted for several reasons.
But I will finish it. Then . . . then I'll write something else. Ninety-
five percent of what I've written has been true, has been about me.
. . . I'm a little tired of Miller now. I'm thinking of trying something
completely different . . . nonsense . . . a la *Alice in Wonderland*
. . . Maybe . . .

*It was time to take leave, and it was difficult to tear oneself away
from the Miller free-state. The two authors embraced spontaneously, and from Olle Länsberg's lips, or rather from the deep
recesses of his heart, came, "FATHER!"*

*We turned our car around and drove toward Hollywood. Some
words of Miller were ringing in our ears:*

*—"We should go naked more often. Naked within. If it gets cold,
we'll have to try to double our love."*

Sex Goes Public: A Talk
with Henry Miller

David Dury / 1966

From *Esquire*, 65 (May 1966), 118–21, 170–72. Reprinted by permission of *Esquire*.

The sexual revolution is over. It ended the day—when four-letter words were used onstage? oral contraception hit the campus? maidens offered up their maidenheads before marriage so their husbands-to-be wouldn't think they were square? heroes of novels were homosexual prostitutes? Well, it happened under our noses, in the full light of day and it is a revolution characterized by the *overt* with nothing unspoken, nothing hidden, in full public view where we watch each other perform and nothing that swings can shock. Even Henry Miller, the Old Man of the Sexual Liberation Front, finds himself, in the interview below, left far behind by the armies of free spirits who once followed him. The salt has lost its savor; bringing us to a moment in sexual history when boredom characterizes the most intimate acts that have thrilled mankind since the beginning of modern times. Sex is an object; the sexy hero, like James Bond, is a collection of posturings living in a world of no human exigency: no marriage, no family, no guilt. He is a machine for pleasure and we watch him fulfilling his sexual ritual only because he promises to introduce a variation that will titillate. He whips himself in a drive for nuance: a seduction with an added dash of sadism, an orgasm just a little bit bigger. And suddenly we sense the strangely familiar current of the sexual activity of the near future:

> "Savage, extreme, rude, cruel, not to trust;
> Enjoy'd no sooner but despised straight;
> Past reason hunted; and no sooner had,
> Past reason hated. . . ."

But, then, Shakespeare lost his cool and we won't do that.
Question: Are you bored with sex?

Answer: One can't get bored with sex. But one is bored with making such a tremendous issue of it. This constant harping on sex all the time is so immature, not just sexually, but socially and politically. It's as though we're a race of adolescents.

Q: But many people would say that you're the one who harps on it in your books.

A: I harped on trying to get at the whole truth of one man: myself. Sex was a big part of that, but no matter how you add it up, in pages or print or words or volumes, it was only a part. It just happened that this was the part that had shock value.

Q: And now you're tired of the shock and the harping?

A: I am absolutely sick of it, and sick of the whole American approach to it, and sick of the way this sexual revolution is going. I'm fed up with the whole thing.

Q: Don't you think that all this talk about sex is at least better than the ignorance and secrecy we used to have?

A: Anything's better than that. There's finally been a tremendous change in our attitudes and America is more daring in the matter of sex and expression about it, therefore more honest, which is all to the good and long overdue. But because in the past we have been so goddamned backward about sex, this revolution is causing sex to become a preoccupation. This I find sad, and even deplorable in many ways. I sometimes wonder if we can even truthfully call it a revolution.

Q: What would you call it?

A: An adolescent rebellion! And one, if I may say, that is going the way of most adolescent rebellions—right into a new *status quo,* a new tyranny, a tyranny of the flesh.

Q: But isn't the usual way out of suppression to go berserk at first and then finally balance out?

A: Yes, but we're far from balanced. Because now you've got the whole *system* getting in on the act. What once was more or less the opposition is finding ways to exploit the sexual revolution by marketing and advertising. After all, this tyranny of the flesh reduces the whole thing to purely material terms, which fits right in with our age-old problem, our exaggerated emphasis on material things. This may have helped our progress in some areas, but it's certainly the source of most of our shortcomings, too, which are unfortunately in crucial areas of the nonmaterial.

Q: So sex becomes a commodity; now that there's more openness.

A: Hell, *people* are becoming commodities, especially women. Sex is the newest status symbol, another asset you need to be sophisticated. I can judge only from my own circumscribed circle, the people I know, what I read, and all the letters and conversations with readers who tell me their most intimate secrets. But I'm sure that by now Americans are probably having more sex than anybody. They're certainly devoting more time to the subject than anywhere I know of. And there's promiscuity everywhere in this country. But I don't sense the passion and vitality of sex. It's not in the air here, as it is, say, in France. Here it's more like everyone's trying to prove a point.

Q: But it's still better than it was in your time, in the Twenties and Thirties, isn't it?

A: There's more quantity, more frequency, sure. Opportunities for sex are so much more at hand than when I was young. Cars, motels, apartments. During my time, the girls were so shut in, and you were always being watched. Now everybody's free about sex, but they're shut in in other ways. In the old days the great difference was that when we were committing these—What are they calling them? Adulteries? Fornications? Illicit-sex? Ridiculous words! When we did it, we did it! We didn't sit around and talk about it first, intellectualize it. There was always pleasure involved. I mean, great fun! For everybody! Joy, do you see? That's the big difference, that element of joy! Joy in sex! You'd have to be a blind man not to see it. In my time, either they weren't having *any* sex because of too much guilt, or they were having wonderfully joyous sex. Now everyone's having sex, the guilty ones probably more than anyone—but it's so joyless, so much of it.

Q: The way you depicted it in your books like *Sexus* and *Capricorn,* was that an accurate picture of the way it was?

A: Sure, but I must say that when I started out and wrote these books which caused such a turmoil about sex, I never thought of myself as an exponent of sex, a sexologist, a professor of that kind of thing, no! With me it was all incidental, like eating and drinking,

but an important part of a much bigger thing, a much bigger
freedom. I don't think it was ever my aim to make sex itself an
important issue. It was always more the *total liberation* of oneself
that I was concerned with, not just sexual liberation alone.

Q: Then do you think this sexual revolution is premature?

A: I don't know about premature, but they can never expect to
be truly free in sex until they've liberated themselves in the larger
perspective. This new standard may be a thrill to some at first, but
in the long run it will be just as insufficient and ruinous as the old
standard. What we never get at is the most important goal in life.
It's what I call spiritual liberation, and that's a religious thing.
Which doesn't have anything to do with churches. It's beyond any
church! At bottom, it's really like awakening in the true sense,
yes, awakening, *spiritual awakening, spiritual liberation!* How can
they so consistently, so completely miss that over and over again?
It reminds me of the famous saying of the Marquis de Sade just
when the Bastille was being torn down and he was being freed at
last, a glorious moment for him, and then he says such a classic
thing—he says, *"Français, encore un tout petit effort. . . ."* Do
you see it? He's saying, "That's fine, Frenchmen, now just one
more little effort!" And so it is with this business of the sexual
revolution, there's one more little effort needed for Americans to
be really free people, and that is *the* effort. Sexual freedom and
the effort toward that should only be one aspect of a movement
toward much larger freedom, to think and act freely and creatively, in every domain! Just as with all the other freedom movements or revolutions, the civil-rights question, the teen-age thing,
the anti-war protests, the academic-freedom fight—all of it is fine
but ultimately pointless if they're not each tied in toward a total
spiritual freedom and awakening.

Q: How do you think we can do that?

A: By concentrating only on the big issues and forgetting all the
petty trivia.

Q: Do you consider sex without love to be harmful?

A: There's nothing wrong with sex without love. But much more
is needed, because just to have a good sex fling isn't enough,
there has to be something more. A man has to fall in love. He has
to want something more of the woman and see more in her than

an object to be used. Though I've talked about sex without love, it never was my thought that this is the supreme goal. In the final analysis, for man or woman, an extended life of loveless sex will be ruinous, it ruins the psychic health.

Q: What exactly do you think men are missing in the way they relate to women sexually now?

A: They're missing a lot of things. For one, there's no adoration for women! Now there's another word I would like to emphasize—*adoration!* Where do we have *any* adoration today in our talk about women and sex? I believe in adoration, not only in relation to women, but in relation to men as well, where the man above you is someone you adore and admire and want to emulate, the adoration for a master. This is completely lost in our society today. Instead of adoration for women, men now seem to be just always on the chase.

Q: Should we be more passive?

A: No, not passive, but receptive. I mean, once the situation presents itself, then one can be the initiator. My approach is to be ready for anything, open to all things, whatever comes along and is meant to be. I believe that when the right thing comes along, whether it's a sex partner or whatever, there's really no struggle, it takes place naturally, and I think this is the wise thing. The only active action one must take is to be ready and put oneself out there in as many times and places as possible, and in the fullest and most honest way possible. Why should you go bucking your head against a wall that's immovable, nine times out of ten, anyway? Why not just wait for that tenth time when the wall crumbles before your eyes the moment you look at it? Beyond that, I don't formulate anything in my head about approaches. I think things would happen to people generally much more often if they adopted this attitude, if they just *let* things happen, instead of having to force them. All sorts of things happen to me, sexually and otherwise.

Q: But that's passivity, isn't it? Things happen *to* you, rather than you *doing* them. Unless you mean that once the wall does crumble or the opportunity without struggle presents itself, then you're a *doer.* Is that it?

A: More or less, and it's also the idea that how often I have sex, or anything else, is unimportant. But when something arises, then it is important and I do become the doer, yes. But in sex, you see, I never have considered myself the Don Juan type I'm made out to be by some people. I think I'm much less so than the average guy. Why, when I hear fellows talk nowadays, old friends from my life and new friends I'm around, hearing what they say and seeing the way they behave, why they're on the make much more than I ever was! It's only because I wrote about it, it's down there in black and white. Actually, I think if anything I was always below today's norm, not oversexed, do you see?

Q: What about the change in the roles of the sexes that is accompanying the changing standards—where the female is gaining more equality and even self-sufficiency? Is this bringing things more in line with your ideals?

A: It should if the woman doesn't become too aggressive, too much of the demanding bitch. If she remains the seductress, all this development could make her that much better *vis-à-vis* the male. I think the woman derives a lot from her submissiveness, but only if she has a lot to give and is giving voluntarily, not because she's dependent or dominated. But the female situation is so complex that she needs to be almost a little bit of each of these things we talk about. Except for the bitch! I mean, it's similar to her having to be mistress, lover, wife, mother, all rolled into one. I can appreciate the woman's role in life and her whole place in the system of things.

Q: And men?

A: Well, the whole thing about male supremacy has always been a myth, an illusion from the start. You might say we possessed the strength to put ourselves in seemingly superior positions, as rulers, and we can dominate in that way. Which is sort of a pseudo-masculinity. But there never were any masters of their own fates anyway. Where in the hell are they, I'd like to know. Even the great heroes of history are rather ridiculous in many ways, aren't they? So this delusion about the almighty male is being shattered now, with the individual becoming so much less important in a worldly way. Which should be another step toward more honesty between the sexes, if the male will face it and concentrate on mastering himself. Anyone who truly knows male and female knows that it's the woman who is always the deciding factor. The man only makes a show. He's a blusterer, but she's really the one who's pulling the strings.

Q: You never did care much for the idea of the dominant male, did you?

A: I never cared for any kind of domination. There's no future in it. You can never really dominate another person, another sex, another country. Who's the worse off, the master or the slave? I say the master. He gets it in the end from the slave, one way or another. Just as man has gotten it from woman, as revenge for subjugating her. She has bent his whole psyche, twisted his outlook on life.

Q: That sounds a little like "momism," doesn't it?

A: Maybe so. Except I think men deserve it. I feel sorry only for later generations who pay for the sins of their forefathers. Your generation, you're innocent, but guilty by inheritance. It's up to you to change it. And for your own good—because a woman can't develop as a person if she's being subjugated. It either saps her, or she wastes too much energy in devious retaliation.

Q: The old pretension that a sexual relationship is supposed to lead to marriage has almost vanished. Is this a healthy sign?

A: Why sure. It always was a very phony terminology anyway. Out of our dictionary of puritanism. I think any of these new tendencies which are leaning toward a more realistic approach to sex or marriage, and to life, are very healthy signs.

Q: How is marriage itself being affected by these changes in our sexual mores?

A: Marriage looks like a lost cause. I suppose marriage as an institution has its own *raison d'être,* but I don't feel it belongs with people who know themselves, who are perfectly mature. They don't need to go through the ceremony in the first place, religious or civil. And even though a lot of people aren't mature, I think the conventional form of marriage probably just helps them stay immature. The basis for marriage should not be what the clergy wants, this immature myth of eternal love and the phony vow of the everlasting; *or* what the state wants, the legal contract and all of its ramifications. We're bound to it now because of these legal considerations of property and child support, but that should be taken care of without legalizing the union itself.

Q: Then you approve of the growing trend in living together as husband and wife without going through the legal proceedings, at least not until there are children involved?

A: Oh, yes. They don't have to wait for any revolution or legislation to change the laws. People are breaking laws in all directions, wherever they can get away with it. Many of our laws long have been obsolete and ridiculous. Intelligent people don't regulate their lives by outmoded laws. After all, if we try to define what a real marriage is, isn't it basically a completely voluntary union? If it's real, there should be no need to enforce it. If the union has to be legally enforced, then there never was a marriage in the real sense. Marriages are made in heaven, and they are unmade in heaven, and then they are over! They last only as long as there is beauty in them, a validity and a reality to them. The important consideration should be to see that the children are taken care of. There's less need now for marriage than ever, and the family itself is so broken, practically disintegrated as an institution. But the adult problems are nothing compared to the damage being done to children. It's sad! So sad that it gets to be laughable when you read all these pompous articles by sociologists and child psychiatrists saying that what children need is love! That's wonderful, but how are they going to get it from these imbeciles who are their parents, who don't even know the meaning of the word love, who don't show any love, even to each other, or to mankind in general. Whether the family stays together or not, the children are still suffering. More true attention should be devoted to them. So it's a great big question, but again it brings us back to this problem of spiritual lethargy.

Q: Yes, but I was wondering why you ever found it necessary to become legally married four times yourself? Was it to please the women, to conform at the time, or for your own security in the relationship?

A: Oh, god, that's a funny one, isn't it? I suppose it was a little of all of that. Different things in each of the four. And children, too.

Q: Do you think that your four marriages were failures?

A: I suppose insofar as any attempt at an everlasting marriage is a failure, then they were failures. But I don't think of them that

way. If failures in any sense, you see, they were very fruitful
failures. . . . The idea of any permanence is an absurd illusion.
Change is the most permanent thing you can say about the whole
universe. So why should we try to fix things? A thing is as good
as long as it lasts. I mean, what is our value? Growth, right? Well,
does permanence stimulate growth? I doubt it, except perhaps in
rare cases where the husband and wife are growing together at the
same rate. On the other hand, I think we are inclined to demand too
much from marriage sometimes, as well as too much from everything else. We have to be more realistic and less idealistic. A great
mishap for Americans is this idealism that rules them, the fantastic
idea that everything must always be the best, the most, the
greatest, the highest, the most spectacular. I don't mean you should
resign yourself to an irreparably bad situation, but this idealism
of ours causes trouble on every side, in all relationships, asking for
the impossible, instead of trying to do something with what is in
hand, if you can. If you can't, then fine, move on to that unknown
something better around the corner—but try first!

Q: Some people say one way to try is with this new wife-
swapping idea, the switch clubs. How does that strike you?

A: It seems to me that if I were involved with a woman, deeply
involved, I wouldn't be very much in favor of that. That would be
my first reaction. But there's another side, of course. Where there
is a good marital relationship, but it's cooling off sexually and they
want to stimulate it; then this swapping might be a very good thing.
Except that again it smacks a little of a commodity being ex-
changed, doesn't it? And anything that reduces a human being to a
commodity, well, what could be worse?

Q: Do you think the erotic content of your books still speaks to
young people?

A: I think there will always be a response from young people
because the books are new to them; each new crop of youngsters
coming up gets the impact fresh.

Q: Do you still get any responses like the violent old pornography charges?

A: Well, you know, we talk about the revolution being established, but it is only because a relatively small vanguard segment is
establishing it. And the vast middle section of people, the apathetic

and disinterested ones, they aren't opposing it. But there's always the fearful maniacs who oppose anything they consider radical.

Q: How do you feel about the way the sexual revolution is being reflected in the arts, in novels, in movies, the theatre?

A: My impression is that there's a great deal more pornography today . . . and a great deal less obscenity. Pornography is the round about, a leering or lecherous disguise which only adds to the mark: but obscenity—even though it may offend because of its frankness—is forthright, the whole truth, coming out with it cold, shocking if necessary. Obscenity is cleansing, because whenever a taboo is broken, something vitalizing happens, another step toward greater truth and honesty and openness. But pornography exploits the taboo and just serves to reinforce it.

Q: And there's more of the latter?

A: That's the way it looks to me. There also seems to be a lot of cuteness about sex in all the arts too. This might be amusing in a sexually healthy society, but in one that's still basically sick, it's repulsive. The only forthrightness I've seen is devoted to all these perverse and sadistic books and films and plays. They're being fairly straightforward in what they're doing, these more abnormal people. But what are they doing? They're dealing with a very limited area, you know, perversions and dope and all the rest of it. I'm not condemning them. I was just never interested in perversion or sadism of any kind. We're just different types, myself I mean, and someone like Burroughs or Genet.

Q: Do you see any hope on the literary horizon then, either in sex or the spiritual liberation you speak of?

A: No, I sure don't. Too much is derivative. There's nothing new being said. It's kind of a masturbation: they're not going beyond what has already been done. A few writers broke the ice, giving today's writers the liberty to express themselves. But they're not doing anything new with this liberty. They should be finding new liberations in a thousand different ways, new ways! What's the good of writing more sex novels? They have their place, and always will. But to do it because it's the thing to do, it's the fashion, it's the mode—I deplore that.

More than anything else, I'd like to see someone throw a bomb in the spiritual realm! Open us up that way! Yes! There you are!

That's what's needed now, a spiritual explosion! We don't need to read any more about sex! We're already surfeited with this. The sexual revolution is a *fait accompli,* an accomplished thing. We're not going to retrogress. . . . The point is, there are grandiose problems to be solved, and to be written about, instead of continually writing either about sex or about sadism and masochism and spiritual meanness. Let's tackle the new things! Let's quit telling sad old stories or merely entertaining one another. Let's get going! . . . Though I keep reading and hearing about new talents, who is there on the horizon? Everything seems so childish. Even in magazines, for example, one feels insulted by this "girlie" approach, the nudes they display, children, one-dimensional playthings, mannequins, beautiful and well appointed, but I don't think they're erotic at all, except maybe for teenagers. And the other crap, the stories, the cartoons, this sex-as-a-commodity idea we talked about, I think it's more for a twelve-year-old. Once in a while there's some worthy editorial writing, but the bulk of even the most sophisticated magazines of this type is pretty shallow. Some say my female characters weren't fully depicted; well, look at *their* depiction of women, purely physical, and they're not supposed to be just picture magazines, so that's no excuse. That's a reverse sort of puritanism, isn't it? Glorifying the female body, but ignoring or denying her as a person. The whole peep-show approach is meant for adolescents from sixteen to sixty, I think. But it's very revelatory. Their attitude is true to the contemporary adolescent reality all around us. Because we aren't mature, the audience isn't mature, so the product is immature. It's too bad publishers can lead, instead of following like this. But of course when we talk about better approaches, there are always the obstacles that have to be torn down first, the tested interests, the bourgeoisie, the church.

Q: How would you compare the *cool sex* of today's youth with the *metaphysical sex* you talked about so often in your books?

A: I must tell you that the word *cool* is a word I don't like. To play it cool, to be cool, to cool it. The use of that word goes against me. It already has in it the opposite of passion. It means cunning, wise, clever, detached—above all, detached! I'm all for attachment, involvement . . . and the misery resulting from it.

Q: How about all these dance crazes—frug, watusi, jerk?

A: What I call the nonsexual dances, where you stand apart and gyrate, or masturbate. This to me is a passing phenomenon. I only feel sorry that they're dancing apart. Savages can do it wonderfully, but savages make it very sexual. Whereas here it seems just athletic, gymnastics, you don't feel anything erotic. And it seems so narcissistic and egocentric in a bad sort of way. It's like the atom splitting, a break in the polarity; instead of coming together, they're going apart. It's just more evidence of isolation and alienation. In my time, dancing was what you might call a good excuse for sex with your clothes on, that's what dancing was then! The great dance halls on Broadway—O my God!—the lights were dim, the bands were marvelous. And that's all anybody was doing then, this true sex dance, the element of sex was the strongest part of it. Now dancing is almost asexual, it's so palsy-walsy. I've watched my kids doing it. Two men could be dancing these things.

Q: How have you raised your kids? . . . If you forced some moral code on them, they'd just waste a lot of time rebelling against it, is that it?

A: Yes, probably so. I like to keep it as natural as possible in such an unnatural world as this is.

Q: You don't feel as if you've ever given them any guidance about good and bad?

A: Not much. I've never had to. They live their lives and I watch them. Now they're teen-agers, caught up in this sexual revolution themselves. And they're not doing too badly. The only kind of training I ever consciously set out to give them is to awaken them to spiritual values, to think more clearly, to think above all the petty issues of the day—that's what I call most of these problems we're fighting about today, petty problems, ignoble ones! I try to get them to think about life itself.

Q: What about when they come to you with questions?

A: I don't advise, unless I am asked a lot of serious questions or one very blunt direct question. Then I only say, this is what I think, or, this is what I would do, this is the way I think it should be done, or how life should be approached. But it's not necessarily saying that you have to accept what I say as the final answer. I feel that people have to find their own answers anyway.

Henry Miller's Real Woman
David Dury / 1966

From Mademoiselle, 64 (December 1966), 90–91, 150–51.

Henry Miller has become famous for, and been accused of, many diverse tendencies with respect to women. Sympathy and understanding have never been foremost among these.

He has been charged with misogyny and masochism. He has been said to exploit women sexually and to ridicule them savagely. His concentration on mammae, genitalia, and glutei has been called a denial of the woman as a person, which, says one critic, is ironically consistent with the Puritan tradition. His frantic bouts of transitory copulation have been defined by other commentators as his failure to find any deep, warm, and lasting communion with a female.

As Miller's neighbor in West Los Angeles, where he lives now in a Pacific Palisades town house with his two teen-agers, my getting to know him over the last few years has naturally involved many long conversations about everything from astrology to French food. But we never seemed to get around to any real revelations about his actual feelings toward a central aspect of his life and work: women.

Then finally, after a dinner with my new bride and me at our Malibu apartment not long ago, Miller turned his white-fringed, monkish head toward my ear, and startled me by whispering with the most serious intent:

"You know . . . this woman could be your salvation!"

That Henry Miller would think of any woman in such revered terms was an immediate surprise. Sensing my confusion, he reached across the table to grasp my wrist and begin an all-night conversation that would reveal many little-known dimensions of himself. Filled with the intimate assurance of wisdom gained from experience, he explained:

For a young man like you, just starting out, trying to be creative and all—there couldn't be anything better than a real woman, an all-woman woman, one who really has IT, you know, a woman who exudes the life-force with obvious warmth and feeling, the true

earth-mother with a romantic spirit, not a shallow, painted-on
glamor girl.

*You mean to tell me that you, Henry Miller, think of a woman as
an "earth-mother"?*
Sure, what's wrong with being mothered? I spoke of this in a
piece I did about love a while back [MLLE, January 1964]. What's
a woman's value, if it isn't a force tying men to life, inspiring them
to be vital and creative, soothing them when they come home, as
they often do, with their tails between their legs? There's something
ridiculous about the way so many pompous men regard women as
helpless things who need protection from the world. A real woman
needs no protection. She doesn't live in a man's shadow. She
turns on the light. And having such an all-woman woman can make
a life-or-death difference in the way a man lives.

*But I never thought you would think of a woman as being
so important.*
Why, sure! Why not? It's like a fact of nature. Underneath it all,
the woman is in control, or can be, in a mystical or spiritual
sense. After all, in the final analysis, it's the woman who picks and
chooses. She just sits back, watching the show being put on for her
benefit by men, and then she chooses her victim.

Her victim?
Yes, well, with quotes on, you know, facetiously.

*But that idea—man as "victim"—that sounds like the misogyny
which the critics always try to pin on you. And if you really think of
women as victimizers, your incessant involvement with them would
support the masochism charges, too, wouldn't it?*
I suppose so. Masochism, misogyny—there's a little of both in all
of us, isn't there? And sadism, too, eh? I remember that as I
wrote about all the suffering, or what I thought was such tremendous suffering, which I had endured at the hands of people and
the world and whatnot, I was also struck by all the hurt that I had
inflicted. Before a person really wakes up spiritually, really gets
with it, expands himself through liberation, he is so taut and tense
that he has all these destructive traits running through his personality. The one big masochistic trait that I see in myself is that I

know I can never give a woman some of the things she usually demands; so, *I* always end up getting burned. But even knowing this, I can't stay away from them.

You've written before about this inability to give a woman some of the things she wants. What do you mean?

Oh, the main thing is the fact that women are so inclined to demand proof. They say: *Prove* to me that you love me. Well, this throws me completely. I've never been one to prove or disprove things—be it love or anything else. For me, things are either obvious or entirely beyond any rational justification. It's a rare woman who will take the time to understand that idea in the first place. They have a hard time tolerating this basically flexible quality of mine; it's something that most men hide behind their authoritarian veneer. But I refuse to hide it. And so, as I always explain, my attitude is often a combination of strength and weakness, and my answers are often yes-no, instead of either-or. I see both sides of everything and find myself unable to take the didactic stands they seem to want. And so women often consider these incorrigible aspects of my behavior as sadistic.

You're describing a pretty basic conflict between the sexes, aren't you?

Of course. It's always been with us and still is—beneath the thin little role-playing façades men and women think they have to put on to gain each other's acceptance. As I've said before, and will say again even at the risk of repeating myself, basically men are obsessed with truth, but women demand that men compromise this or play games with it. Because women, you see, are obsessed with life. A woman will go to any extreme of untruth in the name of life—and good for her! She simply does not possess the male penchant for truth. For her, life equals love and vitality, not truth. But I'm not saying that this makes women evil.

Just as women demand from men the didacticism that any real truth seeker could never have, so also men try to impose unnatural compromises on women. Men have long been, and still are, committing much more terrible atrocities and wars in the name of one would-be truth or another than women have ever thought about committing in the name of life. But the big difference I see is that

a woman dedicates herself completely to love, while a man always
reserves a certain facet of himself—that part which his ego
pretends must deal with the world. Males and females merely have
different angles of approach—which is the *real* beauty of the
"delicious difference," if only we could learn to accept and appreciate this, instead of each sex trying to make the other like itself.

*You're now beginning to sound less and less like the misogynist
you say you're not.*

I should hope so. All that's just because I've been so critical of
women, anyway. Of my mother, my wife, the dumb dames I've run
across. I know a bitch when I see one, and I call her by her right
name. But obviously I have no misogynistic feelings in the true
sense. That's absurd! I've always spoken out about my dream for a
better woman, just as I have about my dream for a better man.

*Is your "better-woman" dream still what you call the all-woman
woman?*

Yes. Yes!

*Do you think she will try to be independent and strive for equality,
as most enlightened and emancipated women seem to be doing
nowadays?*

Why, sure, up to a point. The all-woman woman would draw the
line where that involves taking on the male role, becoming the
aggressor. These aggressive females, particularly the American
type, aren't improving their situation vis-à-vis the male. The idea
that women are getting more self-developed is good, because they
can be that much more of a comfort and inspiration to a man that
way—or even to the world, if they happen to have the capacity for
some kind of worldly life's work. But I am sincerely convinced
that a woman's greatest reward comes from the role of—what shall
we call it?—stimulator and comforter. Now, if she takes the
greater independence and equality necessary for her own development, and becomes masculinized by it, then she is the tragic
loser, as much or more than the man. She loses her powers as
seductress when she becomes masculinized. And I do still believe
deeply that woman has got to be the seducer. That's the other side
of her role. She's best when she's that way. And it's also best for
the man. It brings out all that is masculine in him.

But isn't it quite possible that independence and equality could make her a better seductress?

Yes, it really should. But if it makes her equally aggressive in the male sense, instead of truly seductive, then it will be like two machines coming together . . . put a coin in the slot and bang! bang! You see? The poetic prelude and the art of it all will be gone. Just get it over with, bim-bam! I still believe a man really wants to woo a woman. It gives him great satisfaction, don't you think?

Sure, provided she's worth wooing, but so often—

That's virtually an archaic word nowadays, isn't it? To woo. It'll be a misfortune if that's lost in all these changing roles.

Many people think women are losing their old qualities of help-lessness and submissiveness. How do you think this will affect wooing?

It should be good, shouldn't it? After all, there will be more to it if the woman is on her own two feet. It will be more of a challenge to the male. She will be more attractive, and he'll want to woo her all the more. It's much more exciting to woo a woman who really is something than one who is just a helpless nothing.

You mean you'd like to see an end to the submissive woman?

No, wait a moment! It's good for a woman to be submissive, but not the way the beach down there submits to the waves, being moulded by them. No. More like the way the sea gives life to all the things that live in it and spring from it. Now, if a woman becomes more of a person, as we've been saying she should, then she'll have that much more to give, won't she? She should only be submissive insofar as she's receptive and responsive and giving. That's where her real happiness comes from.

Yes, but isn't there a danger she'll get so involved in being her own person that she won't be receptive?

No, not a true woman. She'll never become so involved in herself that she can't respond and give. I believe this kind of submissive-ness is the greatest quality in true woman. Obviously, she can hold a man better with this than she can if she's a demanding bitch. The important thing is not so much giving of her time and attention, but giving stimulation by giving truly of her*self*. Either way, it would

seem that outwardly the man is getting a good break, being waited
on or being stimulated. But what it does to the woman is much more
important and beneficial. It's very much like, say, the attitude the
Hindus have toward the beggar. Why do they permit public begging,
even encourage it, while we are trying to eliminate such things all
the time, make them unseen with welfare programs? It's for the
benefit of the giver! The Hindus understand that. It opens up
his heart.

And so when a woman gives herself completely in this way, in
the kind of submissiveness I've been talking about, she's inflating
her own heart and spirit, and she's going to win more from that man
than the woman who is demanding everything.

The demanding one is the opposite. She wants everything but
really gives little in return for it, though she might try to make it
appear she's giving, which to her means giving up, sacrificing, you
see? I would say that's the American type, more than any other
in the world. If these American women could pick up some of the
best qualities of Oriental women—not the overly slavish aspects, but
the abilities they have to please the man—we could have the perfect
woman in America. The Oriental female knows how to make a
man feel like a lord, and the American male knows how to make a
woman feel like a queen—if she's worthy of it. That's how you have
a wonderful relationship. That's how it should be, the man treated
as a lord and the woman as a queen. Ideal!

But this "true woman" is so rare. We usually have to choose
between the thinking type who's pretty unyielding otherwise, or
the submissive one, who doesn't offer much of a full personality to
relate to.

Yes, I know, and I would say that those who desire the thinking
woman have a healthier, and more mature attitude, and a real
appreciation of the full woman. And, in the long run, she'll unbend.
But I doubt if that's a very common attitude, the idea of valuing
a woman's mind, relating to her full personality. Most men still like
to think they're ruling over their women, because the men themselves aren't mature yet, which obviously isn't good, either. But
my main caution about a man being attracted only to a thinking
woman is the danger of the relationship becoming too cerebral, too

calculated, too analytical, which can destroy the balance between thought and feeling and sensuality. If this happens, you run the risk of losing the elements of passion and of adoration, and the honest, spontaneous kind of giving.

Well, what about the men who don't want their women to be so giving?

The bastard who wouldn't be able to accept this gift of the woman—he's a worthless individual in my mind. Worse than a miserly man is the one who cannot accept generosity when it's given him. And we know that type in this country, the materialistic capitalist, who wants tit for tat all the time, both ways. The type I'd like to see is the man who will give everything, and who'll take anything that's given him, and do them both in the same spirit. That's a bigger thing.

But some men feel that submissiveness isn't really a gift, that actually it's more of a burden than a blessing.

My vision of this romantically submissive woman is not some weak, helpless, leaning thing. Sure, a man would find that unappealing and reject it. I'm talking about true giving, the giving of the self. If he can't accept that, then he has a miserly soul.

What about mutual need and reciprocity? Maybe he just doesn't want whatever she's giving.

Well, we're assuming that her gift is something, not nothing, and that there's a strong basic attraction or love to begin with. If he doesn't want what she's giving, then why is he with her?

Maybe it was mutual attraction at first, but then things changed.

Then it's up to both parties to try to restore the situation somehow—if they can. And if not, well, it was good for a while. Be thankful for that, not bitter. It can't last forever! But generally speaking, there is a terrible lack of gratitude today, which really lies in the heart, doesn't it?

The sense of grace, one of the biggest words in the Christian religion—but like the rest of it, worthless and useless today—is almost totally dormant. And isn't this what we have to learn, in relation to all these things we speak of, to have a sense of grace, learn how to accept from the fates the grace that comes to us? And

it does come. Every day, some grace comes to everyone, but it
goes unrecognized and unaccepted and, worst of all, unappreciated.

It all has to do with littleness or bigness of the heart, of the mind,
of the outlook on the world. We're talking about love and women.
That's only part and parcel of a greater problem: *the whole attitude
toward life!* And when that attitude is bad—as it is now—when
it's at its most ignoble, then every aspect of life is going to be
diminished and denied and crucified and perverted. It's all tied up
with the whole plexus of things. In all these things we speak of
specifically—each one is only an aspect—we've got to learn to be
more accepting and less demanding.

*What about the man with the roving eye? That's pretty hard for
most women to accept.*

It's true that we do have a tendency to turn our eyes, even when
we have the most wonderful woman by our side. Sure, a man
does that. He should! The whole male instinct is to do that. But
there's got to be some compromise and reconciliation, you could
say, between his instincts and his understanding, his higher nature.
With the right man and the right woman, those little sallies won't
disrupt anything. When everything's right between two people, an
awful lot of latitude is possible. You don't necessarily have to
practice it, but it has to be there in spirit.

If a relationship is bad, you have to alter whatever is making it
that way. It's a creative task, the responsibility of both parties.
And then, too, a man must evaluate, think in terms of what is best:
maintaining this relationship he has, or finding a still more ideal one.
This is good, isn't it, like self-improvement? Improving one's lot in
life is a sign of health and growth. But, we've got to be careful about
always demanding some nonexistent perfection and learn instead to
appreciate, to enhance what is in hand. There is no excuse for the
indifference we see in so many relationships today.

*Even though women are so much more free and open now, the
indifference thing seems to be growing. Is this because the lure and
peril of the forbidden, which you've always had in your books, is
gone? Because women are today more sexually accessible?*

I suppose that would be one reason, although I think it only
applies to certain types, say the smugly stuffy middle class. There,

it's terribly true about the growing indifference. But I don't think it's true for the whole male population. You can be damned sure of that.

Still, the fact that so much indifference does exist says something about the inauthentic way many Americans are brought up to relate to love and sex. Now that it's more acceptable, the kick is gone. Again, they're missing the whole point, aren't they? Whether it's the kick of this forbidden thing, the drive to conquer, or the new materialistic compulsion to acquire sex as another asset, to possess it, to GET it! It'll all lead to indifference in the long run, if authenticity doesn't take over. And this indifference proves that men have to relate to their sexual partners more truly as women, as people, if they are to be stimulating.

What about the shattering of the myth of all-powerful, authoritarian male supremacy? This should affect the way women think about men, shouldn't it?

Certainly. Women believed in this male myth, too, didn't they? And males tried to prolong the myth as long as they could to impress the females. But now women can see that there isn't anything like the all-powerful father figure anywhere—at home with Daddy, or in bed with husband, or anywhere. We're all just aspects of this over-all cosmic picture. Our value lies in what's inside, and what we can creatively bring out from within. And woman, being more of a biological creature, living more on instinct and intuition than a man, is thrown off balance by all this modern illusion-shattering. She's going to have to assert herself now as an entity in herself, as, let's say, a biological specimen, too. The race is in *her* hands, not in men's.

When you stop and think about all this male-dominating business, the male towering over the submissive woman in the novels of certain periods and all around you in your own childhood, that submissive, helpless creature got her way in many ways, didn't she? Subtle, underhanded ways. But I don't think anyone can completely dominate another person, nor can one sex—or one country!—dominate another. Marriage is a two-part harmony, not a ruler and a subject.

*Do you think the current trend toward cohabitation, making
marriage more of a voluntary union and less of a legal one, is a
step toward this harmony?*

Well, that's a hard one to prophesy about. Possibly so. But while
we can see this problem of stagnancy in marriage very clearly
because it's before us, when we take a step to solve it we don't
know for sure what new problem will be contained in our solution.
It's all part of a very much bigger problem.

*Women seem to like living with a man for the first year or so, but
then, if you're going to go on from there together, they get more
anxious to legalize it, right?*

Of course, because women end up with the children, which is a
good enough reason to feel that way. After all, the children should
be the main concern here.

*No, even without considering children, I don't know many women
who would go for it beyond a couple of years without getting the
itch for a license.*

Women tend to be more conservative and, therefore, much more
interested in a lasting arrangement, even if it's only an illusion.
Legal marriage gives them this illusion, and until women become
truly self-developed and independent, until they have better legal
protection for child support without legalizing the union itself, they
are always going to want it. Also, the whole concept of marriage
and family is still wrapped up in our seemingly phony capitalistic
structure. That's the reason we're still operating in so many
outmoded ways, with all the pretense and hypocrisy and misplaced
values.

Capitalism will put up one hell of a fight before it acquiesces to
socialism or some new kind of social reform we haven't thought
of yet. Despite the fact that something new is needed, something
that would be best for all the people, capitalism will resist, just as
the rigidity of outmoded communism in Russia will do likewise.
And as long as this resistance by such a controlling force remains,
all the other obsolete facets that go with it will hang around long
beyond their usefulness.

*You've said before that people should abandon the myth of
permanence in marriage and just be able to enjoy it for as long as it*

*lasts. But don't you think many people have trouble doing this
because of guilt when the breakup comes?*
Isn't that just another hangover from the idea of a heavenly,
everlasting union? It's the guilt coming from that. If there were
an absolute faith that time didn't matter, and the cause of the
breakup didn't matter, and the only important thing was that you no
longer wanted to be together as man and wife, and if you could then
part in that way but still remain good friends, maybe even sexual
friends, wouldn't a lot of these things dissolve into thin air?

*Yes, but the breakups are hardly ever mutual. They're usually
one-sided. One is dissatisfied, then the other one feels rejected, often
bitter and hostile—which makes the initiator of the breakup feel
guilty, as well as harassed, right?*
The bitterness and hostility are very rarely justified or necessary.
They certainly don't serve any kind of constructive purpose! But
you cannot eliminate sorrow and grief. And yet, regardless of that,
you don't have to be put on the crucifix of an everlasting marriage.
No one does. There'll always be pain and anguish in human relations, because people don't behave the way other people expect
them to. But they shouldn't be expected to meet the other's demands. And if everyone doesn't get what he wants, it's up to him
to grin and bear it, bear the suffering, but smile, and not be hostile
about it. Men suffer this way every bit as much as women. There
may be a woman we want, we think we have to have. And we don't
get her. So we suffer. But let's not be children about it, let's be
mature men or women.
I think it's time we learned to let things come and go as they will,
without being so clenching and forceful and possessive, without
having childish tantrums or hostility, or feeling, "I've been victim-
ized." Let life flow! People need a larger *raison d'être* than just
their love relationship, anyway. Something they're doing together—
or even separately—but some worthwhile, engrossing pursuit
they can both share in some way, even if it's only in conversation.
When you feel that "my whole life revolves around this man or
woman," it's very nice, except that it's invariably followed by
"therefore, he or she had damn well better behave the way I demand,
or my whole world will fall apart and I myself will be annihilated as

a person." This is what causes the destructive hostility when the breakup occurs.

You say that, but in much of Sexus, *especially the end, you were displaying many of these destructive tendencies. You were seemingly destroyed as a person by Mona, because she evidently wanted to leave you and take up with a lesbian.*

Yes, I suppose so. My grief and disappointment were genuine, but I overreacted to the consequences in a sort of self-defeating, immature way, perhaps. But still not hostile, you see? Maybe the intense need for someone we're involved with is just a human thing we'll never change—and maybe shouldn't—but hostility must be eliminated.

With me, in that *Sexus* situation you mention, well, I picked myself up and outgrew it, didn't I? I overcame it quickly enough, by saying, "Listen! I am a person in my own right. I am going to say the hell with this whole mess, this whole country which has been so oppressive to me in so many ways, for so many years, and go to Paris and become myself, concentrate on *becoming,* and write it down for others and myself to see." That's what I did: I wrote *Tropic of Cancer.* And then all the other books went counterclockwise from there. Back over all the pain and mistakes, the discoveries and adventures—and joys!—in retrospect. But we all fall into the trap of outraged hostility sometimes, don't we? It's very bad for us, and for the one we love . . . and for love itself.

Many critics have chastised you for never portraying love itself in your books.

Sure they have. And these are almost always the ones who are criticizing just one book, not the whole of my work. It's all right if they want to say that about one book, wherever it applies, but in saying Henry Miller is all negative and never shows any love, they display their ignorance.

Critics are just people, after all. They criticize, because you didn't write the kind of book *they* wanted. It wasn't like Flaubert or Tolstoy or whoever is their favorite. The characters don't evolve, or whatever it is they say. No, of course they don't, it was all written *en passant,* so to speak. But other critics rave because you wrote *just* the kind of book they wanted. So what does it matter?

I don't write for the critics. I write for myself and the reader, whoever he or she may be.

As for love, well, this is something almost sacred to me. I don't have to explain everything. A thing of beauty sometimes is so perfect and complete that you don't have to write about it. In the autobiographical novels, I was more interested in showing the scoundrel in myself than the good side, more interested in misfortune. Maybe I went a little overboard in that way. But often I think we can learn more about God by studying the work of the devil, and more interestingly, too, I might add.

The main thing with love, as any woman will tell you, is to experience it . . . and the greatest contribution literature can make is to free people sufficiently so that they are able to love!

Henry Miller: A World of Joy

Sandra Hochman / 1968

From *The New York Times,* 118 (November 3, 1968), II 33.
Copyright © 1968 by the New York Times Company. Reprinted
by permission.

The house that he lives in is tucked away on a quiet street in a
suburb of Los Angeles. It is a fairly large white house but not
very different from the other houses on the block. One enters the
house and suddenly it is as if one has entered an enchanted world
of color, joy and imagination. A house that exists at the end of a
rainbow—rooms filled with paintings, watercolors, books, graffiti.
The feeling that one has in the center of this house is one of
exuberance and love of life.

Henry Miller enters the living room. He is 77 by the commonplace
standard of age, but he has nothing to do with these mortal
markings of time. He is ageless. His step is bouncy and young, he
resembles a pixie, a wizard, a sage. I look at his face—his eyes are
glittering and clear—they are slanted upwards and might be the
eyes of an Oriental emperor—his mouth curves easily into a smile
that is Chaplinesque—he is both a visionary and a clown—his head
is bald—and he touches his head often—he speaks quickly and
listens carefully. His step is light and boyish.

Quickly he passes over introductions and begins to ask me about
my poetry. He asks many questions. There is nothing that he has
to hide and he assumes that no one else has anything to hide either.
He has a quality that is so often found in children: an openness
that does not judge, a delight in meeting someone that he has not
known before.

On a table in the living room is a small black Chinese cap. He
holds the cap in his hands now, explaining that he always wears this
cap after swimming, to keep his head warm. I can just imagine him
wearing the cap—walking around the house like an ancient Chinese sage. He sees that I am looking at a group of his watercolors
hanging on a wall and he says, proudly, "Those are my insomnia

paintings. I just couldn't sleep. You see, I had sprained my toe. My
little baby toe and every night, just like a clock, my little toe sent
me a message and woke me up. So, every night I awoke to paint
these pictures. It all came from that message. But that is what
has happened to me all my life. I find enjoyment in difficult situations.

"About California. When I came back from Europe I wrote *The
Air-Conditioned Nightmare,* but I didn't have a cent. I came to
California to live for two or three years—primarily because of the
climate. When I lived here first, in Los Angeles, I used to go
everywhere on foot. People used to stop me and try to offer me a
ride. They just couldn't understand someone *walking.* Then I moved
to Big Sur. Every day—would you believe it?—up to 25 people
came to visit me. I didn't have a telephone. I don't know how
they found me. But they found me and I couldn't get any work
done. Then, when my marriage broke up, my children were living
in Los Angeles with their mother and I came to be near them.

"This year my friend Lawrence Durrell came to California to see
me. I was writing to him for years saying 'Don't come to America,
Larry, you'll hate it.' When he came to California, to my surprise
he loved it. He's coming back here next year with a trailer."

Miller finds enjoyment in writing, painting, astrology, eating,
playing Ping-Pong. "I keep the Ping-Pong table handy for people
I don't want to talk to. You know, it's simple. I just play Ping-Pong
with them."

Hoki, Henry Miller's beautiful young Japanese bride, is intro-
duced into the conversation. Hoki is in the next room, wearing a
cotton dress and a plaid kerchief around her black hair. She offers
us some cold drinks and welcomes me, then disappears. There is
a portrait of her in the living room, painted by Miller, with an
inscription that says "To Hoki, a Princess from the Far East,"
and certainly there is a spirit in Hoki which suggests both worldli-
ness and timidity.

"I had a hard time courting Hoki," Miller says with a smile.
"She was singing in a cafe in Los Angeles and I just kept hanging
around waiting to see her."

He skips from the courtship to the present. "Hoki just came back
from Japan where she was recording. She called me from there and

asked me to write a song for her record and I wrote one called 'At the Garden Wall,' but they changed the title because it wasn't right in Japanese.'' Then he adds, ''Too corny.

"Don't ask me about politics. I'm against war. And I never voted in my life. But I'll tell you one thing—I'm living with this hope: that the youngsters will get rid of all the old birds and wiseacres. In this country the ordinary man, you know, is dead inside before he's 40. It's not his fault. It's the fault of mechanized things. There's a lack of individuality. Everything is made for comfort and ease.

"You want to know what I believe? I believe in giving the poor everything. The good people of the world? They don't need money. I could go back to sweeping floors and I wouldn't mind. In fact, I try to sweep the floor here but nobody lets me. I cook my own meals. In this country you have to fight to get the *pleasure* of doing dirty work. But don't you see? It's when I'm washing the dishes that I get my illuminations. I learned long ago the secret of the Chinese—to empty your mind. I empty my mind for writing. I never know what I'm going to write until I sit down to write it.''

Watercolors are the passion of Henry Miller. He has been painting all his life and has written a book called *To Paint Is to Love again.* I asked him if he would show me his paintings and happily he led me into his studio where he works. In the studio were huge bookshelves filled with copies of his books translated into almost every language. There were copies of *Tropic of Cancer* in Japanese, Serbo-Croatian, Russian—and beneath the bookshelves were tables upon which he keeps his paints, his brushes in jars, the stacks of white bond paper upon which he paints.

He began a spontaneous watercolor lesson: "The most important thing is not to be afraid to make mistakes. You see here all my mistakes which have been painted over and over. I use a sponge. If I do a watercolor that I don't like, I take the sponge and wash it off. Then I begin all over.''

He passed his hands over the smooth white cocoon of empty paper upon which he would plant his nude colors, working like a gardener to make reds, yellows, blues, greens, bloom into huge watery visions. Then he led me to another table where some of his paintings, just returned from exhibition in Paris and Tokyo, were piled neatly on the table. He picked one up after another—there

were clowns, landscapes, portraits, abstracts—explosions of forms
and color. I said that some of the paintings reminded me of the
drawing of Grosz, of his humorous and cruel drawings of misplaced
people. "Yes—Grosz is one of my favorites. How did you know
that?" He continued lifting up the pages of paintings. "I also like
Klee very much. His humor."

The pictures were all different and made me suddenly emerge in
a world of sunbursts, carnivals, landscapes of the impossible. "I
often try to copy the Japanese landscapes." We continued through
the reams of drawings and pictures, with Miller showing me how
he used the sponge, the brush, the colors. I thought of Rimbaud,
and how he described colors in a totally new way, redefining the
meanings of yellow, red, blue, green. Watching Miller take pride in
showing me his images in watercolors, I understood why he felt
so close to Rimbaud, and why he had chosen to write a book about
him. Miller, like Rimbaud, deals in the material of apocalypse
through color. He paints the sun, heat, electricity, the air and
sulphur of his world. He has painted almost all of his life and it is
obvious that painting has meant as much to his life as writing. He
breathes in his own pictures as if they possessed a quantity of
fresh air. His work is filled with color, eruptions, humor, darkness,
wit—all of the qualities that are in his cosmology of writing.

But as he shows his work, it is as if he can hardly believe that he
has painted all that joy; there is something that says, "I, Henry
Miller, have reverence and humility for the world of joy, exuberance, love. Therefore I am. Therefore I paint."

The walls of Miller's painting studio are covered with wild hand-
writing—a huge mural circles the room: funny sayings, bits and pieces
of Oriental wisdom, swear words, an ulets, poems, autographs,
maxims, drawings and childish pictures of faces. It is as if one were
back in the first cave of man, where everything that was to be
turned into historical documents was written or drawn on the wall.
The graffiti are marked in crayons, the watermarks of friends,
angels, passing acquaintances, saints, old cronies from Paris,
children. Some of the sayings are larger than others and jump out at
me from the wall:

DON'T LOOK FOR MIRACLES. YOU ARE THE MIRACLE!

GUNS EXIST IN THE WORLD TO COME. BUT THERE ARE NO TARGETS.

In large letters the word "ZAP" is blocked out. Other words: "FATIMA." "VIVA-ZIVA" and "KILL THE BUDDHA." "Yes," Miller smiled, "I enjoy this wall-writing. There's one quote that comes from a letter written to a friend of mine from a girl in Japan. She wrote to him 'Take care of yourself. Repeatedly.'

"And how do you like this one?" He points to a marking on the wall that says "LOVE, DELIGHT, AND ORGAN ARE FEMININE IN THE PLURAL." 'That was written by my friend Blaise Cendrars. It's true. You know, in the French language they are all feminine.

"The older I get, the more I think of myself as a clown. A clown who enjoys everything. There is nothing on earth that I want. Nothing that I want to do that I haven't done. But as you get near the end, there isn't much time left. Each moment is precious— there is so much I like to do, and must do."

He smiled at me—the smile of a man who insists on being an acrobat of the imaginary world, a juggler of paints, words, songs, visions, countries and friendships. "Now," he said, "I have a favor to ask of you. Will you write something on my wall?" He handed me a magicmarker. I remembered that I once read, several years ago, a book by Miller called "The Angel Is My Watermark" and I had borrowed the word "watermark" for a poem. I wrote:

> To Henry Miller,
> We follow, like insects in our innocence,
> The watermarks of each miracle.

It is time to leave. Miller walks with me to the front of his house, stands on the doorstep, waving and bending, just a little, in a bow. He looks like one of those Chinese masters on an ancient screen who knows the secret of the universe.

Henry Miller Is Appalled
at His Offspring

Bob Thomas / 1969

From *Richmond Times-Dispatch* (June 29, 1969), F-5. Reprinted by permission of *Richmond Times-Dispatch*.

PACIFIC PALISADES, Calif. (AP)—He possesses the benevolent air of a retired priest. The rheumy eyes narrow into slits, and he speaks in freshets of monologue about his concern for America, the generation of youth and the future of literature.

In this seaside suburb of Los Angeles he resides in a two-story white stucco house surrounded by businessmen, doctors and other members of the upper middle class.

It seems a strange place for the great bohemian, Henry Miller, hailed by some as a liberator of American language and morals, assailed by others as a literary pornographer.

His early novels paved the way for the whole stream of sexually explicit works now coming off the printing presses. Like many a father, however, he is appalled by what he sired.

At 77, Henry Miller is finally being accorded honors he and his adherents long have felt were due him. His once-banned books are now sold in most communities.

The relaxed standards of films now permit his literary works to reach the screen. His *Tropic of Cancer* is being filmed in France by Joseph Strick, who directed the movie version of James Joyce's *Ulysses*. A Scandinavian company is bringing forth *Quiet Days in Clichy*. Miller himself is starring in a full-length documentary, *The Henry Miller Odyssey*.

"All this happens so late, so late," laments Miller, shaking his head. "Why couldn't it have happened sooner, when I could have enjoyed it more? Why does recognition come 30 years afterward?

"Perhaps it was just as well. Success is much more destructive than failure. I've seen men ruined by success.

"I wrote *Tropic of Cancer* in 1931, and it was three or four years

135

before the publisher in Paris dared to print it. Not until 1961 was
it printed in America.

"When I meet with young writers today, I hear them complain
that they have a wife and family and they can't make a living from
writing. I tell them that it is unfortunate, but any serious writer
must wait 20 years before his work will be recognized. Perhaps that is
speeded up today, because there are more avenues for an author's
work. But most of us must wait."

Speaking of *Tropic of Cancer,* poet Ezra Pound once exclaimed:
"At last, an unprintable book that's readable."

Serious critics have agreed with Pound on both scores.

Said novelist Lawrence Durrell: "American literature today begins and ends with the meaning of what he has done."

Does Miller feel responsible for today's frankness in books?

"Yes, I suppose I am, along with Joyce and D. H. Lawrence. But
they liberated the novel more in a literary way, while I did it for
the man in the street."

And what does he think of the result of this "liberation"?

"I am appalled. I could be a censor, but only on matters of taste
and values. That is what is lacking in today's writing. But, of course,
I would never impose censorship for any reason. I feel that any man
is entitled to express himself with complete freedom. In time,
perhaps, the writing will achieve taste and sensitivity. But it is liable
to get worse before it gets better."

And what of Philip Roth's *Portnoy's Complaint?* the runaway
best seller dealing with sex.

"I have no reason to read it," says Miller.

For Henry Miller, the waiting for fame began in Paris in 1930. He
had known a harsh childhood in Brooklyn, studied at City College
in New York and at Cornell, then bummed around the United States
in odd jobs before seeking the bohemian life of a writer in Paris.

But even in prewar France, Miller's writings were considered too
avant garde. He scrabbled for a living from magazines and the
meager sales of his books, *Tropic of Cancer, Tropic of Capricorn,
Black Spring, The Cosmological Eye,* and others. They were too
far out to achieve wide readership, as well as too explicit in sexual
acts and language to gain entrance to puritanical America.

The war sent Miller back to the United States and greater poverty. His total assets on arrival: $10.

He settled in the mountainous Big Sur country near Monterey, Calif., living a primitive life as he tried to continue serious writing.

"Whenever I run down America, it is the institutions and customs that I attack," he reflects. "I find that if I ever go directly to the people, I am never disappointed."

"From 1940 to 1952 I never had a checking account," he says. "I lived on credit most of the time. The man who delivered the mail also delivered groceries and other things, and he allowed me to charge everything. I even bought my stamps on credit. He did that for many artists at Big Sur, and you know something? He never lost money on any of them."

The war helped a change of fortune. American GIs discovered his works in France, and his reputation began to spread. After the war, his publisher had amassed $40,000 in royalties, but Miller didn't go to France to collect the money.

"I was having a fight with my wife and I didn't want to take her," he explains. He is now wed to wife No. 5, Tokyo-born entertainer Hiroko Tokuda, 30.

When Supreme Court rulings loosened laws against obscenity, Miller's books finally were printed in his native land. *Tropic of Cancer* was published in 1961, and others followed, too quickly, he believes.

"After a year, the sales dwindled. Now I rely on foreign publishers for my income. In France and Germany and especially in the Scandinavian countries, my books are very popular. There you find a much more literate population," he said.

When prosperity finally overtook Henry Miller seven years ago, he moved from Big Sur to his home here. He is oblivious to the affluent neighborhood but devoted to his house, particularly because it affords space for his four great interests—writing, painting, swimming and table tennis.

Miller talked with an interviewer on a Sunday afternoon, after he had engaged in a rigorous table tennis game with Robert Snyder, producer-director of *The Henry Miller Odyssey*. The author gives few interviews these days.

Despite his reluctance, he delivered numerous opinions in response to questions about his life and the world around him. Such as:

What is the state of the novel?

"I stay away from reading them. I've thought for some time that the novel died 30 years ago with Joyce. I don't get any nourishment from reading any of today's novelists, except for one: that fellow who writes Yiddish novels, Isaac Bashevis Singer.

What does he see as the future of writing?

"I believe that writing will some day give way to another mode of expression. Eventually I think that we will communicate without words. This could be done by feel or by another breed of human being who can develop extrasensory communication. Then we won't have to talk so much. There is entirely too much talk in the world.

"There is also too much written today. Ninety per cent of all writing—in fact, 90 per cent of all the arts—is junk. It could be wiped out entirely with no loss to civilization. This mass of junk becomes a burden to young people, who must sift through it to find something of value."

What do you think of the young people today?

"I think a lot of what they are doing, particularly on the campuses, is stupid and harmful. But I find them to be less bad than the adults. The young people may be going about it the wrong way, but at least they are trying to attack the hypocrisy and injustice in American life."

What is your view of America today?

"I think that in literature, in politics, in almost every phase of its existence, this country is going through a process of deterioration and disintegration. I see very little left of what inspired the founding fathers."

Tropic Revisited

Newsweek / 1969

From *Newsweek*, 74 (August 19, 1969), 10. © 1969, Newsweek, Inc. All rights reserved. Reprinted by permission.

Life has gotten easier for Henry Miller since the days in the '30s when he shacked up with Bohemian friends in the Montparnasse garrets described in his once banned novel *Tropic of Cancer.* Cleared by U.S. Courts in 1964, *Cancer* is now being filmed in Paris by Joseph Strick, who directed the film version of James Joyce's *Ulysses* in 1966. Miller, 78, is back in Paris for the summer, ensconced in fashionable sixteenth-arrondissement digs. From time to time he drops in benignly on the set, but mostly, he says he longs for the days when no one knew his name. What with publishers pestering him for blurbs, young authors asking for advice and money, and newsmen clamoring for his views of the filming of *Cancer,* Miller complains he has no time to himself.

Still, he has done some work on a documentary film of his life, and he hopes mime Marcel Marceau will star in a movie version of an unpublished new story about a clown. "But what I really should be working on," Miller says, "is the second half of *Nexus,*" the last book of the *Rosy Crucifixion* trilogy. "I doubt I'll ever do it," he confesses, grinning, "because I'm getting that wonderful sensation, the delight of leaving it unfinished, leaving it a mystery, saying f— you, guess it."

Last week, he took time off from an afternoon of lunching and girl watching at the Cafe du Trocadero, across from the Eiffel Tower, to give his views on this and that.

On the filming of *Tropic of Cancer:* "There were chances to have done it many times. I always said no because I knew they could never do justice to it. Well, all those problems have disappeared; you can do anything today. I have a feeling it may look a bit innocent."

On sexual freedom and food: "Now they have this complete liberation in the realm of sex, but we're a long way from having

freedom, don't you think? How can you talk about freedom when
you don't have money to buy food?''

On what a young writer should read: ''Novels are the least
nourishing; novels don't contribute anything to a writer. He
should read chemistry, astronomy, everything.''

On pornography: ''I don't read pornographic literature. I can't
read the stuff. I never do. I don't like the Marquise de Sade . . . What
is my definition of pornography? I would say that is that when it
touches on sex in a slimy way—to tickle you—whereas I make a
distinction between it and obscenity. Obscenity is direct and has a
purity about it.''

His favorite writer: ''Isaac Bashevis Singer. There's no Jewish
blood in me, but I dig his stuff: it's just like I'm eating pie. I
understand perfectly. And if I'm not a Jew, I ought to have been
one . . . because any writer who's been in exile, suffered, has been
ignored, humiliated, knows a little of what the Jews went through.''

If he could relive his life? ''It sounds terrible, but I'm satisfied
with what I did.''

Henry Miller: I Wonder Who the Hell I'm Writing for

Julie Burns / 1970

From *Mademoiselle*, 71 (May 1970), 162–63, 198–202.

Henry Miller is a small man, deceptively frail-looking, strutting and still defying the world like an imp in his endless search for truth. He reminds me of the little boy in "The Emperor's New Clothes"; he is perhaps the only one in town who admits they don't exist.

We met for the first interview in the Special Collections Department of the UCLA Library, 15 minutes from his Pacific Palisades home. He was looking through a faded green clothbound volume filled with his characteristic scrawl—the "notebook" he used during his 1941 *Air-Conditioned Nightmare* tour of America.

What was the nightmare that was air-conditioned?

I'm not sure I can tell you. Maybe . . . yes. The horrible monotony . . . the *monotony* in America. One place is like another—no quality, no character to any town or city. I can't think of one American city that really has character, and I've seen all the major cities and many of the towns. People mention San Francisco, but I've been there and I'm not moved by it.

There are paintings in here with your notes. Is it true that you now spend more time painting than writing?

Yes. Well . . . yes and no. If I spend more time painting, it's because I spend so little time writing, you might say. But I don't do either continuously. I'm frankly lazy now, and negligent and indifferent about both, you see. I only do things now when I feel like it.

To what do you attribute this?

Maybe to old age? Probably. Well . . . there are other factors, of course. My life is always an interruption, a constant interruption.

There are visitors that I don't expect, projects, telephones—every sort of annoyance possible, which is, they say, the price of fame.

You say annoyance. I would have assumed you'd enjoy that spontaneous kind of life—where you don't know from one moment to the next what you will be doing.
I would . . . if I were always doing what I like. But NOT when I'm at the mercy of others who are trying to get me to listen to propositions, sign this, and so on.

When I asked you to talk with me today, you said that you always hesitate to talk directly "on the air," whether it be tape or film. Is this because you like to edit what you're saying?
It's probably because I'm a writer, and the only way for me to express myself fully is in writing. When I *talk,* I'm another person—I'm more imperfect in the handling of my thoughts. Take most of these programs—Johnny Carson, Joey Bishop, Merv Griffin—what do you call those men? Interviewers? Personalities? *Whatever* they are, they are very adroit and adept and have a fluency and facility and flexibility that I think is wonderful, because that's what *I* lack. But sometimes in these interviews a guest star—often a very important personality—becomes nervous. You wouldn't expect that, would you?

But the star is out of his element, too, since he would normally have a script to work from.
But I like it when these big personalities occasionally grope and fumble and stumble. Just as I love that book Picasso's mistress wrote about him, which made him so angry. Some people said it was a dirty thing to do. But it showed his human weaknesses, which are adorable because we *all* have them. But as to interviews . . . I'm certainly not at my best in that realm, and why should I make an ass of myself in front of the public?

When you said a moment ago that you neither paint nor write as much as you previously did, it reminded me of your statement in To Paint Is to Love Again . . . *"The surest way to kill an artist is to supply him with everything he needs . . . every conceivable gadget, every last comfort, every useless luxury." You wrote that*

when you were in Big Sur. Do you think that life in the Palisades is too comfortable for real creativity?
But I'm *constantly* uncomfortable there. I'm working in a tiny room at a small desk, and there's not enough room on this desk to paint.

Then you still believe that the surest way to kill an artist is to give him a full supply of everything?
Oh, yes. I think that only a master could survive that sort of thing. And I don't think he would want it. An artist always wants to make himself a bit uncomfortable.

You also seemed reluctant to talk about your painting. Why was that?
Because I think people are giving undue importance to my paintings . . . to the *fact* that I'm painting and to the paintings themselves. I don't put myself in the category of a real painter. I'm painting for pleasure. And now, against my better judgment, as it were, I'm getting dragged into exhibiting my work.

But doesn't it give you pleasure to know that people are interested in your paintings . . . that they're even interested enough to buy them?
I can answer that for both my painting and my books. I would say that perhaps less than 10 per cent of my readers are the only ones I'm interested in having read me. The others are worthless. My books don't do them any good or me any good. You see, I believe that over 90 per cent of *everything* that is done in the realm of music, drama, painting, literature—any of the arts—is worthless.

You certainly don't put your own work in this category.
Some of it.

Then you really don't care or even think about your audience?
I don't care about it at all. It doesn't mean anything to me . . . because I have a contempt for all my readers and buyers. Only a few people mean anything to me. The rest, the mob who buys or admires or writes letters . . . fans . . . they don't mean a damn thing to me. They're bores. They bother me, in fact. And sometimes I'm horrified. I say, "What! . . . so that guy is one of my readers . . . so that's the kind of idiot I have reading me!"

*But wouldn't you have the public in mind when you are in the
process of creating?*

Many people ask me that. I don't, really, at the time I'm writing.
Except sometimes, during a certain passage, I might think of a friend
and say to myself . . . "He'd like that. If he knew I was writing this,
he'd enjoy it." But I don't have a vision. You can't. Who is this
public? It has a million faces. I don't know who my public is. . . .
And I don't care!

*I understand you receive thousands of letters from people who
say, "I learned this or that from you." Don't you feel gratified that
you are able to open doors for people?*

I tell you something . . . I don't feel at all touched by it. I don't
think anybody *can* open doors for people. It's an accident. . . . I
believe that anyone who came along and hit that person at the right
time could have done it. He was ready to be opened, do you see? And
I don't care about opening doors. That's not why I write. Writers
and creative people shouldn't be proud. How shall I say it? They are
only instruments in the hands of unseen forces. They shouldn't say
"I . . . my signature . . . Henry Miller . . . Jean Cocteau" . . .
whatever it be. It's not important. We are only instruments.

Of God?

Of whatever you want to call it . . . unseen forces . . . the
greater beyond.

*Do you feel that anyone has had an important influence on
your writing?*

There have been plenty who affected me. I even wrote a book
called *Books in My Life* where I talked about the men who
influenced me. My greatest influence, I suppose, was Knut Hamsun,
a Norwegian writer. Nobody ever saw any connection. No critic
ever realized that I even tried to write like him. Deliberately. But I
don't think I succeeded. I would love it if I could. Even to this
day. If I could write like Knut Hamsun, I would be a happy man. I
would think I accomplished something.

How would you describe your own writing?

I'm a special case as a writer. Once again, I don't think I'm what
is generally called a writer. That is, I'm outside that category in some

ways. I decided to write only about my own life. And I've adhered
to that pretty much.

Why did you make that decision?
Because it was easier for me. And it was more truthful. Why
should I try to write about imaginary characters and situations,
when my own life, seemed so much bigger and more important than
anything I could invent? It would come out of my guts, out of my real
feelings and experiences.

When did you make this decision?
In 1920 . . . or was it 1927? I was working for the Parks
Department in Queens County, New York. I sat down at my desk
one afternoon and began a notebook. I wrote the whole story of my
life in that notebook, in telegraphic notes . . . sort of an outline . . . in
about 25 or 30 pages, I've worked out all of my personal books—
Black Spring, Tropic of Cancer and *Capricorn,* the three volumes
of the *The Rosy Crucifixion,* and so on—from these notes, and I've
never exhausted them. They mean a lot to me. I can unlock them
and expand. I think for *Tropic of Capricorn* I used only one-and-a-
half pages of the notes.

*You just go back to your notes when you're ready to write
another book?*
If it's a book that falls into the pattern of the *Tropics* or the trilogy
. . . yes. Otherwise, no, of course not. If I'm telling about my life
in the past, it would be a continuation of those books.

How many pages of notes are left?
There are about seven or eight pages. I haven't done anything for
several years with them. I should . . . there's a lot yet to do. But
I'm beginning to have the feeling that I'll *never* do it, that I'll leave
the seven or eight pages unfinished . . . purposely, deliberately,
and maliciously. Because I think I want to slap my readers in the
face for being only prurient and curious and avid for sensations. I
want to say to them, "Look, I'm not going to tell you the whole
thing. You can dope it out for yourself."

You've written things that aren't autobiographical, haven't you?
Yes. A play called *Just Wild About Harry.* . . . that was taken

from a song title, you know. And I'm working on another one.
And, of course, there's *The Smile at the Foot of the Ladder*, that
little book about the clown. There was a big opera done on it,
produced in Germany and now in France and Italy. It's a fantasy.
It's one of the most well-liked things of anything I've done. Now
that had nothing to do with my life. I actually wrote it to please a
painter named Fernand Léger. He'd said to me, "I'm going to do a
book on the circus, paint the illustrations. Would you write the text
for it?" It's generally the reverse, you know. But I was intrigued. I
sat down and wrote from the top of my head. I didn't think. I don't
know where it came from. But Léger was disappointed. He said he
expected something like *Tropic of Cancer*.

Actually, you've written many more essays than novels, haven't
you?
I never wrote a novel. *Tropic* is a slice of life.

Do you have a favorite book?
Sure I do. The Greek book . . . *The Colossus of Maroussi*. That's
my favorite.

Is there any book you'd like to re-treat, re-write?
No. Because that's not in my style of thinking. Whatever I do,
that's the best I could do at the time. And I say, "Fine, let it go at
that." I don't believe in rewriting. I'm against perfection . . . so
there wouldn't be anything I could achieve in a rewrite. Just as I
wouldn't want to rectify an error in living. I've done lots of bad
things in my life. And if you asked me, "Would you want to
change it?" I'd say no. Because I see that the good things and the
bad things level off, as it were, and out of good comes bad and out of
bad comes good. I take things as they are.

A friend of mine has a page from a little-known book of yours
called Into the Nightlife *framed and on his wall. Why haven't we*
heard more about this book?
Well . . . it's a book we did in 1948, my brother-in-law and I. He's
an Israeli artist. It was a limited edition with silk-screen production, all of which he did himself. It's my writing and his illustrations.
We brought it out for $250 a copy, I think. Beautiful book. Quite
unique.

Can it be purchased anywhere?
I have about 45 copies. They're for sale. But, no, you couldn't find them in a bookstore anywhere, if that's what you mean.

Have you ever illustrated any of your books?
I don't think I could. I'm not gifted as an illustrator. I'm not gifted to be a script writer for the movies, either. I wouldn't mind if I could write a wonderful script, but I can't do it. I'm limited. And I think everyone is limited, and that he ought to know what his limitations are.

Are you writing anything now?
Yes . . . I'm *supposed* to be working, put it that way, on several articles for magazines. And then a book about a very special series of watercolors—*The Insomnia Series,* 11 paintings I did at three o'clock in the morning, whenever I woke with insomnia.

What is your emotional response to painting . . . as contrasted to writing?
Well . . . I enjoy painting. I enjoy the physical act itself. I enjoy being surrounded by my own paintings, looking at them. They give me pleasure doing them. Secondly, as a half-assed painter, so to speak, I don't worry and fret as a great painter perhaps would. For me, it's either hit or miss . . . and if I'm lucky I hit all right, according to *my* standards.

Then you say that your attitude is different because your writing is your life work?
Partly that . . . and partly the fact that writing is harder. It takes more out of you, I believe. You're thinking of ideas, and they're abstract—thoughts and words do not come as easily as brush strokes.

Do you think that painters are earthier people, freer people, than writers?
They give me that impression . . . as though they loved life and enjoyed it more. Whereas writers usually give me a feeling of being sickly and neurotic and unhealthy.

Do you consider training to be helpful to the creative person?
I don't believe so. That is, for me. And I would almost generalize

about that. I think that all training has to be unlearned again, all
the disciplines you get in school. I don't believe in *education*. If I
had my way, I would never have sent my children to school. I
think children should learn haphazardly. If they ask a question, I
answer it as best I can. If they're more interested, maybe I'd
suggest a book to look up. But going to school so many hours a
day, learning all that nonsense, is what I call utter garbage. The
only part of education I approve of is kindergarten. The rest cripples
you, makes an idiot of you. I know this sounds crazy, but I
believe that we're all born creative. We all have the same creative
instincts. Most of us are killed off as artists, as creative people,
by our schooling. The real education, in my mind, would come from
a master to a disciple, and we don't have any such thing in the
Western world. Except now and then, rarely, in the world of
painting, let's say, or music. I mean a master not only of the
medium, but a master in the spiritual sense. You see, all that is
called knowledge here in our world, in our civilization, doesn't mean
much to me. What is it Picasso said not long ago? It made my heart
jump, it was so wonderful! He was looking at an exhibition of
children's works somewhere and he said, pointing to the work,
"Think of it . . . it's taken me all these years to get back to where
they are." To be able to do as they do, spontaneously, fearlessly,
colorfully, with utmost liberty. Do you see? When you go through
"discipline," you get cramped, inhibited, thwarted, and frustrated.

You're going to France. Do you find the country more industrial-
ized now and the people more stereotyped—closer to what we are
accused of here in the U.S.?
Well . . . the influence of the U.S. all over the world is a bad one,
in that sense. We are destroying people everywhere with our way
of life. I think we have the worst way of life conceivable.

In what way?
In what we do each day. The work we indulge in, how we drink,
smoke—our attitude toward love, sex . . . ALL these things.

Would you say that our life is superficial?
It's WORSE than that. It's monstrous and absurd. EVERY-
THING is wrong with it in my mind. COMPLETELY wrong.

*To what do you attribute this? Our outlook . . . our American
point of view?*
I don't know. Who knows what brings about these things?

Power?
Well . . . of course, our whole money system . . . using people,
exploiting people, underpaying them, starving them.

*You have in the past criticized America for making things too
easy. You felt that life became stereotyped as a result, and that
none of us are truly involved in living—in the experience of life, of
love, of living.*
That's right. But don't forget that we WORK to make things
easy. This is what we are all working at—making these gadgets,
improvements, and so on. But we make ourselves miserable doing
it. Nobody makes shoes any more—alone—does he? Or a suit of
clothes? Or builds his own house? He makes *part* of a shoe.

*But is there a way to turn back time? Isn't this all just a
consequence of the Industrial Revolution?*
That's what they would like to have us believe, the powers-that-
be. But I can think of going back. Sure. Why not go back as well
as forward?

How would you do that?
Just do what you like . . . as the young people are *trying* to do
today. Show that you don't have to do what you're *supposed* to
do. You don't have to belong to the Establishment and follow this
way of life that's laid out for you.

*I've heard it said many times that the values of the French people
are also changing, as their industry is expanded; that the Frenchman is now only concerned with his car and his television set.*
It's true that the car and television alter people. But it's not just
France . . . this is universal. In my mind, wherever there's
progress there is deterioration . . . degeneration. All these inven-
tions and discoveries that are supposed to be good for man, in my
opinion, are working toward his destruction.

What is it about France that you like so much?
Qualities that will always be there, all the qualities that I don't

have . . . which I like. They're very hard to make friends with . . . which I like. They stand off; you have to seduce them. Then . . . the food is marvelous! There's also a great spirit of tolerance and freedom there that I don't see anywhere else in the world. And they're good to be with. They know how to live. And I don't think people in America, or Germany, or Sweden, or any of those countries do.

Speaking of French tolerance and freedom, wasn't your book Sexus *banned there for many years and only recently released?*

Yes . . . it was banned for 15 years or more . . . from the time it was first published. And it was published then in a castrated edition . . . every line that was censorable taken out. Then it was banned altogether. I was brought to court. It's a court we don't have here in America. You go before a judge, and he discusses the whole thing . . . what do you think about it . . . how you feel . . . this and that. I must have spent an hour there with this judge, who greeted me warmly when I arrived and told me I'm in the best tradition . . . Villon, Balzac, Zola, Rabelais. I said everything I wanted. The last question he put to me was . . . "Mr. Miller, do you really think that a writer should have the liberty to say anything he chooses in a book?" I thought . . . for a good long minute . . . and I watched the clerk who was transcribing and who was looking at me anxiously. Then I said, "Yes, I do," and the clerk, under the desk, went like "bravo" . . . clapped his hands . . . do you see? I was really in a special position . . . the only man still banned in France. I can't think of any other author whom the French have banned . . . the Marquis de Sade . . . but that was over 200 years ago . . . and now all his work has been permitted.

Do you think the U.S. is growing up . . . in its attitude toward censorship?

Without a doubt. We're already permitting everything and anything to be published. Anything, I would say. *Sexus* is published in the United States. To be honest, I think most of the stuff today should be censored . . . if I believed in censorship, which I don't. Because it's so bad . . . such horrible writing. I don't mind the obscenity. I think that's all right . . . that's healthy. But if that's all

they're aiming at . . . there I would say simply that that's bad literature.

*Would you still consider your work sensational, comparing it with
the things being written today?*
Yes.

You think you can still outdo *what they're doing now?*
Yes . . . I can. Because it isn't just use of pornographic material.
It's the drama behind it, the force, the meaning. But I'm at the
point where I don't care any more. There are so many idiots among
my fans that I wonder who the hell I'm writing for.

*Would you say that the new attitude toward censorship actually
creates bad writing?*
When you have freedom, everybody uses it . . . anybody and
everybody. So the poor writers enjoy it as well as the good
writers. And, of course, since this country has been so puritanical
for so many years . . . since its birth . . . well, everybody is jumping
overboard now with the new freedom. Actually, the invention of
the printing press has turned out to be a misfortune for mankind.
I would like to see books eliminated. We have a plethora of them.
And 90 to 99 per cent of them are not worth reading, in my
opinion.

Then what form of communication would you advocate?
I don't know. We have movies . . . television . . . and we could
invent things. We're not creative in the realm of communication.
We're still in an archaic, medieval stage. Technologically, we do
wonders. Culturally, we're baboons. It's a shame to ruin your
eyes reading page after page in order to extract a little kernel of
something. And most books don't even have that little kernel.
Morons can write books. And they do! I would say about 50 per
cent of the books written are written by morons. High-grade
morons.

*If you say books should be eliminated . . . does that mean that
the good books should be outlawed with the bad?*
I'm not talking about outlawing. I'm talking about hoping for
another way to communicate. We should soon get to the point

where we know without talking what is in the other person's mind. It's an extra sense. But it can be developed. If we *wish* it. We can have anything we want in this world, if we wish it. You know the cardinal sin in Catholicism has to do with laziness . . . spiritual laziness. Sluggishness, spiritual sluggishness. I think we're living in a world of sleepwalkers. People are not awake. Because if they were, they couldn't stand what's going on. They would either vomit their guts out, or they'd kill one another.

Perhaps this explains the dichotomy which I detect in you. You seem very pessimistic about civilization, yet very positive about the world.

I'm in favor of life. And I say civilization represents a death influence, not a life influence. Civilization is rigidity . . . it's ossification. And when I say I'm against it, I mean I'm against all that we are made to learn, to study, to know. The first thing we should learn is how to live together. Nowhere do they teach us that! We're all murderers at heart . . . or willing to be. Any time the Government drums sound, we're willing to take up the gun and kill whomever we have to kill. The first thing man ought to do is to learn to live in peace with his neighbor.

Do you have any ideas about how this might be accomplished?

Yes. To *be* at peace. If you *are* at peace, then you don't have to fight for peace.

Then it's an individual thing?

Sure. It will never be settled politically or economically. Never by governments. Each individual must wish it that way.

I think the hippies would concur with you on this. Do you have great hope for the young people of today?

I see *some* hope . . . I don't say great, because I think it takes much more than anything they are doing. It might take a complete revolution. I can't even guess how long it might take to begin to live as real human beings.

What do you think of the hippie philosophy . . . generally?

Everything the hippies stand for is a weak presentation of profound things. Don't ask me to prove it. That's how it impresses me . . . I can't always give you logic.

Would you say that the hippies themselves are falling into a pattern, much as the generation before did?
I have the hope that they may make a breakthrough and show us a different pattern . . . that, for once, the ideas of young people will remain and have some effectiveness. Always, in the past, as soon as they become adults they join the Establishment. They become conservatives. The radical always becomes a great conservative. And the revolutionary becomes a tyrant, just like the one he overthrew. This time, I'm hoping for a new kind of human being to arise, with an entirely different consciousness. All the ideals they talk about . . . I don't see them accomplishing them. It isn't ideals we lack. As far back as we know there've been men of ideals, and they've never succeeded.

Then you think we're headed for disaster?
In my opinion, civilization is already doomed.

What signs do you see?
Listen . . . we've had three world wars, haven't we? Social conditions don't improve . . . they get worse. Hatred increases. Persecution. Tyranny. All over the world, there's nothing but fighting going on. There's no peace with one another, one nation with another. All are on edge, waiting to spring at each other's throat. What a world! And the world of money. What a farce! We don't need money to live. And we don't need men to be robots . . . working at insignificant jobs, as most everybody does. I don't see any meaning in anything that anybody's doing, except the very few creative individuals.

Who are they?
You can name them. Everybody knows. Everybody has a few that he can name. He can be an inventor. He can be an artist. Anything. But he's creative. And there are only a few dozen in the whole world.

How would you describe creativity?
It's godlike. It's a life-giving thing, instead of the death rhythm people are exhibiting. It's getting out of the mould. It's using the mind, the imagination, the heart, the spirit . . . things we don't see in daily life. Who shows his heart? Who shows imagination?

*Is this, then, the advice that you would give to the youth of today
. . . to be creative in their thinking and living?*

I wouldn't say anything. I don't give advice. You can't tell
anybody what he should do. One should just go on living and
doing what he feels like doing . . . whether it's right or wrong. I
don't discourage anybody from doing what he wants to do . . . even if
he wants to be a whore, or a murderer, a thief or a saint. This
doesn't mean that you should follow me, that you should take my
word as gospel.

*But what about young people starting out in a creative field such
as writing. Don't you have any advice for them?*

I don't know, because it can vary with each individual. Now it is
true that to some I would say, "Forget it, you're not meant to be
a creative person. Drive a truck, be a thief, a pimp, or something.
It's not your field." I've told that to people who tell me they're
writers or would-be writers or painters. There are only a few of the
elect that are made to do things. Most of them fall by the wayside.
And this seems perfectly normal to me, and natural. In order to be
a creative individual in any medium, it's not just skill that you
need, not just the ability to write or paint. You also need to be a
very strong, tough individual who can withstand the blows and buffets
you'll get from society. Because it takes years and years before a
man gains recognition, and in order to wait you have to make
tremendous sacrifices. Few people have the strength to do that. It's
almost unholy, ungodly, to ask it of human beings. And there are
so very few who make it. What are you going to do for the others?
Can you endow them with powers they are not born with? This
typical Western and American way of giving them a pep talk is very
nice . . . and sickly, too. Give them the right doctrine . . . the right
medicine . . . and they'll come through. I don't believe that
nonsense at all.

Where does the strength to wait for recognition come from?

Well, I suppose it comes from God, to tell you the truth. But
that's not a good answer. There are many, many factors involved—one's health, one's vitality, one's background, heredity,
social environment. . . .

You know, I don't want you to get the impression that I'm a very pessimistic individual. I consider myself neither a pessimist nor an optimist. I don't like either term. I *like* to think that I'm a realist—that I see things as they are and tell them as they are. I think we're asking for destruction, and I see ourselves destroying ourselves. But I still say that life is marvelous. We simply have not learned how to live, and therefore we create our own misery. The moment we wake up, the moment we *want* it differently, we can have it that way. I believe that there's nothing greater than life. That's all there is. It's marvelous. But it isn't just beautiful. It's all things. It isn't just good or bad, one way or the other. It's everything. All at the same time.

Henry Miller in Conversation
Georges Belmont / 1971

From *Henry Miller in Conversation* (Chicago: Quadrangle Books, 1972), 20–37.

Georges Belmont: What is striking about your work, in fact, is that what you call acceptance of the world has no hint of passive acceptance, either of things, society, or individuals. On the contrary it seems to me to be an extremely active, generous acceptance of everything: life, things in general, and in particular human beings.

Henry Miller: And even of my enemies. And that I reckon is the most important thing, because it's said—and rightly so—that the enemy is within, inside you, and not outside.

I have finally absorbed this fact and understand that I myself am the enemy as well. Likewise, in my view, it is very important to accept the 'other', the person who is not *for* you. This is why I like St Francis of Assisi so much . . . because he accepted everything, up to and including atheists. In a way I find him better than Jesus.

Georges Belmont: That is precisely what I call your generous acceptance of the world.

There's one question which readers of your work often put to me. It's this: 'Do the people who live and speak in his books (for one *is* directly involved with life and speech in them, and one has the impression of being immersed in lives as they are lived, and in words as they are really spoken), do these characters really exist, or did they exist the way they're described? What have you to say to that?

Henry Miller: Why, yes, they really were like they are in my books. Sometimes of course there is a distortion, an exaggeration, but this is more to bring out the truth; not to disguise things, but to go into them in depth.

When a man speaks to you, there are a great many things behind what he says that are important. That is what I try to put across. Not only the talk but what is behind it, whether concealed spontaneously or not.

Georges Belmont: What seems to me of prime importance—and I remember this was one of the first things I thought of when reading your books in the past—is that this desire to get inside people comes, in your case, not from curiosity, but from integrity . . . that above all it comes from the heart. The heart is essential in your work. It's heart that leads you to inflate, to exaggerate aspects of someone that are often only potentially present in him.

Henry Miller: Yes, I think that's true.

Georges Belmont: You act as a revealer of people.

I remember that two years ago I was in New York and one evening I met a professor from an American university. A short time before this he had himself met one of your characters at a friend's house . . . a character, incidentally, from what you told me was a favourite among your own books: *The Colossus of Maroussi*. The name of this character is Katsimbalis. He is the 'colossus'. And he too now has a professorship at an American university, in Florida I believe. And this other professor who had met him told me most ingenuously, and I'm sure with the greatest of honesty, that he recognized nothing of your 'colossus' in Katsimbalis. He was very disappointed.

Henry Miller: Wasn't that *his* fault? Not Katsimbalis', nor mine.

Georges Belmont: Doubtless. Nevertheless it is a fact that you have a tendency—once again through generosity—to exaggerate your subjects, to exaggerate what seems to you to be the best and richest sides of them.

Henry Miller: Yes, that's true enough—at least as far as characters I like are concerned.

You know, there is one thing in life that upsets and distresses me about people: it's that they never want to acknowledge greatness in others. They always want to demean . . . 'A giant? Oh no, not a chance! Impossible!'

Having said that, perhaps I also exaggerate the characters I don't like, but in the opposite way.

Georges Belmont: I wonder. In fact, I doubt that one could discover a trace of malice in your books; I don't feel that any of them portray someone over-drawn in a derogatory way.

Henry Miller: Perhaps the price I make others pay—those whom I don't like, or feel contempt for, or even hate—is that I often

portray them in caricature. I have often been told that I excel in
caricature, and that's certainly true! It seems to me that I always
see things in two ways: in reality and in caricature.

Georges Belmont: For my part, I submit that even your caricatures come from the heart.

I am thinking, for instance, of a kind of character who appears
fairly constantly throughout your books in one guise or another,
and whom I shall typify as your Doctor Kronsky, the rather grotesque psychoanalyst whom you end up by psychoanalysing
yourself, making him cough up to his patients all the money he'd
taken from them. You surround him with an aura of such affection, for all his grotesqueness, and embellish him to the point of
such opulence, that in his way he's no longer grotesque at all. Or am
I wrong?

Henry Miller: First, I'm going to tell you one thing: I don't much
like psychoanalysts, even the greatest. Jung, for example . . . for
me he's a great awful bore. In one sense I respect him, for his
explorations; he had some brilliant ideas, but he sticks in one's crop,
and he's so ponderous . . . ! Ah, yes, he's a real Swiss! And Freud!
I read all I could of him, as well as Jung and the rest of them,
when I was young, and I was thrilled by it. But nowadays that
means nothing to me any more. They tell me, apropos of Freud,
that he 'broke down the barriers'. I don't agree at all. In my opinion
he made a good job of dumping new loads on us and our con-
sciences. He has liberated one side of us, and overburdened the
other. We're barely hobbling along.

Georges Belmont: At least it's true to say that Oedipus didn't
have a complex.

Henry Miller: There you are!

As for my Doctor Kronsky, he really was grotesque in real life.
Only he was very goodhearted. I met him at the Telegraph
Company, and we became friends at once. He was part of the huge
circle of friends I had at that period. He wasn't a messenger boy,
he was a medical student. I was fond of him because he was
grotesque and because he had great heart. He would often criticize me. It even got to the point where we'd spar in the street when
we were discussing things of an evening. He'd put up his mitts

and invite me to do the same. And we'd spar away. The oddest
thing was that I was his boss, his *patron*.

Later, at a time when I'd decided at all costs to commit suicide,
he gave me a pill—out of goodheartedness. For a whole year I'd
kept on begging him, 'Give me something so that I can have done
with it and kill myself'. He'd reply, 'Come on now, that's no sort
of a thing to do'. And then one day he said to me, 'Well, all right,
since you're set on it, here you are'. And he handed me a pill.
. . . You know the story?

Georges Belmont: I'd like you to tell it, anyhow.

Henry Miller: Well, I swallowed his pill, then I took off all my
clothes. I was lying naked on the bed. It was the middle of winter.
I opened the window to make sure of doing the job properly. During
the night it began to snow. When I opened my eyes in the morning
I hadn't even caught a cold, but because the window was open I
was covered with snow. The bugger had slipped me a sleeping-
pill!

Georges Belmont: Where did this obsession with suicide come
from?

Henry Miller: Oh, from my hassles with Mona, my failure as a
writer, my relations with my parents—everything. Everything
was desolation, sadness . . . disappointment after disappointment.

You know, not long ago in Venice I thought about committing
suicide again. From time to time it gets me. But now I've got used
to it. I tell myself, 'Right, here we go again! . . .' And I think about
how I didn't kill myself the other times, and how I'll surely find a
way of riding it out again, you see? So, I go to bed and tell myself
that I'll stay there until it's over. Sometimes I stay there twenty-
four or forty-eight hours at a stretch. When it's over I get up, I feel
good, and I'm hungry—a sure sign of good health!

Georges Belmont: Being in good health has always been important to you?

Henry Miller: Essential.

Georges Belmont: Of prime importance, even?

Henry Miller: Yes.

Georges Belmont: Do you still dose yourself with spoonfuls of
liquid paraffin every morning? You used to in the past.

Henry Miller: Yes, because I was constipated. But that went away a long time ago. You know how?

There was a doctor who swore that he could cure me. I said, 'Thanks a lot. What do I have to do?' He replied, 'Don't think about it, even if it comes back, take absolutely no notice of it and it will go away of its own accord.'

I thought it over and it came to me: the remedy is not to worry about it. And that's what I did in the worst disasters—even where constipation wasn't concerned. I stayed impassive, like a Buddha.

Georges Belmont: And that was enough?

Henry Miller: Yes, that's all it takes.

Georges Belmont: Just now you seemed to imply that you'd suffered from a feeling of frustration even in your relationship with your parents. What was that relationship?

Henry Miller: Above all it was my relationship with my mother. She didn't love me. The neighbours say the opposite—that she loved me very much. In any case she never showed me any affection. She never kissed me once. All the time she used to insist that I was a failure, a good-for-nothing, a worthless character. And also that I always missed out on everything. So much so that by criticizing me, she undermined my very spirit. Try as I would, she never expressed a hint of joy over what I did. For her I never did anything right, nor anything good. When I decided to become a writer, she was somehow hurt. In her view it was pure madness. She wanted me to be a tailor and work with my father. Now *that* was madness, stupidity.

From the age of sixteen on, as far as I can recall, the curtain was down between us. My only satisfaction was that she left me entirely free. I could play around in the street until all hours. As a young kid I was already coming home late at night; they never asked me what I'd been up to.

After that I left home. I lived with the woman whom I have depicted as 'the Widow'. She was my mother's age, or nearly. She had a son a year older than myself. Pretty good, eh?

And then I came back home, probably because I was out of money and out of work. I was unable to go on living with that woman. Yes, I went back, and for a period of five or six weeks I tried to write.

I had my typewriter, and I'd tap away on it. And every time a neighbour, male or female, rapped on the window or rang the doorbell my mother would come rushing in and say to me: 'Quick, Henry, quick! Hide your typewriter, and get into the cupboard!' And then . . . oh, the smell of camphor and naphthalene! There were times when I'd stay shut in there for an hour, sometimes two, because my mother didn't want anyone to know that her son was writing. To her it was something shameful.

Over the years she has never read a line of anything I've written. She didn't want to hear even a mention of my books. When, at a much later date, I visited my mother and father, that was the kind of thing one didn't talk about . . . taboo! Only once, after my return from France in 1940, she asked me: 'Have you made any money?' I answered that I hadn't and that it was better not to talk about it. Then she said to me, 'Why haven't you at least written a book like *Gone with the Wind?*' Think of it, what a woman, eh?

Georges Belmont: Do you think this attitude your mother had could have had any effect, however momentary, on your own attitude towards women in general?

Henry Miller: I am often asked that. Yes, many people say so. I suppose there's a half-truth there. Nothing is as terrible as not feeling loved by one's mother, and feeling no love for her—nothing, not even filial respect.

I have described in my books the way she treated my sister, who was backward. Instead of showing her affection, understanding and sympathy, she was constantly punishing her.

I must have been eight when she began to give her lessons, because the school didn't want to take her—she was impossible, too 'retarded'. I was going to school myself and in the evening I used to do my homework in the kitchen. There was a blackboard there. When my mother decided to teach my sister arithmetic I remember she'd say, for instance, 'What do one and two make?' My sister would reply 'Five'. Then my mother: 'No wrong!' My sister would say 'Seven', and so on. In the end she'd become hysterical and would blurt out any number. And each time she did so my mother would give her a slap. And there I was sitting over my exercise books and schoolbooks, taking it all in. It was . . . I'd sweat like mad . . .

Georges Belmont: Your sister was older than you?

Henry Miller: No. Four years younger. And she was an angel. An angel in the real sense, and she's always stayed one. She has never known envy, hypocrisy, lies—none of that. Yes, she really was an angel. She had a nature of the utmost goodness but, like angels, she was not made to live in this world.

Georges Belmont: And your father?

Henry Miller: Oh, he's something else entirely. When I was young I didn't much like him either, because he caused me pain. Every night he'd come home drunk and have constant rows with my mother. There were always scenes at supper, and it wasn't long before the two of them would start to scrap. And I'd begin to gag. It's a disorder I've suffered from for years; I'd start eating and my throat would get constricted. That lasted a long time.

But later, much later, when I came back from France and saw my father again and we chatted together, I discovered that he was a good man, a very good man. It was my mother who plagued him; she'd criticized him all his life. I really think that she was the cause of everything.

Georges Belmont: And how did your father react vis-à-vis your books?

Henry Miller: Oh, he was always happy to know that I'd written a new book, even though he'd only read one of them, *Money and how it gets this way.*

Georges Belmont: That little pamphlet you published yourself in Paris, before the war?

Henry Miller: That's it. And he thought that everything I said in it about money was the truth. And yet it was a satire, a burlesque even, or something near it. But he used to take it dead seriously.

And there's another of his quirks I remember. He'd read one other book, just one, in his whole life. I defy anyone to guess what it was. It was Ruskin's *The Stones of Venice,* which I myself find difficult reading. Why on earth that particular one! I still wonder. But he literally adored it.

Georges Belmont: Did you yourself read much when you were a child?

Henry Miller: Oh, yes. I always had a book in front of me from the time I began to learn to read onwards. My grandfather was a tailor, like my father. I can still see him sitting crosslegged, sewing

on his low table, and I'd sit down beside him and read—I was six
or seven. My mother would lecture him about it, and say 'You
shouldn't allow that child to read like that; it's very bad for him'.

Georges Belmont: What sort of books did you read at that age?
Children's books, I assume?

Henry Miller: Of course. I was no genius, you know. But when I
was about sixteen, I began to immerse myself in all the great
authors. Yes . . . even Balzac!

I remember I read *La Peau de Chagrin* in English. In translation
the title became *The Wild Ass Skin*. But there was a snag. In
English, as you know, the word 'ass' does mean 'donkey' but also
'backside', and when my father saw the title he forbade me to
bring such books into the house. He figured that it was some
pornographic dime-novel.

Georges Belmont: At dinner the other night you told me that you
were at present re-reading certain books from your childhood?

Henry Miller: From my childhood? Not really, no. Mostly from
my early years in Paris. The Salavin stories by Georges Duhamel:
La Confession de Minuit, Le Journal de Salavin. And also . . . oh,
I forget . . .

Georges Belmont: But cast your mind back. You told me about a
book and we realized that we'd both read it when we were
children . . . *Cuore [Heart]* by an Italian author, Edmundo de
Amici, I think, who is completely forgotten these days, I fear.

Henry Miller: Ah yes, you're right. I re-read it six months ago.
The idea just came to me out of the blue. Why, I don't know.

These days I get a stronger and stronger urge to know what used
to appeal to me in my youth. At the time I was full of admiration
for this or that author, and I like to compare whatever I may think
of him now with what I felt for him in the past. The most bizarre
thing is that in that respect I've not changed at all: I still admire
these authors as much now as then. It's extremely reassuring to
discover that, you know.

Georges Belmont: You don't think that you admire these books
because, as with your own characters, you transform them and
add something to them? . . . That you add, perhaps, something of
yourself, in the final analysis?

Henry Miller: No, no, I admire them for themselves. Take, for

instance an author like Rider Haggard—an American writer for
children and young people who is little known in this country, a
kind of Mayne Reid. I've re-read him. Some of his works really
are great books. But everyone laughs at me when I say that. 'That's
for the kids', they tell me, but I don't think so. Mind you, it's a
fact that he's no longer popular with young people in the States
nowadays. The same goes for Jack London; he's not read much
any more. And there's someone else whom I liked enormously,
especially for his revolutionary feeling—he was a socialist at a time
when that was frowned on. He was treated as a 'radical', as an
extremist, or near-extremist. I forget his name . . . wait . . . no,
I've got it: Dreiser.

Georges Belmont: What lead you to read Salavin again? Chance?

Henry Miller: Yes, in a sense. One day I went for a stroll in the
Rue Mouffetard and the Place de la Contrescarpe; I went back
later, and on one of those jaunts I suddenly remembered that in
Duhamel's book Salavin had lived in the Rue du Pot-de-fer, just
nearby. So I thought, 'Well, now I must re-read the story of Salavin'.

The funniest part of it is that I don't know why I got the
feeling—which proves how much my first reading of it struck me. I
had the feeling that the opening sentence of the book was *'Je me
nomme Louis Salavin. . .'*. But I couldn't find that sentence in
the *Confession de Minuit* which I'd just bought. I got really quite
disturbed and uneasy; and kept thinking, 'My word, Duhamel has
cut that sentence from the later editions; why the hell?' And I
floundered around trying to think why. Later on I found it; it was
in the *Journal*. Then I was happy.

Georges Belmont: How did that second reading of it impress you?

Henry Miller: Very forcibly. It's a work of great simplicity, in my
opinion, and not really French in feel; Russian, rather, as though
Duhamel had been influenced by the great Russian writers.

Salavin is an ordinary man, almost a failure, but he's only a
failure in the world's view of him, not the reader's. On the
contrary, for the reader he's a very interesting character who
reveals every side of himself. That's what appeals to me.

Georges Belmont: You mean that he's like so many of Dostoevsky's characters who are failures in terms of their lives, but who make, one might say, exciting reading?

Henry Miller: Exactly. That's why I say that there's an analogy between Duhamel and the Russians.

Georges Belmont: Do you find that you've a special affection for failures?

Henry Miller: Yes. For poor people, failures, the wretched of the earth, everyone like that. More so than for men who are recognized and famous. And for the good reason that I tell myself that I too am still nothing but a failure. I always identify with these people. For the most part I've been a failure all my life, I think. And even today, I still wonder . . .

Georges Belmont: Aren't you exaggerating rather?

Henry Miller: Perhaps, perhaps, but that's how I feel. I can't get the idea out of my head, do you see?

Georges Belmont: All the same, hasn't there been a moment in your life and in your work when, as a writer especially, you felt somehow certain of yourself and what you were doing? Or have you perhaps always doubted yourself a lot?

Henry Miller: No, it would be wrong to assert that I always have doubts. For instance I am now starting to believe in what I'm doing, and basically, I was certain quite early on. Yes, I think I can say this—even outside my books, being certain about what I am and my ideas generally, a strong feeling of certainty, even. I've always fought against 'knowledge', against intellectuals. That's what's important. In my opinion, intelligence alone leads nowhere and intellectuals can never be certain of anything. They're men who are always doubting. They talk as though they 'know' but they don't know—at least I don't think so. Whereas a very simple man who is, let's say, rather religious in temperament, can have that certainty. And for me it's a marvellous thing to meet human beings like that.

Georges Belmont: You have just used the word 'religious'. Now, there are passages in one of your books, one which I think reveals quite a lot about what people call your philosophy—forgive the expression, I know you don't like it much when applied to yourself—certain passages in *The World of Sex,* to call it by its name, in which you insist on the fact that you are a religious man. Could you explain what you mean by that?

Henry Miller: There's nothing I'd like better. It's a subject which concerns me all the more intimately because most people don't believe that I could be religious. Nevertheless, I am. That doesn't prevent me from disliking all religions. To me all religions are idiotic, and a bad thing for mankind.

At the same time I do believe in certain things. It's difficult to explain. Fundamentally I am a religious man without a religion. I believe in the existence of a Supreme Intelligence . . . call it God if you like. I believe there is a bond between myself and this God who is bound with the cosmos. But I also believe it to be a fact that we shall never *know,* we shall never penetrate into the mystery of life. That's a thing you've got to accept, and in that sense I am religious.

I've no need of 'texts'. The Churches, even Buddhism, are only a travesty of religion in my opinion. Often, one is right in calling oneself more religious, more of a believer in that sense, than many who claim they are.

I believe that chance does not exist in the universe, everything follows rules. Life has great significance. If you haven't absorbed that fact, it's not worth a thing, not worth speaking about. The important thing is that man should never lose sight of his link with the universe. Life is a miracle. For me, everything is mystery and miracle. I can't be realistic about life, like so many young people are. For me it is the sacred, holy thing.

Georges Belmont: You've just used the word 'cosmos'. I think that one of the most striking features of your work is that the religious side of you is expressed to the fullest extent—too bad if this term sounds a bit ridiculous nowadays, it still has a meaning—by a sort of pantheism. Your books are shot through with sudden illuminating moments. For example, in the *Tropic of Capricorn* there is an unforgettable passage where you are in a forest, you've been for a swim, and go into a cabin to change.

Henry Miller: Ah, yes!

Georges Belmont: And at that moment a fantastic storm breaks out; you go out into the rain, with the lightning flashing all around you, and indulge in a kind of ritual dance—I can't think of another way of putting it. I refuse to believe that that passage was pure invention?

Henry Miller: No, it really happened.

Georges Belmont: And you called on God . . .

Henry Miller: Yes, but I denied him!

Georges Belmont: More than that: you reviled him.

Henry Miller: Yes.

Georges Belmont: Just as the ancient Greeks were able to revile their gods.

Henry Miller: Yes. What about it? Does the passage seem hard to swallow?

Georges Belmont: Certainly not. On the contrary I see it as a supreme manifestation of your religious feeling, of that union, or at the very least, that bond with the cosmos you were speaking of a moment ago.

Q & A: Henry Miller
Digby Diehl / 1972

From *The Los Angeles Times*, 91 (January 23 1972), 19–23.
Reprinted by permission of *The Los Angeles Times*.

Our greatest living American writer celebrated the passage of his
80th joyous year alive last month at his home in Pacific Palisades.
Since the publication in 1934 of TROPIC OF CANCER Henry
Miller has produced an awesome body of literature comprising some
50 published books and dozens of unpublished or incompleted
manuscripts, many of which are in the Henry Miller Collection at
the UCLA Research Library Archives. In the great romantic tradition of American letters, pioneered by Herman Melville and Walt
Whitman, Miller's writings are an autobiographical journey through
the past four decades of the 20th century—a spiritual saga of
our times.

It is unfortunate that Miller's work is still so in advance of its
time in stylistic candor that he has been ignorantly neglected even
by many members of the literate community, who regard him as
some sort of eccentric pornographer. Indeed, many of his
books—TROPIC OF CANCER, TROPIC OF CAPRICORN,
QUIET DAYS IN CLICHY and the ROSY CRUCIFIXION series—contain some of the most vivid sexual descriptions in the
English language. And these passages are an invaluable part of
the American experience which Miller chronicles in his books.
Other writings, such as THE AIR-CONDITIONED NIGHT-
MARE, BIG SUR AND THE ORANGES OF HIERONYMUS
BOSCH, or TO PAINT IS TO LOVE AGAIN, are barely even
scatological. Curiously, his best book—and his personal favorite—
THE COLOSSUS OF MAROUSSI, is the lyrical narration of his
travels through the Greek isles.

One of the original expatriate writers of the '20s and '30s, a
resident sage at Big Sur for many years, and extraordinary
traveler, Miller's long and remarkable life is impossible to abbrevi-
ate here. A new book, MY LIFE AND TIMES (Playboy Press,

$15.50), contains an excellent chronology and tape-recorded commentary by Miller as well as a beautiful collection of visual Miller history.

Most recently Henry Miller has come under fire from the women's liberation movement, an occurrence which occasioned one of the most cogent critical studies of Miller's writing by Norman Mailer, who said: "He captured something in the sexuality of men as it had never been seen before, precisely that it was man's sense of awe before women, his dread of her position one step closer to eternity (for in that step were her powers) which made men detest women, revile them, humiliate them . . . he screams his barbaric yawp of utter adoration for the power and the glory and the grandeur of the female in the universe, and it is his genius to show us that this power can survive any context or any abuse."

During the several long afternoon and evening visits to his home, when we were often joined by his wife Hoki and his friends Joe Gray and Robert Snyder, I came to feel that I had never met a man with such depth of human understanding and insight into humanity. He seems to me very close to his own ideal conception of the "whole man." Talking in a surprisingly Brooklyn accent, gesturing animatedly with a cigarette or a glass of gin and tonic, Miller is the consummate raconteur. The following excerpts from our conversations give, I hope, some inkling of the extraordinary experience of meeting this legendary figure.

Q: I've noticed the curious phenomenon that people who know very little of your writing seem to regard you as some kind of priapic maniac and those who read you faithfully regard you as a saint.

Miller: The world in general is only captivated by those books in which I relate my sexual experiences. And that's one side of me. And then another person comes along, and he says, "Haven't you always been interested in the Orient? Don't you talk of going to India and Tibet; don't you believe in the Masters?" There are many different points of view about me. Well, they're all equally true. But the physical side, the lecherous, so to speak—that's the one that they're all interested in.

Q: Do you still feel lecherous at 80?

Miller: No, no, as a matter of fact, I never did behave lecherously. I wasn't a lecherous type; I didn't run around with my tongue hanging out, you know—panting.

Q: In *The World of Sex,* you said that your life and adventures were really no different from those of the average man. You've got to be kidding!

Miller: Well, when I speak of "the average" I mean the guys I knew in my life. And, listen, they were greater lovers than I ever was. They made greater lists of names, and so forth. But unfortunately, they didn't expose themselves in writing. It's only because I put it in print that it's made such an impact. You mention 20 or 30 women; that sounds like a thousand when you put it in print. If you'd known Errol Flynn or Barrymore. My God, yes. That was their whole life. My infidelity was always very naked, obvious. I've never made any bones about it. Although I didn't brag about it, either. I always called it circumstance. At any rate, it's not sinful. If we could lose that idea of the sin business, get rid of that guilty thing, you know, then I think that a great many things that disturb people, would be accepted as very normal, and natural, and nothing made of it, you know.

Q: *Tropic of Cancer,* which was banned in the United States in 1961, is now, 10 years later, being shown on the motion picture screens in full color.

Miller: I don't attach so much importance to that. That is, to the idea that "We've made great progress." The pendulum swings, from Victorianism, puritanism, to this other thing, a wild swing. It's somewhere in between that I think would be the right way of living. Today the emphasis is on sex too much, and with it doesn't go the beauty of the sexual relationship. Contemporary books and films portray it like a contest, trying to show how much you can do. That's not it. With the abolition of censorship, that means that anything goes. The rankest, the worst quality, literarily speaking. That's the sad part of it. This will right itself. The pendulum will swing back and forth, and man will right himself.

Q: What about your "sainthood"?

Miller: I've never had any ambition to become a saint. There are a few who are worthwhile in my opinion. Remarkable men. Because, as Rimbaud said, the saints were strong men. But sainthood, sanctity, doesn't appeal to me. Saint Francis is to me the greatest figure that ever appeared in Europe. But we have no other saints, I think, to match him. And he was a true revolutionary. Especially in the sense of his catholicity. He was a true catholic, with the small "c." He wanted to embrace everybody in the various orders that he established. He had the murderer, the prostitute, the atheist, he embraced all humanity. Whereas most religions shut out all humanity, you know? In Saint Francis's kind of catholicism, you have a real democracy for the first time. We've never had a democracy in the world, either. But that would be the closest thing to it.

Q: I guess that takes care of your saint-sinner dichotomy.

Miller: I could give you some other things people see me as. I've also been portrayed as a very bad writer. I mean, one of the very worst writers. Many of the critics, especially the British critics, say that I'm long-winded, monotonous, repetitious, and I only talk about myself. What I'm doing in my writing is ranting about society. Maybe I say what I believe is the right way of life. But it's my creation, my invention. When I do it, they say he's pompous, and raving, but it comes out in my anarchistic and rebellious state of mind, which I still have. I'm still ranting and raving. All I have to do is step outside into the world, and see how horrible it is. There never was a time when the condition of the world was ideal. We've never had an ideal society. It's always bad. But I think you have to learn to accept it as it is. There's no reason you can't suggest other kinds of worlds, other ways of living. You know, learn to be in it, but not of it. But don't wear yourself out fighting it—which I did in the beginning, as a young man. I really thought I could do something to change the world. But I soon found out you don't change the world. You have to learn to live in it. No special group, no particular individual can change the world. I think the world is changed by the aggregate of people in it. By how they live individually. The great changes come by the things they don't do. By their inertia. It's that failure to live up to themselves that creates bad conditions. We always look for some Hitler, some target to blame. They are not the prime cases; the inert mind, the slothful, lazy mind is. There's the quick and the dead, and most of the world is dead. They're not having the kind of life one enjoys.

Q: So what does a man do?

Miller: There's a big difference between living with a thing and accepting it. You live with it in order not to become ill yourself. To protect yourself. But while in it, you're still detached from it—mentally and spiritually. That enables you to endure almost any condition. If you have that kind of understanding you can look at life with that detached viewpoint, and still retain the ability to lead your own life; you won't have the conflicts that people go through. You have a certain immunity, so to speak.

Q: You sound like a man who has found a way to get through life.

Miller: This is an error, to say that I've found the way—I'm getting credit for that all the time. No. I'm still searching. I'm not writing, I'm not expressing it anymore. I don't need to assuage my soul by writing. I'm not a man who knows the answers, and has arrived at that place where he's serene, on the path and skating, you know what I mean? No. It'll always turmoil in me, and chaos, and bewilderment. But in a different order from that, you have another man, on another level. There's another thing that's important, too. I never renounce what I've done, even if what I've said was foolish and wrong. That was a part of me then, and it should not be taken out, you see, and cleared up, cleaned up. In other words, the imperfections of a man, his frailties, his faults, are just as important as his virtues. You never separate them. You can't. They're wedded.

Q: Well, you say you're doing nothing, but I keep hearing about these new projects. It sounds like you're doing a great deal.

Miller: These new projects are not of my creation. They're thrust on me. And maybe it's a kind of vanity, a personal vanity that you don't realize. There's always a way to get to a man. I would like to be everything—or be, just be. Not do. Being, to me, has become more important than doing. In the early part of my life, doing was important. But now it's being. And that's so much better; because by saying that, you realize that you're saying that the activity of men is humbug, it's utterly unimportant. They make it seem important to themselves. And that's why I revere the sage all the time who doesn't need anything, eats very little, has no vices, doesn't need the cigarette, he doesn't need the television, he doesn't need to go to the theater or anything, and he's just himself and he's content with what he is. And it's a whole world, it's an endless, infinite world to him. Now, that's putting it best I can, you know? That's what I'm sort of aiming at in life. But I'm a poor slob of a Brooklynite, and an American, you see? And I'll never attain that. I was ruined at the start.

Q: How do you spend most of your time, now?

Miller: To tell the truth, I spend most of my time doing what the world would say is nothing. I'm busy all the time, it seems, but actually, it's a kind of lazy life I'm leading. And I would like it to be more so. I wish I could cut all the branches, the obstacles and really float. Really do nothing. I mean that. Nothing—just being. That would be my ideal. But I'll never attain it. I haven't got the temperament. I'm too active inside. I cut away as much as possible; but you can't cut it all away. I'm involved; I can't help it. I don't like it, either. I prefer to be unknown.

Q: Really?

Miller: Yes. Being known doesn't mean a thing to me. Man doesn't want fame. All he wants is room enough to move around in and do what he likes. But all the other—the money, the fame, the success, all that—these are just as bad as non-recognition and poverty and hunger. It's the obverse of the coin. The same. I do very little writing. Very little painting even, for that matter. Oh, it comes in spurts, let's say. I remember one year I did about 200 of them. But that's always on the side, don't you know? In a year I always paint 75 or 80 or 100. But I shouldn't boast about that because it's very easy to do them. Doesn't take me very long. If I have the desire, I can do a watercolor in half an hour or less. After all, I'm 80 years old. I've done the major portion of my work. I feel that. I don't want to repeat myself. I don't want to write a single word that isn't necessary. Now I primarily just want to live.

Q: But having had that writing drive for so long—

Miller: Oh yes. And that drive is still there, in me. But it's dying, dying naturally. If one could have determined his life as he wished, I would have stopped long ago, maybe. When I finally began to realize what it means—what does it mean? I wrote— most honest writers would say—you write for yourself. You're not writing for the world. You're not writing for a magazine, a publisher. You're writing for your own self to find out who you are, what makes you tick, where you're going, what it's all about. Well, once I found all that out, I should have stopped.

Q: Not to be Freudian, but writing does seem to satisfy some need.

Miller: Oh, yes. That is its chief function. But the therapy you give yourself also radiates out to the world. People identify with you when they read you. And somehow they also receive the therapy that you meant for yourself. They are liberating themselves as they identify with you. When I was in Greece, I met a soothsayer, who looked into his magic book, and said, "There you are, you have wings. But your feet are imbedded in the earth. You can't fly."

Q: If writing is a kind of therapy, does that imply that a writer puts his whole self or just his neuroses into his work?

Miller: Well, there are writers, and there are writers. The only writers I respect are those who have put themselves completely into their work. Not those who use their skillful hands to do something. This isn't writing, in my opinion. A man who can dash off a book, let's say, and say it's a good novel, a best seller, even of some value, but it isn't representative completely of him, of his personality, then there's something wrong there. This man is a fraud in a way, to me. All he put into his book was his skill. And that's nothing. I prefer a man who is unskillful, who is an awkward writer, but who has something to say, who is dealing himself one time on every page, that's what the writer is, I think. Of course, that kind of thinking about a writer only applies to modern times. In the past that wasn't so. I wouldn't say that about Dante, Homer, Goethe, Shakespeare, I don't think so. I can feel in them a certain detachment. I've never been drawn to the classics, for this reason. The writing is always too professional, too skillful, and following old patterns, it seems to me, improving on them—but the breakthroughs have occurred with rare men who spoke in their own voices.

Q: Doesn't that contradict what you once said about the best writing being the opposite of personal egotism?

Miller: When I read some of my early work, I say it's something good, strong. But it isn't Henry Miller; it's something that came through Henry Miller. I was just a medium to express it, the instrument upon which someone else was playing. You learn how minimal is your ego, this thing you think is Henry Miller. The thing that became great because of you is not you. You're just an instrument. That's all. I talk about myself because I know it's the truth. I can talk more about myself than about a fictional character because I've experienced it. It follows that the man who writes exclusively about himself is the least egotistical person in the world. It is writing in the right vein, the right spirit. To reveal. Not to boast and brag. That's why in the books I enjoy pointing out my weaknesses, my faults. They're far more interesting to me than the virtues are. When I'm sitting there at the typewriter, my antennae are up, and I'm open to the waves, as it were. The ethereal waves, if you like. And therefore, I'm another individual. I'm at my height, very sensitive and aware then. Now that we're talking I'm just anybody, just like everybody. When I get to writing, it's almost like a monk, putting on his robes, preparing. You put yourself in an attitude of prayer almost. "Let the best in me come forth." I type fairly fast, but mainly the typewriter is an aid to me, an inspiration. It stimulates me, the sound. I used to play the piano, and when I'm at the typewriter, I have the same feeling as when I'm at the keys.

Q: I remember that you describe that process of becoming yourself through a process of dying and rebirth in one of your early books.

Miller: In Paris about 1934: I died. I mean spiritually. I took everything on my own shoulders. I decided I was responsible. I didn't blame my parents, my background, society, school—I was the one responsible. And what a relief it was, that day in Paris when I had a vision of how things were. I really saw myself clearly for the first time. I said I can no longer blame anybody. From now on, I take the responsibility. Instead of being a burden, you threw everything off. No more guilt, no regrets, nobody to blame, nobody blames nobody. You have to accept yourself. There you are for what you are, with all your limitations. There are no perfect beings. Once you get that idea, you throw off a lot again. Do you like yourself when you look in the mirror? I always do. I say, "Gee, I look good today." And I meet the most beautiful women— the most beautiful women are the ones who tell you, "I hate myself when I look in the mirror." I hear that again and again.

Q: Why do you figure that is?

Miller: Why? I figure it's because they're empty inside. They're really seeing themselves at heart.

Q: *Tropic of Cancer* was published in 1934. Does that embody in literary terms the sort of free self-expression you are describing?

Miller: Actually, that was a book on which I suppose I did more revising, more altering than any other book. Largely to cut it down: it was too much and it wasn't organized. Anais Nin had a great deal to do with it. By telling me what she thought weak, and so on. Her letters did a masterful job. Like a buzz saw, she'd cut out phrases. She and I used to sit at that cafe, never forget that cafe on the Rue Lafayette, where I worked for the Hindu; it was right near the newspaper place, called Les Trois Cadettes. And there was a little hunchback who used to sit opposite us, and we used to give him drinks, like a clown. And while we were correcting the *Tropic of Cancer,* we were talking to him, and he's gesticulating, and breathing, and that's how we did that job, in the cafe, largely. I learned a great deal about writing from that first published book. I'd written others, but they were no good; they were like what I'm talking against, the "Writer" with a capital "W." Later I became the person writing.

Q: You mentioned three novels you had written before *Tropic of Cancer.* When did you actually begin working seriously at writing?

Miller: When I was with my father in the tailor shop, in 1914 and I wasn't even writing seriously yet, I met Frank Harris, who wrote *My Lives and Loves.* He was buying clothes from my father and he took a fancy to me, always asking questions—what do you do, what do you like? He was a wonderful man, always drew you out. I said to him, I thought I would like to be a writer. He had just taken over editing *Pierson's Magazine,* and he eventually published an article of mine. My very first article appeared, though, in the magazine *Crisis,* published by W. E. Berghard Du Bois. He published my article about India in this Negro magazine. I guess it was about 1913.

Q: So you did a lot of magazine writing at first?

Miller: Listen, if the magazines would've taken me, I'd have been only too happy to do it. I was determined to live by my writing. There was *Smart Set,* and *Snappy Stories,* and some story magazines around, so I tried to write for them. And to my surprise, they accepted one of my stories. And then, I got the brilliant idea—why should I write for them? I'll go through their files, and go 20 years back, pick out a story, change the beginning and end and names, and I sold them four or five like that. They loved them. Their own stories. By the way, most of the time, most of my writing was under my wife's name. Or sometimes the name of my grandfather, Valentine Needing. Never Henry Miller.

Q: I know that you have a phenomenal memory, but did you take notes or anything to use as refresher material for your books?

Miller: I have one notebook that I haven't even finished which is the material of all my autobiographical work. I wrote that in the space of—well, I was working in an office for the park department in New York. I began in the afternoon, and I stayed after work, and finished there around 5 in the morning, slept there on the floor, and did my work as usual the next day. I had written about 40 pages, telegraphic style, and that was the basis of all my autobio-graphical novels: those 40 pages. *Tropic of Capricorn,* I remem-ber, took only one and a half pages out of that book, and that's a thick novel, you know. So I look to that skeleton to refresh myself, but I don't adhere to it. It's just to give a plastic structure.

Q: You still have that?

Miller: I still have it, yeah. I ought to put it in the UCLA Archives, but I keep it because I still think I ought to finish volume two of *Nexus.* See, I need one more volume to finish that whole *Rosy Crucifixion* series. And I can't do it. I think I'm going to leave it like the unfinished symphony. See, more and more I've grown disgusted with my readers. I revealed everything about myself, and I find that they're interested in this sensational life. But I was trying to give them more than that. That's why I write very little.

Q: For someone who supposedly writes very little, I understand you carry on an incredible correspondence—25 to 30 letters a day!

Miller: I'd rather sit down and write a brief note than call someone up. I hate telephones. I owe my beginnings as a writer to the fact that long ago when I worked in my father's tailor shop, I had lots of spare time and I wrote letters, letters galore. Long letters—20, 30, 40 pages. To friends. These letters were talking about the books I'd just read, or the museums I went to, or they were explorations. Letter writing, I think, gave me my natural style. I have what's called a natural style, and I think letter writing was what brought it about.

Q: I know that you have always read voluminously all your life and still do; are there any books of particularly recent interest to you?

Miller: I read only at night. When I was a bum in Brooklyn, broke, and no work, then I'd sit in a chair six or eight hours, and read. When I began to write books myself, I never gave myself that privilege of reading during the day. It's almost a waste of time to me. I've got more important things to do. It might be more important to play Ping-Pong. Now I say to everybody: "Read less and less." The reason for that is I want them to think more and more. To live. And writers don't need to read so much, really. You see what gives nourishment to an ordinary man—he needs a full meal, let's say. But the writer needs only a crumb and he's nourished. Because he ingests it, devours it, whereas the other man has to take in great gulps. But the writer only needs little touches. His reactions are stronger. And yet, for all this talk, I've read a hell of a lot of books. Many more than I should have, I feel. I read many that did me no good at all—only a very limited number counted, were worthwhile. Not very many of them were famous books. That's another thing: it doesn't matter what literary reputation the books had. What matters is how valuable that book was to you. If that book stimulates you, arouses you, starts you thinking, changes your life, that's an important book.

Q: In *The Air-Conditioned Nightmare* and several other of your books, you have consistently attacked the vapidity and vulgarity of American culture. Have your views on this mellowed?

Miller: America has never had anything approaching the aristocracy of France, right? Never. America to me is always the vulgar mob. And the city man—especially in America—is a hideous type of citizen. In America, the deterioration of the spirit looks sharper than it does in other countries. We have yet to come to the new kind of revolution that's going on, that has happened in China, and Java, Indonesia. We are going to have some kind of revolution, but I doubt that it will be an ideological one, based on philosophical

or ideological principles. I think that the new revolution will come
from the young, and that they still don't know what it is—they
can't give us the structure of a new society. They just know that
this one has to be abolished. I agree with them thoroughly. Didn't
Plato cover this fully? Didn't he discuss every kind of government
that man could have? And what was his conclusion? That it was a
vicious circle. You go round and round. Plato, of course, believed
that in the perfect society, you should banish the artists and the
poets. He believed that the poet's creative qualities are too chaotic
to order a world. Now, my belief is that if you trust the artist,
you'd have a crazy world, maybe, but a delightful one. An insane
one, maybe. But it'd be far better than this one that we have now.
Over the years, we've tried every possible kind of government.
Except this poetic one.

Q: Don't you think that America, in its technological unpoetic
way, has made a lot of progress . . .?

Miller: Progress? World-polluting airplanes, that's their idea of
progress. Now we can be a few hours from this city to that. And
it's the most abominable way to travel. It's killed the joy of travel.
It would be nice to set out on a donkey like Stevenson did. That's the
way to see a country. But what's wrong with our world? It's our
industrial life. Manufacture. Business. Commerce has ruined everything. It allows us to sit here, in comfort, but it has its bitter
compensations on the other side. For every bit of progress we
make I always feel we lose something in our soul. We gain one inch
and step back two feet. With progress. Progress is a phony word.
You may evolve, but progress, in the sense we use it—that's an
unthinkable thing to a real Master. Because with him, everything
that is regarded as progress is actually a withering away. He wants
less and less. What he's getting down to is nudity. Nothingness.
Nothing. As little as possible. That's the idea, don't you know?
Instead of a multiplicity of things.

Q: Many young people profess allegiance to you, your books and
to your ideas—

Miller: That's one of the reasons I'm dubious about them. They
shouldn't have allegiance to anybody. They shouldn't derive from
anybody. I want them to be original. I don't give a damn about
disciples; no man of any stature wants followers. I want anarchy,

real anarchy, but in the highest sense of the word. In real anarchy, each man is an individual, is himself. He's eccentric, and there are no rules to grapple with, and deal with him. That's the great dangerous risk, in that nobody wants to plunge into it.

The whole society from time immemorial has always worshipped youth. Youth is the great word, isn't it? Now we all know, who've been through youth, that it isn't such a glorious world. And I don't know how they got all those qualities that they attribute to youth. Youth is used wrongly, you see. I mean, I think that the young men of 80, see, are the men who could do things. And they have a youth which is the real youth. Do you see what I mean? It isn't a physical youth, it's greater than that—it's a spiritual youth, the youth of the mind and spirit which is eternal.

Q: Do you really feel younger, spiritually, now that you've reached "four score" years?

Miller: As you come near the end, your wonder increases, and maybe you get a little more sense, too—a little more wisdom. When I die, if you were to say, "What is your last word?" I'd say "Mystery." Everything is more and more mysterious to me. Not more and more familiar, but more and more mysterious. I think that scientists would say the same thing. The more and more they get into their particular realm, the more mystified they are. Knowledge is like cutting into a limitless cake. Cut a chunk, it's bigger. Cut another, the cake is still bigger. That's why knowledge is so relatively unimportant. No one has real knowledge. All you can have is wisdom. Wisdom to live. But not knowledge about the universe.

So what is the most important thing in life? It is the spiritual after all, because that is what makes everything else. Because without the Spirit—again, with a capital "S"—you're nobody, and nothing you do physically is of any consequence. I'm not running about asking questions anymore. What I have will do me for the rest of my life.

Reflections of a Cosmic Tourist
Jonathan Cott / 1975

From *Rolling Stone,* 181 (February 27 1975), 38–46, 57.
© Straight Arrow Publishers, 1975. All rights reserved. Used
by permission.

*But you have so refined our sensitivity, so heightened our
awareness, so deepened our love for men and women, for
books, for nature, for a thousand and one things to life
which only one of your own unending paragraphs could
catalogue, that you awaken in us the desire to turn you
inside out.*
Henry Miller on Blaise Cendrars
    The Books in My Life

Henry Miller—"confused, negligent, reckless, lusty, obscene, boisterous, thoughtful, scrupulous, lying, diabolically truthful man
that I am"; author of many famous and infamous books "filled with
wisdom and nonsense, truth and falsehood, toenails, hair, teeth,
blood and ovaries" (his words)—has been called everything from
"a counterrevolutionary sexual politician" (Kate Millet) to "a
true sexual revolutionary" (Norman Mailer); an author who ne-
glects "form and *mesure*" (Frank Kermode) to "the only imaginative prose writer of the slightest value who has appeared among the
English-speaking races for some years past" (George Orwell).

   Now 83, and in spite of recent illnesses still painting and writing,
Miller is still accepting what he once called our Air-Conditioned
Nightmare with joyful incredulity, still continuing to find out and
tell us who he is. This past year marks the 40th anniversary of the
publication of the first Paris edition of *Tropic of Cancer*—Miller's
first published book—and it is now indisputably clear that Miller's
more than 40 subsequent volumes must be read simply as one
enormous evolving work—a perpetual *Bildungsroman*—
manifesting the always changing, yet ever the same, awareness and
celebration of the recovery of the divinity of man, as well as of
the way of truth which, Miller says, leads not to salvation but to

181

enlightenment. "There is no salvation, really, only infinite realms
of experience providing more and more tests, demanding more and
more faith. . . . When each thing is lived through to the end, there
is no death and no regrets, neither is there a false springtime; each
moment lived pushes open a greater, wider horizon from which there
is no escape save living."

Gentile Dybbuck (as he once called himself), patriot of the 14th
Ward (Brooklyn), American anarchist, Parisian *voyou,* cosmic tourist
in Greece, sage of Big Sur, Henry Miller is today an inhabitant of
an improbable-looking Georgian colonial house in Pacific Palisades, Los Angeles—a house teeming with posters, paintings,
sketches and photographs, all tokens and traces of Miller's ebullient,
peripatetic life.

There are a number of his radiant "instinctive" watercolors
hanging in the living room. ("If it doesn't look like a horse when
I'm through, I can always turn it into a hammock," he once said of
his "method" of painting in *The Angel Is My Watermark.*) On
one wall is a hand-inscribed poster listing the names of scores of
places Miller has visited around the world—with marginal comments:

    Bruges—the Dead City (for poets)
    Imperial City, California (loss of identity)
    Pisa (talking to tower all hours)
    Cafe Boudou, Paris: Rue Fontaine (Algerian whore)
    Grand Canyon (still the best)
    Corfu—Violating Temple (English girl)
    Biarritz (rain, rain, rain)

In the kitchen, posted on a cabinet, is his Consubstantial Health
Menu, which announces favorite dishes: e.g., Bata Yaku! Sauer-
fleisch mit Kartoffelklösze, Leeks, Zucchini ad perpetuum, Calves'
Liver (yum yum) . . . and a strong warning: Please! No Health Food.

Across one end of his study is a floor-to-ceiling bookshelf contain-
ing hundreds of his own works translated into scores of languages,
while two other walls are completely decorated with graffiti and
drawings, all contributed by visitors, friends and by Henry himself: "Kill the Buddha!" "Let's Case the Joint!" "Love, Delight

and Organ Are Feminine in the Plural!" "The Last Sleeper of the
Middle Ages!" "Don't Look for Miracles. You Are the Miracle!"

Most fascinating of all is the author's famous bathroom—a verita-
ble museum which presents the iconography of the World of
Henry Miller: photos of actresses on the set of the filmed version of
Tropic of Cancer, Buddhas from four countries, a portrait of
Hermann Hesse ("Most writers don't look so hot," Miller says.
"They're thin blooded, alone with their thoughts."), a Jungian
mandala, Taoist emblems, a Bosch reproduction, the castle of
Ludwig of Bavaria, Miller's fifth wife Hoki (from whom he's now
separated and about whom he wrote: "First it was a broken toe,
then it was a broken brow and finally a broken heart"), the head of
Gurdjieff ("of all masters the most interesting") and, hidden away
in the corner, a couple of hard-core photos "for people who
expect something like that in here." (Tom Schiller's delightful film,
Henry Miller Asleep and Awake—distributed by New Yorker
Films—is shot in this very bathroom and presents the author taking
the viewer around on a guided tour.)

"I really hate greeting you like this, in pajamas and in bed," Miller
says as I enter his bedroom. Smiling and talking with a never dis-
carded bristly, crepitated Brooklyn accent and a tone of voice
blending honey and *rezina,* he continues: "I just got out of the
hospital again, you see. They had to replace an artificial artery
running from my neck down to the leg. It didn't work, it developed an abscess, and so they had to take out both the artery and
the abscess. I'm really in bad shape, no?" Miller says, laughing,
"And this is all attributable to those damned cigarettes. I was an
athlete when I was young—don't you know? I was good at track and
a bicycle rider. I didn't smoke until I was 25, and then it was
incessant. And all my wives smoked, too. If I start again it means
death. My circulation will stop, and they'll have to cut off my legs."

Again a smile and a gentle laugh. "Always Merry and Bright!"—
Henry's lifelong motto.

"You'll have to speak to my left ear—the other one doesn't work.
And I've lost vision in my left eye."

"Can you see me?" I ask.

"I certainly imagined you differently," Miller responds. "When

I heard that someone named Jonathan was coming, I thought you'd be some tall, uptight Englishman with blond hair. But I'm glad I was wrong.''

Henry, unlike his fellow expatriate novelist and namesake Henry (James)—it is impossible to think of two more wildly opposite types—is well known for his caustic Anglophobic attitudes. (Miller in a letter to Lawrence Durrell: ''The most terrible, damning line in the whole of *The Black Book* is that remark of Chamberlain's: 'Look, do you think it would damage our relationship if I sucked you off?' That almost tells the whole story of England.'') But strangely, it is the English Lawrence Durrell who, as a 23-year-old writer and diplomat living in Corfu, wrote the then 43-year-old Miller an ecstatic fan letter after reading *Tropic of Cancer,* calling it ''the only really man-sized piece of work this century can boast of.'' They have been close friends and correspondents for almost 40 years, and in fact Durrell and his wife are expected this evening for dinner. (Durrell taught this past year at Cal Tech, one of the main reasons being to keep in close contact with his friend.)

Hanging on the wall alongside Henry's bed is a dramatic photo of a saintly looking Chinese man, whose face bears an uncanny resemblance to Miller's own.

''That's a photo of a Chinese sage I found in a magazine 30 years ago,'' Henry says, noticing my interest. ''I framed it and kept it ever since. I regard him as an enlightened man, even though he wasn't known.''

''You yourself once characterized the French writer Blaise Cendrars as 'the Chinese rock-bottom man of my imagination,' '' I mention, pulling out my little black notebook to check the quote.

''I'm sure Durrell christened me that,'' Henry says. ''Are you sure I said that about Cendrars?''

''Absolutely, it's in my book here.''

Henry looks at me bemusedly. ''That's really something,'' he exclaims. ''I should have realized this before. But with that book you really look just like that guy Columbo on television. Peter Falk plays him, and he seems a little half-witted, you know, a little stupid . . . not conniving but *cunning*. Yes, I'd like to be like that. That's my idea of a man! . . . Go right ahead with . . . what is it you want to ask me? . . . Amazing just like that guy Columbo.''

"This isn't really a question," I say, rummaging through the book, "but speaking of the Chinese, I'd like to read you a little story by Chuang-Tze, the disciple of Lao-Tze. I wrote it down to read to you because to me it suggests something very deep and basic about all of your work."

"Just read it loudly and slowly, please," Henry says.

Chuang-Tze writes: "The sovereign of the Southern Sea is called Dissatisfaction (with things as they are); the sovereign of the Northern Sea, Revolution; the sovereign of the Center of the World, Chaos. Dissatisfaction and Revolution from time to time met together in the territory of Chaos, and Chaos treated them very hospitably. The two sovereigns planned how to repay Chaos's kindness. They said, 'Men all have seven holes to their bodies for seeing, hearing, eating and breathing. Our friend has none of these. Let us try to bore some holes in him.' Each day they bored one hole. On the seventh day Chaos died."

"That's a fantastic story," Henry says. "And it's interesting that you see that in my work."

"I was thinking of your idea of chaos as the fluid which enveloped you, which you breathed in through the gills. And of the fertile void, the chaos which you've called the 'seat of creation itself,' whose order is beyond human comprehension. And of the 'humanizing' and destruction of the natural order. And I was thinking, too, of your statement in *Black Spring:* 'My faltering and groping, my search for any and every means of expression, is a sort of divine stuttering. *I am dazzled by the glorious collapse of the world!*' "

"Yes, that's wonderful," Henry says. "I don't even remember some of these things you say I've written. Read some more from your notebook."

"I've been thinking about your obsession in your books with the idea of China, and that photo on the wall made me realize how much you look Chinese. 'I want to become nothing more than the China I already am,' you once wrote. 'I am nothing if not Chinese,' and you've identified *Chinese* with that 'supernormal life such that one is unnaturally gay, unnaturally healthy, unnaturally indifferent. . . . The artist scorns the ordinary alphabet and adopts the symbol, the ideograph. *He writes* Chinese.' And in many of

your works you point over and over again to the fact that our verb
'to be,' intransitive in English, is transitive in Chinese."

"Yes, yes, that's become my credo. To be gay is the sign of
health and intelligence. First of all humor: That's what the Chinese philosophers had, and what the Germans never had. Nietzsche
had some, but it was morbid and bitter. But Kant, Schopenhauer
. . . you can look in vain. Chuang-Tze is a genius, his marvelous
humor comes out of all his pores. And without that you can't
have humor. My favorite American writer, for instance, is the
Jewish immigrant I. B. Singer. He makes me laugh and weep, he
tears me apart, don't you know? Most American writers hardly
touch me, they're always on the surface. He's a big man in
my estimation.

"But speaking of the Chinese, I have intuitive flashes that I have
Mongol and Jewish blood in me—two strange mixtures, no? As far as
I know, I'm German all the way through, but I disown it. I believe
that blood counts very strongly—what's in your veins. I've had
that feeling. Because I'm a real German, and I don't like that. Not
just because of the war . . . long before that: I was raised among
them in a German-American neighborhood, and they're worse than
the Germans in Germany. . . . Of course, there's Goethe, Schiller,
Heine, Hölderlin, the composers. . . . Naturally they're wonderful.

"You know something? I was recently reading Hermann Hesse's
last book, *My Belief.* And the very end of this book has to do
with Oriental writers. He mentions how his perspective on life
changed when he became acquainted with Lao-Tze, Chuang-Tze
and the I Ching, of course. And I discovered these writers when I
was about 18. I was crazy about the Chinese. I have trouble, however,
with the novels like *All Men Are Brothers*—too many characters
and there's no psychology—everything is on the surface."

"One of my favorite books of yours, Henry, is *Big Sur and the
Oranges of Hieronymus Bosch.* Your meditations on and descriptions of your friends and life in Big Sur are so serene and lambent,
like some of the great Chinese poems. I wish it had gone on
and on."

"The poets who retired in old age to the country," Henry
reflects. "Yes, that's right. I've tried to model myself on the
Chinese sages. And they were happy, gay men. I've heard that the

old men in China before the Revolution used to sit out on river
boats and converse, drink tea, smoke and just enjoy talking about
philosophy or literature. They always invited girls to come and
drink with them. And then they'd go and fly a kite afterwards, a
real kite. I think that's admirable. . . . We flew kites in Big Sur,
but there we had big winds in canyons with birds being lifted by the
updrafts. The kites got torn and smashed."

"I especially remember," I mention, "that passage in *Big Sur*
where you describe the morning sun rising behind you and throwing
an enlarged shadow of yourself into the iridescent fog below. You
wrote about it this way: 'I lift my arms as in prayer, achieving a
wingspan no god ever possessed, and there in the drifting fog a
nimbus floats about my head, a radiant nimbus such as the Buddha
himself might proudly wear. In the Himalayas, where the same
phenomenon occurs, it is said that a devout follower of the
Buddha will throw himself from a peak—*into the arms of
Buddha.*' "

"Yes, I remember that," Henry says. "Your shadow is in the
light and fog, overaggrandized; you're in monstrous size and
you're tempted to throw yourself over."

"That reminds me of Anais Nin's comment," I mention, "that
the figures in your books are always 'outsized . . . whether tyrant
or victims, man or woman.' "

"That's true," Henry responds. "That's because I'm enthusiastic
and I exaggerate, I adore and worship. I don't just *like,* I love. I
go overboard. And if I hate, it's in the same way. I don't know any
neutral, in-between ground."

Henry Miller's enthusiasms and exaggerations have led many
persons to hold on to a distorted picture of the author as a writer
only of six supposedly epigamic "sex" books (the *Tropics, Quiet
Days in Clichy,* and *Sexus, Plexus and Nexus*) for a reading
constituency consisting primarily of GIs in Place Pigalle, existential-
ist wastrels or academic "freaks" like Karl Shapiro (who called
Miller the "greatest living author").

Of the above mentioned works, *Tropic of Capricorn* is certainly
one of the most original works of 20th-century literature. And the
fact that Henry Miller has been stereotyped so disparagingly is a
peculiarity of American literary history, since his work is one

that consistently evolves, perfectly exemplifying the ideas of rapturous change, metamorphosis, surrender and growth.

"The angels praising the Lord are never the same," the great Hasidic Rabbi Nachman once said. "The Lord changes them every day." One of Henry Miller's favorite statements is that of the philosopher Eric Gutkind: "To overcome the world is to make it transparent." And it is as if with the transparency of angels that Miller reveals an unparalleled literary ability to disappear into the objects and persons of his attention and thereby to allow them to appear in an unmediated radiance. Miller's heightened identification with everything he notices is made even more powerful by means of an astonishing descriptive presentational immediacy and an attendant sense of magnanimity.

Consider his meditation on his friend Hans Reichel's painting, *The Stillborn Twins:*

> It is an ensemble of miniature panels in which there is not only the embryonic flavor but the hieroglyphic as well. If he likes you, Reichel will show you in one of the panels the little shirt which the mother of the stillborn twins was probably thinking of in her agony. He says it so simply and honestly that you feel like weeping. The little shirt embedded in a cold prenatal green is indeed the sort of shirt which only a woman in travail could summon up. You feel that with the freezing torture of birth, at the moment when the mind seems ready to snap, the mother's eye inwardly turning gropes frantically towards some tender, known object which will attach her, if only for a moment, to the world of human entities. In this quick, agonized clutch the mother sinks back, through worlds unknown to man, to planets long since disappeared, where perhaps there were no babies' shirts but where there was the warmth, the tenderness, the mossy envelope of a love beyond love, of a love for the disparate elements which metamorphose through the mother, through her pain, through her death, so that life may go on. Each panel, if you read it with the cosmological eye, is a throwback to an undecipherable script of life. The whole cosmos is moving back and forth through the sluice of time and the stillborn twins are embedded there in the cold prenatal green with the shirt that was never worn.
>
> —"The Cosmological Eye"

Or read Miller's descriptions of the Paris photographs of the French photographer Brassai:

> What strange cities—and situations stronger still! The mendicant sitting on the public bench thirsting for a glimmer of sun, the butcher standing

> in a pool of blood with knife upraised, the scows and barges dreaming in
> the shadows of the bridges, the pimp standing against a wall with
> cigarette in hand, the street cleaner with her broom of reddish twigs, her
> thick, gnarled fingers, her high stomach draped in black, a shroud over
> her womb, rinsing away the vomit of the night before so that when I pass
> over the cobblestones my feet will gleam with the light of morning stars. I
> see the old hats, the sombreros and fedoras, the velours and Panamas
> that I painted with a clutching fury; I see the corners of walls eroded
> by time and weather which I passed in the night and in passing felt the
> erosion going on in myself, corners of my own walls crumbling away,
> blown down, dispersed, reintegrated elsewhere in mysterious shape and
> essence. I see the old tin urinals where, standing in the dead silence of the
> night, I dreamed so violently that the past sprang up like a white horse
> and carried me out of the body.
>
> —"The Eye of Paris"

Most persons seem to have forgotten (or have never known) not
only passages like these but also: the great reveries on Brooklyn,
the pissoirs in Paris and the madness of Tante Melia (all in *Black
Spring*; the hymn to Saturnian effluvia and the talking-blues Dipsy
Doodle passacaglia which tells the story of Louis the Armstrong
and Epaminondas *(The Colossus of Maroussi);* his dreamlike
discovery of the secret street in "Reunion in Brooklyn"; the letters
to Alfred Perlès and Lawrence Durrell; the prose poems describing Miller's obsession with painting *(To Paint Is to Love Again, The
Waters Reglitterized);* the *Hamlet* correspondence with Michel
Fraenkel (long out of print); and the essays on Balzac, D. H.
Lawrence, Cendrars and H. Rider Haggard. All of these have
been overlooked in the still raging debate concerning Miller's prob-
lematic attitude toward women.

The recent Mailer/Miller/Millet literary fracas presented Kate
Millet, in her book *Sexual Politics,* accusing Miller of depersonal-
izing women with his virulent and fear-ridden sexual attitudes, while
Norman Mailer in *The Prisoner of Sex* defended him as a "sexual
pioneer." There is little question, as Mailer points out, that Millet
distorts Miller's escapades and determinedly overlooks the author's omnifarious, picaresque humor. But in terms of getting to the
roots of Miller's sexual attitudes, neither Millet nor Mailer comes
close to the perspicacious criticism of Miller's friend of more than
40 years, Anais Nin, nor to Miller's own comments on these
matters in his correspondence with various friends.

In her diaries Anais Nin often mentions the paradox between
what she sees as her friend's gentle and violent writing, his
veering from sentimentality to callousness, tenderness to ridicule,
gentleness to anger. And she suggests that because of what she saw
as Miller's "utter subjection" to his wife June (Mona, Mara, Al-
raune in his novels), Miller used his books to take revenge
upon her.

Miller himself has written: "Perhaps one reason why I have
stressed so much the immoral, the wicked, the ugly, the cruel in
my work is because I wanted others to know how valuable those
are, how equally if not more important than the good things. . . .
I was getting the poison out of my system. Curiously enough, this
poison had a tonic effect for others. It was as if I had given them some
kind of immunity."

Sometimes, in his letters, we find Miller protecting himself,
describing himself as "a little boy going down into the street to
play, having no fixed purpose, no particular direction, no special
friend to seek out, but just divinely content to be going down into
the street to see whatever might come. As if I did not love them!
Only I also loved others, too . . . not in the way they meant, but in a
natural, wholesome, easy way. Like one loves garlic, honey, wild
strawberries."

But he is unsparing of himself as well: "The coward in me always
concealed himself in that thick armor of dull passivity. I only grew
truly sensitive again when I had attained a certain measure of
liberation. . . . To live out one's desires and, in so doing, subtly
alter their nature is the aim of every individual who aspires to
evolve."

The idea of self-liberation—what psychologists today like to call
"self-actualization" or "individuation"—has always been Miller's great concern in all of his books, which progress from the *via
purgativa* to the *via unitiva*. And even as his novels work counterclockwise (*Tropic of Cancer* tells of Miller's life in Thirties Paris,
Tropic of Capricorn and *The Rosy Crucifixion* of his earlier life in
New York City), Miller gives, as he tells us, in "each separate
fragment, each work, the feeling of the whole as I go on, because
I am digging deeper and deeper into life, digging deeper and deeper
into past and future. . . . The writer lives between the upper and lower

worlds: He takes the path in order eventually to become that
path himself."

This path is often filled with the "strong odor of sex" which, to
Miller, is "really the aroma of birth; it is disagreeable only to
those who fail to recognize its significance." And it is a path which
leads to his rebirth at the tomb of Agamemnon—described in *The
Colossus of Maroussi* as "the great peace which comes of surrender"—and to his rebirth at the conclusion of *Tropic of Capricorn:*
"I take you as a star and a trap, as a stone to tip the scales, as a
judge that is blindfolded, as a hole to fall into, as a path to walk, as a
cross and an arrow. Up to the present I traveled the opposite way
of the sun; henceforth I travel two ways, as sun and as moon.
Henceforth I take on two sexes, two hemispheres, two skies, two
sets of everything. Henceforth I shall be double-jointed and
double sexed. Everything that happens will happen twice. I shall be
as a visitor to this earth, partaking of its blessings and carrying off its
gifts. I shall neither serve nor be served. I shall seek the end
in myself."

And this amazing passage suggests—if not that Henry is a proto-
type of Norman O. Brown—at least something quite different from
what Millet and Mailer are arguing about.

Henry Miller is hardly an enthusiastic supporter of psychological
criticism. "This seeking for meaning in everything!" he once
exclaimed. "So Germanic! This urge to make everything profound.
What nonsense! If only they could also make everything unimportant at the same time." But I decided to ask him about the woman
question anyway.

"Henry," I say, "Anais Nin wrote in her diaries that in *Tropic of
Cancer* you created a book in which you have a sex and a
stomach. In *Tropic of Capricorn* and *Black Spring,* she says, you
have eyes, ears and a mouth. And eventually, Anais Nin suggests,
you will finally create a full man, at which point you'll be able to
write about a woman for real."

"I don't remember her writing that," Henry responds. "That
should have stuck in my head. That's quite wonderful. But it's
interesting, isn't it? It's like that Chuang-Tze story you read me,
about the drilling of the holes into Chaos, don't you know?"

Henry smiles. "But if you saw Anais today I think she'd give you
the feeling that I *am* a whole man today.

"Tom Schiller told me that there was a bomb scare in Copenhagen
when they were going to show his film about me *(Henry Miller
Asleep and Awake)*. A woman's lib group called up the theater to
stop the film from being shown—they showed it anyway—but I
want so badly to write a letter to the women who are against me.
The woman I could write it to would be Germaine Greer. I adore
her—the others I don't know—and I'd like to say: 'My dear Germaine Greer, isn't it obvious from my work that I love women? Is the
fact that I also fuck them without asking their names the great sin?
I never took them as sex objects. . . . Well, maybe I did at times,
but it wasn't done with evil thought or with the intention of putting
the woman down. It just so happened that there were chance encoun-
ters—you meet and pass, and that's how it sometimes occurred.
There never was any woman problem in my mind.' "

"You've been criticized, perhaps validly," I say, "for portraying
women either as phantasmagoric angels disappearing into the
clouds or as down-to-earth whores. Or do you think I'm distorting
the picture?"

"I don't think that's true. I really don't," he replies. "To talk
jokingly about it: They're all layable, even the angels. And the
whores can be worshiped, too. Naturally. That's what Jesus did.
The famous religious leaders always spoke well of whores."

"Again, Henry," I say, "Anais Nin has said that in *Tropic of
Cancer* you seemed to be fighting off the idea of Woman because
there was a woman inside of you whom you couldn't accept."

"It was my mother," Henry replies without hesitation, "whom I
couldn't accept. I was always the enemy of my mother and she of
me. We never got along—never. Not till her dying day. And even
then we were still enemies. Even then she was berating me and
treating me like a child. And I couldn't stand it. And I grabbed her
and pushed her back on the pillow. And then I realized the
brutality of it—I didn't hurt her—but the very thought of doing this
to such a woman! And then I went out to the hall and sobbed
and wept."

"I saw a photo of your mother recently," I mention, "and she
looked like a strong, handsome woman."

"You really think so? Is that so?" Henry says with interest. "I always think of her as a cold woman. . . . But sometimes I think Anais analyzes everything too much. She believes so much that she's had such great help from psychoanalysts, and I'm always saying: Fuck the analyst, that's the last man to see, he's a faker. Now he isn't a faker, he's honest, and there are wonderful men. I read Jung and I know that Hermann Hesse said he was indebted to Jung and Freud. I can't read Freud today, but when I was 19 or 20 I fought a battle for him. Today I don't think it was worth wasting time on, but that's a prejudice again, and I don't deny that. I don't see why we haven't got a right to be prejudiced."

"But psychologically there are so many interesting things in your books, Henry," I say. "The conclusion of *Tropic of Capricorn,* for example, where you say that from then on you'd be both male and female—everything that happened would occur twice. Or the earlier, even more amazing 'Land of Fuck' interlude, which is a reverie about the purity and infancy of sexual desire, in which you seem to become the sexual process itself in an out-of-body journey."

"Yes," Henry agrees, "you're lifted out of the body of the narrative, you're floating somewhere and sex is something like x,y,z— you can't name it. You see, that was a windfall. Every so often you get a gift from above, it comes to you, you have nothing to do with it, you're being dictated to. I don't take credit for that inter- lude. . . . And the last part of *Capricorn* . . . yes, that was a wonderful passage. Sometimes I don't know what these things mean. They come out of the unconscious. It's interesting, these questions. No one picks these things out."

In order to lighten things up, I innocuously ask Henry about rock & roll—something I assume he likes.

"I detest rock & roll," he retorts passionately. "To me it's noise, I miss the beautiful melodies. But I suppose it's an omission. What rock & roll musicians do you like?"

"I like Bob Dylan for one," I say, "and I was thinking that some of your work must have influenced someone like Dylan. Like that passage in 'Into the Night Life' from *Black Spring.*"

"Do you have it there in your book?" Henry asks. "How does it go?"

I read:

> The melting snow melts deeper, the iron rusts, the leaves flower. On the
> corner, under the elevated, stands a man with a plug hat, in blue serge
> and linen spats, his white mustache chopped fine. The switch opens and
> out rolls all the tobacco juice, the golden lemons, the elephant tusks,
> the candelabras. Moishe Pippik, the lemon dealer, fowled with pigeons,
> breeding purple eggs in his vest pocket and purple ties and watermel-
> ons and spinach with short stems, stringy, marred with tar. The whistle
> of the acorns loudly stirring, flurry of floozies bandaged in Lysol,
> ammonia and camphor patches, little mica huts, peanut shells triangled
> and corrugated, all marching triumphantly with the morning breeze.
> The morning light comes in creases, the window panes are streaked, the
> covers are torn, the oilcloth is faded. Walks a man with hair on end,
> not running, not breathing, a man with a weathervane that turns the
> corners sharply and then bolts. A man who thinks not how or why but
> just to walk in lusterless night with all stars to port and loaded whiskers
> trimmed. Gowselling in the grummels he wakes the plaintiff night with
> pitfalls turning left to right, high noon on the wintry ocean, high noon all
> sides aboard and aloft to starboard. The weathervane again with deep
> oars coming through the portholes and all sounds muffled. Noiseless the
> night on all fours, like the hurricane. Noiseless with loaded caramels
> and nickel dice. Sister Monica playing the guitar with shirt open and
> laces down, broad flanges in either ear. Sister Monica streaked with
> lime, gum wash, her eyes mildewed, craped, crapped, crenelated.

"What a passage!" I exclaim. "That's certainly rock & roll
to me."

"I'm glad you liked that," Henry says, "but I have no way of
knowing whether Bob Dylan was influenced by me. You know,
Bob Dylan came to my house ten years ago. Joan Baez and her
sister brought him and some friends to see me. But Dylan was snooty
and arrogant. He was a kid then, of course. And he didn't like me.
He thought I was talking down to him, which I wasn't. I was
trying to be sociable. But we just couldn't get together. But I know
that he is a character, probably a genius, and I really should listen
to his work. I'm full of prejudices like everybody else. My kids love
him and the Beatles and all the rest."

At this point, Robert Snyder walks into the room. Snyder is the
director of an excellent two-hour film entitled *The Henry Miller
Odyssey* (distributed by Grove Press Films, which also handles
Snyder's films on Buckminster Fuller and Anais Nin)—a film in

which Miller is shown in his swimming pool reminiscing about his childhood, playing Ping-Pong, bicycling around Pacific Palisades, revisiting old friends in Paris and conversing with Durrell, Anais Nin and other friends.

Henry has been a film buff ever since his days in Paris, and his essays on *Ecstasy,* Buñuel's *L'Age d'Or* and the French actor Raimu are marvelous pieces of film criticism.

"Do you still see a lot of movies?" I ask.

"Well, as you can guess, I'm a little behind. Bob brought over a film to show here recently—a film that made me sob and weep: Fellini's *Nights of Cabiria.* I could see it again and cry again. And I just saw the original *Frankenstein* again. And of course, the original story ends at the North Pole where everything is ice, and that's the only proper ending for that monstrous story. It's really a work of art."

"There are films that you detest, Henry, aren't there?" Snyder asks.

"*Bonnie and Clyde!*" Henry exclaims. "Did I hate that! I was clapping to myself when they machine-gunned them to death at the end. Dynamite them! Blow them to smithereens! It was so vulgar, that film. I love obscenity but I hate vulgarity. I can't see how people can enjoy killing for fun. Also, there was a perverse streak there. There was a suggestion that the hero was impotent. I don't like that, I like healthy sex. I don't like impotence and perversion."

"What's perversion?" I ask.

"Well . . . what is it?" Henry laughs, confused. "You got me stumped for a moment. Perversion. Now you've got me stumped. Now I'm moralizing. Well, to get out of it nicely, I'd say it's what isn't healthy. I think you know what I mean, don't you?"

"Not exactly."

"Have you become so broad-minded—I'm not being sarcastic— that to you there's no such thing as perversion?"

"I have my preferences, but I wouldn't make a definite judgment."

"I once asked someone what he'd rather be: ignorant or stupid," Henry explains. "I'd rather be ignorant, but I've done stupid things every day of my life. I think we all do, don't you? Every day we're wrong about something. But I have no remorse, no regrets. That's what I call being healthy."

"Just to take you back for a minute, Henry," I say, "someone told me that you knew Gurdjieff when you were living in Paris. Is that true?"

"I wish I *had* met him," Henry replies, "because I think he's one of the greatest figures in modern times, and a very mysterious one, too. I don't think that anyone has ever come to grips with him yet. I was going to make a tour of France with one of my wives, and she didn't know how to ride a bike. So we went out to the park in Fountainebleau—and we drove around Gurdjieff's place, never knowing he was there. What a misfortune!"

"You often write about how it's possible to become aware and awake in the flash of a moment. This concern with being 'awake' was also important to Gurdjieff."

"I think there are two valid attitudes to this," Henry comments. "Because even in the Zen movement in Japan there are those who think you have to work at it, meditate, study hard, be ascetic. And then there's another group, whose attitude is exemplified by the story of the Master of Fuck. It was written by a famous American living in Japan, and it's about a young man whose parents sent him to become a Zen monk. He's a good student, disciplined, but after ten years he's not getting anywhere—he's not enlightened. After 15 years he feels he'll never make it and so he decides to live the worldly life, leaves the monastery and runs into a prostitute who looks wonderful. And in the middle of the fuck he attains satori. . . . I never thought of such a thing and naturally he didn't either, and that's why it happened. Do you know the quote from the Buddha: 'I never gained the least thing from unexcelled complete awakening, and for that very reason it is called that.' "

"Once you're awake, how do you keep awake?"

"I can't answer that question really. But: Do you believe in conversion and that it's sincere? Well, I do, I've seen it in people, and they don't have to struggle every day to hold on to it. It remains with you. I don't know if it ever really happened to me. But I think perhaps it did in Paris in 1934, when I moved into the Villa Seurat and was reading the books of Mme. Blavatsky. And one day after I had looked at a photograph of her face—she had the face

of a pig, almost, but fascinating—I was hypnotized by her eyes
and I had a complete vision of her as if she were in the room.

"Now I don't know if that had anything to do with what happened
next, but I had a flash, I came to the realization that I was
responsible for my whole life, whatever had happened. I used to
blame my family, society, my wife . . . and that day I saw so
clearly that I had nobody to blame but myself. I put everything on
my own shoulders and I felt so relieved: Now I'm free, no one
else is responsible. And that was a kind of awakening, in a way. I
remember the story of how one day the Buddha was walking along
and a man came up to him and said: 'Who are you, what are you?'
and the Buddha promptly answered: 'I am a man who is awake.'
We're asleep, don't you know, we're sleepwalkers."

Henry is showing Robert Snyder some photographs. "Some fan
of mine wanted to cheer me up," Henry says, "and so he sent me
these postcard photos" showing the house in Brooklyn where I
lived from the age of one to nine. I spent the happiest times at that
age, but these photos are horrible, they're like insanity. The whole
street I grew up on has become like a jaw with the teeth falling
out. Houses uprooted . . . it looks so horrible."

"What was your first memory of Brooklyn?" I ask.

"A dead cat frozen in the gutter. That was when I was four. I
remember birds singing in the cage and I was in the highchair and
I recited poems in German—I knew German before I knew English.

"I had three great periods in my life. Age one to nine was
Paradise. Then 1930–1940 in Paris and Greece. And then my
years at Big Sur."

"Why are you living here, Henry?"

"L.A. is a shithole. Someone selected the house for me and told
me to move in. But it doesn't bother me because I have nothing
to do with it. I'm in this house, this is my kingdom, my realm. It's
a nice house, I have a Ping-Pong table, and when my leg was okay
I used to play every day."

"Tell Jonathan about the new book you're working on," Bob
Snyder interjects.

"It's called *The Book of Friends* and it's an homage I'm paying
to close, intimate old friends. It begins when I was five years old—
what happened 75 years ago is so fresh and vivid to me!—and it

starts off with childhood friends. I always made friends easily—all my life, even now. And in this book I'm repeating myself often, overlapping, covering ground I've already written about, but from a different angle. It goes up to Joe Gray—a ex-pugilist, a stuntman and stand-in for Dean Martin. An uncultured guy but a great reader. After reading my books, he started to read everything else. He died two years ago, and he was a great friend. With each friend, you know, I was different."

"The last thing I wanted to ask you about, Henry," I say, leafing through my little book, "was the initiation ordeal imposed by the Brotherhood of Fools and Simpletons—an ordeal you've humorously written about in *Big Sur*."

"The Brotherhood of Fools and Simpletons?" Henry wonders. "I've completely forgotten what that was all about."

"Well, the Brotherhood asks three questions of the initiates. The first is: 'How would you order the world if you were given the powers of the creator?' The second: 'What is it you desire that you do not already possess?' And the third: 'Say something which will truly astonish us!' . . . How would you answer these questions?"

"Ah ha!" Henry exclaims. "That third question I borrowed from Cocteau and Diaghilev. They met in the dead of night and Diaghilev went up to Cocteau and said: '*Etonne-moi!* Astonish me!' The second question was a rhetorical question because there isn't any such thing. And the first question about ordering the world: I would be paralyzed. I wouldn't know how to lift a finger to change the world or make it over. I wouldn't know what to do."

Lawrence Durrell and his wife have arrived for dinner and are now chatting in the living room with Henry's daughter Val and his son Tony and Tony's wife. Henry appears in his bathrobe and speaks to Durrell with the generosity and gentleness that one might imagine a younger son would feel toward an adored older brother. And I am reminded of that beautiful letter Henry wrote to his younger friend in 1959:

Ah, Larry, it isn't that life is so short, it's that it's everlasting. Often, talking with you under the tent—especially over a vieux marc—I wanted to say, "Stop talking . . . let's *talk!*" For 20 years I waited to see you again. For 20 years your voice rang in my ears. And your laughter. And there, at the Mazet, time running out (never the vieux marc), I had

an almost frantic desire to pin you down, to have it out, to get to the
bottom. (*What is the stars?* Remember?) And there we were on the poop
deck, so to speak, the stars drenching us with light, and what are we
saying? Truth is, you said so many marvelous things I never did know
what we were talking about. I listened to the Master's Voice, just like that
puppy on the old Victor gramophone. Whether you were expounding,
describing, depicting, deflowering or delineating, it was all one to me.
I heard you writing aloud. I said to myself—"He's arrived. He made it.
He knows how to say it. Say it! Continue!" Oui, c'est toi, le cher
maître. You have the vocabulary, the armature, the Vulcanic fire in your
bowels. You've even found "the place and the formula." Give us a
new world! Give us grace and fortitude!
  —*A Private Correspondence: Lawrence Durrell and Henry Miller*

As they sit down at the table, Henry says to Durrell: "This guy
here mentioned three terrific questions asked by my Brotherhood of
Fools and Simpletons. I'd really forgotten them."

"What were they, Henry?"

"What were they, Jonathan?"

"I repeat them."

"I bet I know how you'd answer the first," Durrell says, "about
how you'd order the world."

"What would you think?"

"Like a Gnostic," Durrell says, "you'd wipe it out."

"I said that I wouldn't know what I'd do, I'd be paralyzed,"
Henry replies. "But sometimes I do think the world is a cosmic
error of a false god. I don't really believe things like that but I like
the idea. Life is great and beautiful—there's nothing *but* life—but
we have made of the world a horrible place. Man has never handled
the gift of life properly. And it is a crazy world, everything about
it is absurd and wrong, and it deserves to be wiped out. I don't
think it's going to last forever. I think there is such a thing as the
end of the world or the end of this species of man. It could very
well be that another type of man will come into being.

"You know," Henry turns to me, "Larry recently gave me a
book to read called *The Gnostics*. It's written by a young Jesuit,
of all people. And you know something . . . you were asking me
before about rock & roll and the happenings with young people
in the Sixties. Well, when all that was happening, I wasn't aware
that it was a revolution. Now they look back and they call it that.

But the hippies are like toilet paper compared with the Gnostics. They *really* turned the world upside down. They did fantastic things. They were deliberately amoral, unmoral, immoral, contra the government and establishment. They did everything possible to increase the insanity.''

A toast is proposed to insanity.

Even in his early days in Brooklyn, Henry Miller saw through the Social Lie as easily as through Saran Wrap, embodying the alienating Lie as the Cosmodemonic Telegraph Company in *Tropic of Capricorn*. While gainsaying Ezra Pound's dimwitted social-credit economics in a famous essay filled with sublime truisms (''Money and How It Gets That Way''), Miller rejected any and all ''political'' paths (for which he has been often criticized), preferring instead to lambaste every irruption of corporate mentality in any number of pasquinades—one his most delightful being his attack on American bread:

> Accept any loaf that is offered you without question even if it is not wrapped in cellophane, even if it contains no kelp. Throw it in the back of the car with the oil can and the grease rags; if possible, bury it under a sack of coal, *bituminous* coal. As you climb up the road to your home, drop it in the mud a few times and dig your heels into it. When you get to the house, and after you have prepared the other dishes, take a huge carving knife and rip the loaf from stem to stern. Then take one whole onion, peeled or unpeeled, one carrot, one stalk of celery, one huge piece of garlic, one sliced apple, a herring, a handful of anchovies, a sprig of parsley and an old toothbrush, and shove them in the disemboweled guts of the bread. Over these pour a thimbleful of kerosene, a dash of Lavoris, and just a wee bit of Clorox. . . .
>
> —*Remember to Remember*

And in *The Colossus of Maroussi,* he writes: ''At Eleusis one realizes, if never before, that there is no salvation in becoming adapted to a world which is crazy. At Eleusis one becomes adapted to the cosmos. Outwardly Eleusis may seem broken, disintegrated with the crumbled past; actually Eleusis is still intact and it is we who are broken, dispersed, crumbling to dust. Eleusis lives, lives eternally in the midst of a dying world.''

Miller has always chosen reality over realism, action over activity, intuition over instinct, mystery over the mysterious, being over healing, surrender over attachment, conversion over wishing,

lighthouses over lifeboats, enlightenment over salvation and the
world-as-womb over the world-as-tomb. Strangely, cosmologists
have recently given credibility to the intuition that we probably
all exist within a universe composed of space and time created by
the original, erupting, fecundating ''big bang''—all of us and all of our
worlds trapped inside the gravitational radius of a universe from
which no light can escape.

In the Forties George Orwell criticized Miller's idea of passive
acceptance as it was revealed in the image of the man in the belly
of the whale (world-as-womb)—an image which Miller first presented in his impassioned introduction to and defense of Anais
Nin's then unpublished diaries. Miller wrote:

> We who imagined that we were sitting in the belly of the whale and
> doomed to nothingness suddenly discover that the whale was a projec-
> tion of our own insufficiency. The whale remains, but the whale becomes
> the whole wide world, with stars and seasons, with banquets and festivals,
> with everything that is wonderful to see and touch, and being that it is no
> longer a whale but something nameless because something that is
> inside as well as outside us. We may, if we like, devour the whale
> too—piecemeal, throughout eternity. No matter how much is ingested there
> will always remain more whale than man; because what man appropriates
> of the whale returns to the whale again in one form or another. The whale
> is constantly being transformed as man himself becomes transformed.
> . . . One lives within the spirit of transformation and not in the act.
> The legend of the whale thus becomes the celebrated book of transforma-
> tions destined to cure the ills of the world.
>
> —''Un Etre Etoilique''

''The stars gather direction in the same way that the foetus moves
toward birth,'' Miller has said. And his own books of transforma-
tions are remarkably in tune with the new cosmological perspectives
of the universe. Rather than regressing to agoraphobic passivity, his
books continually open themselves up to include and become a
perpetually metamorphosing personality which itself becomes a
''creation.'' ''You have expanded the womb feeling until it includes
the whole universe,'' Miller wrote Durrell after reading *The Black
Book* for the first time—generously praising a fellow author, yet
also accurately describing the direction of his own work.

Henry Miller has continued to foster his ''cosmic accent'' and his
mantic gift but, like the Greek poet Seferiades whom he praises

in *The Colossus of Maroussi,* his "native flexibility" has equally responded to "the cosmic laws of curvature and finitude. He had ceased going out in all directions: His lines were making the encircling movement of embrace."

As the world falls rapidly on its measured ellipse, Henry Miller is writing, painting and dreaming his life away in Pacific Palisades: "Some will say they do not wish to *dream* their lives away," he writes in *Big Sur.* "As if life itself were not a dream, a very real dream from which there is no awakening! We pass from one state of dream to another: from the dream of sleep to the dream of waking, from the dream of life to the dream of death. Whoever has enjoyed a good dream never complains of having wasted his time. On the contrary, he is delighted to have partaken of a reality which serves to heighten and enhance the reality of everyday."

Henry Miller
Ginger Harmon / 1976

From *Publishers Weekly,* 209 (March 8, 1976), 10–11. Reprinted
from the March 8, 1976 issue of *Publishers Weekly,* published
by R. R. Bowker Company, a Xerox Company. Copyright ©
1976 by Xerox Corporation.

Henry Miller, at 84, lives in a nicely trimmed Los Angeles community, Pacific Palisades, in a house he occasionally refers to as a
mausoleum. But he creates his own country within his house, and
the country called Henry Miller may be visited by his Swiss astrologer, by Lawrence Durrell, an old friend, or by Erica Jong, a
newer friend.

Those who want something from Miller seek him out, even to the
point of knocking on his door; his son Tony, who works in the house
during the day and serves as a personal secretary and traffic
manager for callers, usually turns them back. Miller estimates
that most of those who come seeking an audience are looking for
the secret of life or some such profundity. "As if I had a recipe for it.
. . . Well, there's no such thing, don't you know?"

Miller values his heart more than his brain. He accepts his own
intelligence only reluctantly. In response to an observation by his
present publisher and friend that he has constructed his latest book
with a new simplicity of style, he replies that, beyond writing
simply, "Sometimes I would like to write . . . like an idiot. . . .
Because I don't have too much regard for intelligence. I don't
have great regard at all for great thinkers, because I don't think it's
thinking that's ruling the world. It's action. And feeling most of
all, feeling beyond everything."

Miller gave *Henry Miller's Book of Friends,* his latest, to a
Western publisher, Capra Press in Santa Barbara. The book is
Capra's first hardcover book. Author Miller and his publisher, Noel
Young, have a long-standing relationship, their camaraderie dating
back to Big Sur days, when Young was offered a job keeping the
author's grounds in order, in exchange for food, lodging and good
talk for a summer. His principal publishers are New Directions and

Grove Press, he explains; "Why," he interrupts the *PW* interviewer, "are you asking me about publishers?"

Miller, who is fond of small publishers, is often annoyed by the workings of their larger counterparts and likes to tell stories against them. Doubleday, for example, paid an advance years ago on a project which was to feature Miller's observations about America. After a preview of some completed chapters, they turned the book down. Some weeks later, Miller recalls, another editor from Doubleday called, asked after a book about America, and requested an advance look at the manuscript. Miller says the first Doubleday editor was pleasantly stunned when he returned the advance money. (The project was later revived by New Directions, which published the book as *The Air-Conditioned Nightmare*.)

Miller receives the *PW* interviewer in his sleeping quarters, where he passes part of his days. The interviewer sits on a chair next to the bed, and Miller explains that his energies limit his talks to an hour. "Please speak as loud as you can," he requests. He points to a mechanical aid in his right ear, and he explains he has a hearing loss in his left ear. Miller moves at will about the house, but can no longer venture outside it.

In an interview broadcast in tribute to his 80th birthday, the author revealed that his early childhood days were one of the two happiest periods of his life. Asked why he had chosen the friends of those years as the subject of his new book, he says it was done on impulse. "I said one day, listen, I ought to write about my friends, very good friends of mine, but who never arrived, never became known. But they sometimes were better friends than the ones who became known, do you understand?"

Miller's daily life is improvised, his writing likewise. If friends say he writes at a rate of about two hours a day these days, Miller himself refuses any such description—or to talk about anything in his life that implies a discipline. "I am full of chaos, but that chaos is very fructifying."

It is by his extreme expression of the writer's freedom that Miller is best remembered by a generation of booksellers who fought for the right to sell his books in civil suits of the 1950s. Miller's first book, *The Tropic of Cancer,* was published in Paris more than 40 years ago. With *Lady Chatterley's Lover,* the book was one of the landmark cases in freedom to publish in the United States. Miller takes no credit for his efforts in behalf of the writer's freedom. He says he was "writing against the grain, against the times, against everything"—because he could not do otherwise.

Miller's own favorite book, *The Colossus of Maroussi,* is his choice because, in his view, it is his greatest celebration of life—"a joy." In fact, he says, he would still be in Greece today if his passport had not been invalidated by an American consulate official.

Miller's production as a writer has been enormous. It includes voluminous correspondence and many literary essays, as well as the publicly-known works like the *Tropics, Black Spring* and *Nexus, Sexus* and *Plexus,* known collectively as *The Rosy Crucifixion.*

Miller feels writing is an act of self-discovery. "I think that real writing comes from the same source as the dream. We don't write these books. Somebody else writes them. 'It' writes them, whoever 'It' is. We are being dictated to, when we really write with honesty and with soul, and don't just sit down and write out a planned book, as people do."

In his published reflections on writing, Miller has referred to the process as turning himself inside out until he is empty. He extends the same thought to knowledge. "I'm trying to get rid of it. As time goes on, I want to become more ignorant. What good does knowledge do me? I can't help the world. How do you help people? . . . You can't. I push them away. I don't want to catch this disease of misery and loneliness and sickness. We have to help ourselves. There is no other solution."

Miller is constantly pestered for his opinions on sex, love and marriage as if he were an aging movie star. He lives separately from his current Japanese wife, and asked about his preferences in a choice between common-law and legally sanctioned marriage, he elects the former. He says he was "a fool to have married five times," looks dimly at marriage ("It's the death of love"), but treasures love itself. "My God," he says. "It's the only thing in the world—the only thing. Oh, without love we are dead, dead."

Miller always seems to have contradicted America's popular vision of itself: instead of wanting to move west to new horizons,

he traveled east toward Paris; instead of being charmed by the
vastness of the American landscape, he discovered variety in the
tiny islands of Greece. America in its Bicentennial year perplexes
him as much as it always has. America, says Miller, is "a baby.'
He compares the years of its history ("200 *years*") to China ("How
many thousands of years?") or to Egypt ("40,000 years, they
say").

As he grows older, he finds that the visual details of childhood
grow more vivid. He remembers specially happy days in Brooklyn
long ago. What was the second of the two happiest periods of
Miller's life? He says it was in the womb.

"I believe that's a natural longing of man, to want to be back in
the comfort of the womb, where everything was taken care of.
The plumbing was there, the heat was just right, the water always
on tap, you understand? Picassos on the wall, good cigars to
smoke, and so on. You had everything you needed, and you never
lose the sense that this was your first paradise."

Henry Miller at Eighty-Four
Roger Jones / 1977

From *Queens Quarterly*, 84 (1977), 351–65.

When I visited Henry Miller in the spring of 1976 he still looked facially much as in photos taken twenty to thirty years earlier, despite his having passed the age of eighty-four the previous December. The body was frail, shrunken onto its frame, an old man's loose sagging skin around the neck. But the head—with its longish face, taut skin over forehead, and humorous, slightly cynical world-tolerant eyes, crinkled and creased at the sides—was very much like that of the younger Miller.

There before me was the author of *Tropic of Cancer, Tropic of Capricorn, The Rosy Crucifixion* trilogy, *The Air-Conditioned Nightmare* and many others. The old egoist and anarchist in the flesh, amazingly like the man I had imagined from his books and letters. The man whose books had advanced explicitness in literature a significant step, who in Big Sur attracted a colony of followers and later became something of a guru to the flower-power and hippy-type movements in the sixties. And who—this most important of all—signifies freedom in art and life, strength to accept all of life including aging and dying.

Having corresponded several times with Miller, I had his address. I decided to visit and hope he would see me, despite his having written, when I was still in Wales, that he was sorry he could not see me as he was "full of infirmities, and bed-ridden most of the time." When I arrived in Pacific Palisades, I was at first disconcerted to find Miller living in a handsome rectangular white house on Ocampo Drive, respectable boulevard in this middle-class suburb. Ruggedly grand Big Sur seemed more characteristic of Miller than this tamed suburbia with its neat houses, clean sidewalks, and carefully-tended front gardens running into each other. Here the lawns and flowerbeds and shrubs had an order maintained only by intensely careful attention to detail. What was the legendary Free Spirit doing here?

But this was the day after my first call at the house. For getting
to see Miller had not been straightforward. On first arriving I'd
been unable to get any response by knocking on the door. Then a
girl in her early twenties arrived by car and told me Miller was asleep
and anyway did not see visitors. It seemed she did the cooking and
generally looked after him. After a while she agreed to show
Miller a note so I left a few sentences on a scrap of lined paper torn
from my notebook, to the effect that I had come from Wales and
across the continent to see him. I went away, checked into a hotel,
then phoned the hotel phone number to the girl and went out to
buy a cheap meal without any real hope that my call would be
returned. When I returned I was amazed to find a message saying
Miller would see me the next afternoon.

That next afternoon the girl led me into the house. The main
room was dim after the bright sun and I was too preoccupied to
observe properly, but it registered as very tidy and tastefully
decorated, with modernish good-quality furniture. Beyond the
main room we passed through a small hall and entered a medium-
sized room at the end of the house. A bed, just turned down, stood at
the center of one wall. Beside it in the corner was a wash basin.
Against the wall opposite the basin a chest of drawers, the walls
above the chest and over the bed covered by framed photos and
prints of and by artists, including Picasso. And at the desk,
Miller, wearing a dressing gown, tottering slightly as he rose to
shake my hand warmly. Beside me he stood so small and frail I was
embarrassed that he rose for me.

Miller asked me about my journey and about Wales, the country
and people, and the language. Soon he was talking about Dylan
Thomas and the impression Thomas had given Miller of Welsh girls:
"That they were easy to make. Ruddy, robust, vigorous. Not so
feminine. More . . . healthy. But then I didn't put much stock in
what Dylan said. First place he was half drunk all the time."

Miller had no objection to my recording our talk and it made no
detectable difference to the way he talked when I laid the micro-
phone on the desk and recorded the following conversation. It is all
down as it came, except for the gap marked by asterisks. This is
where my cassette ran out, and I was so spellbound by Miller's
words I did not notice for over half an hour.

Part of Miller's genius is in his character, and his voice is a part of that. As I read through the transcription I hear his pleasant Brooklyn monotone again, fluently ranging over his attitudes and experiences, like a spoken continuation of *Nexus* or *Plexus*. I hope that something of Miller's voice, and the spontaneous reality of the talk that May day, comes over to readers now.

Jones: *Do you have many letters from readers and fans?*
Miller: I have an enormous correspondence.

Do you answer them all?
No, many I throw in the basket, most of them I would say. The fan letters, you know. I do answer many though.

Do you write rapidly?
Well I am writing with the hand now. I no longer can type. I write I would say fairly fast. Everything flows easily. I don't have any trouble.

I can imagine you get enough letters to fill an entire day replying to even a small proportion.
No, no, I wouldn't dream of doing that don't y'know. I have enough sense. I have enough sense to survive. Just like if people sit and begin to smoke in front of me I ask them not to. Because its a question of my life you know. *(He coughs expressively.)* Like, people come here to see me, I don't even know them, and they take, they'd have the skin off my back, they'd pick the flesh off my bones, don't y'know. *(Miller gives a throaty chuckle.)*

I was going to ask you: replying to one of my letters asking if you'd help me write a biography of you, you wrote you'd rather see an imaginary biography of yourself written. You've mentioned this several times, why does it interest you?
Well I'll tell you why, easily I think. Because I place imagination above everything. The word "realism" is something I hate almost, abominate. *Reality* is another matter, do y'know? *Reality.* To me that has a great ring. A metaphysical ring. And there's no end to reality, to the meaning or the depth of it or the extent of it. But "realism" such as you get in writing, like certain of our American writers, to me is like the scum on water, you see? So anything that

springs from the imagination, that's poetic, and that disregards
fact—facts to me are only stumbling blocks

*How would you rate a standard factual biography? Such as the
one Jay Martin is writing of you?*
Jay Martin? He's a louse to me! This is a man I'd like to cut his
head off. He's been here, he came here in the beginning to ask
me if he could have my permission and I said No. And he said
Why? And I said, For two reasons. First I don't like you. Right
off the bat. And I don't trust you. And I don't know anything about
your ability to write. Then he begins to tell me all he has done.

Did you see his Nathanael West biography?
I didn't. No, because I hardly read at all now. I have no sight in
this eye. To me it is not so important any more, to read, though I
do miss it. But it hasn't got the value it used to have. But Jay
Martin, yes, that bastard, he went all over Europe I understand,
searching in libraries, visiting people he thinks I know, got every
crumb of information he could. And that's how he fashions
his books.

Perhaps he'll make some money out of it anyway.
Well it hasn't been published. He's got it done, its been finished,
but he hasn't published it. I think largely because he wants
my sanction.

*To go back to the idea of an imaginary biography. Do you see
this as arriving at some more essential truth than a factual biography?*
Oh yes! Oh yes! I would say if you close your eyes and you are a
poet you get more out of a meeting with a man than would one of
these reporters who's a trained journalist and observer. Because
you'd sense your subject with all your being. You see I never worry
about the faults, the mistakes, the errors of fact. That doesn't
bother me. It's the insight, the man's penetration of the other's
character that matters.

*How do you feel about details of grammar and the "importance"
of correct spelling?*
Listen, if I could start all over again from the beginning I would

pay no attention to any rules of writing whatever, not even the
grammatical rules or the spelling. I happen to be a good speller
actually, but it's not important.

Perhaps its easier to say that because you are a good speller.
Listen, I had a marvellous letter a few weeks ago from a French
writer whom I think is the best French writer today. Joseph Delteil,
who lives in the Midi: Montpelier. Do you know him?

No I don't.
He is to my mind the most wonderful. And he's got that rhythm
and the lilt and the verve of a Provençal poet. This is a man who's
galloping like a cavalier on a horse, and taking jumps and leaps and
frisking and doing everything he wants: he is a man who has
complete liberty in his writing. That's the point.

*When you write about your past do you write from notes kept at
the time?*
I did keep notebooks and I refer to them. But I don't necessarily
take it straight from them. In fact I would say I never do. One
phrase might spark off a page, or an entire chapter in the book
I'm writing.

*You said in your letter that nobody knows much about your past,
other than what you've written.*
That's right. Who knows?

The hundreds of people you knocked round with?
They don't know my past, the important part of my life, the
beginning. The childhood, then the first ten years in America
when I'm trying to write and not succeeding.

From when to when was that?
Well wait a minute, I began at the age of thirty-three to write.

As late as that?
Late as that. It was the last date—I mean they say if you don't do
something by thirty-three you might as well give up, you're a
failure. And it's based somehow on Christ's life and death.

So it felt that critical?
Yes. So it was a very late beginning as you can see. My first book

came out when I'm over forty. I'm forty-one and two, *Tropic of Cancer,* easily, easily.

Of course you were doing some editing, so you had pieces published before that.
No! No! All after that! I had three things published, and they were very minor things, in magazines in this country, before I went to Europe. Three things in ten years.

Did you think sometimes, Oh what the hell, I must be mad to go on.
Oh many times, oh sure! Well in fact I know I must have been somewhat daffy, you know, but in the best sense. Mad as a poet is mad, don't y'know? There's a difference isn't there? *(He chuckles.)* Ya know what I mean? All my life symbolizes that I had the guts to stick it out, and do that *(he puts up two fingers)* all the time.

Are you as much of an anarchist in your . . .
Even more I would say, today, though I lead what you would call a respectable life. The other day, just reading about Prince Kropotkin, who was my great favorite[1] . . . of course, "anarchist," nobody here in America is an anarchist, you know. It's an utterly meaningless term here. They confuse it with "anarchy."

Are you saying you are an anarchist in spirit?
No, I'm an anarchist but I'm not an active one, demonstrating and fighting. I never was that, I never had any political affiliations or leanings.

It's a fascinating anomaly that you are noted as a very gracious man, and then there is this spirit of anarchy.
That, and so I couldn't be an anarchist, right?

Yes.
This is so untrue, because I believe Kropotkin was a wonderful figure of a man. From what I've read of his life. And I knew Emma Goldman, and though she tried with a man, to kill a man, for the sake of the movement, for a strike that was on, still she was a gentle and wonderful woman. I've got a whole education listening to her lectures.[2] You know I had started at twenty-one to become a cowboy, do you know that?

You have mentioned it in your writings.

Alright, well I was beginning to have eye trouble, I was getting to wear glasses, at eighteen or nineteen, and I hated to wear glasses. It made me a sissy, I thought. So at twenty-one I pick up and come out West here with the idea of becoming a real cowboy, and leading an outdoor life. I'm finished with books, finished with all that intellectual stuff. I'm on a ranch, a lemon orchard it is, and I'm burning brush with a jackass and a sled. I'm getting all the dry brush with a pitchfork. It was a hell of a job because I had to keep a big fire going, on which all those dead branches were thrown, and I had to overturn this big sled with all that stuff on it and dump it on the fire. In doing all that I got so close to it all my brow was singed off, my nose was swollen, my lips were like blubber. I stood all that. I think the worst thing was the bed bugs in the bunk house. That got me down more than anything. Well anyhow, I was in love then with this widow whom I write about. She was in Brooklyn, and I had run away and not told her anything. I missed her very much. And I told her to send me a wire in my mother's name saying to come home at once, I'm very ill. So I come home. First I had wired my mother saying I'll be home very quickly and don't worry. Then when my mother opens the gate I could see by her face that she had seen through the thing, what a liar I am, what a hypocrite.

But anyhow, at this time I met Emma Goldman. She was giving a series of lectures on the great writers of the nineteenth century. I think it began when I was there with D'Annunzio. And that night I was on my way to a whorehouse when I happened to see the poster and I saw all these writers, Nietzsche, Gorki, all my favorite writers' names. And I stop and go to the lecture instead. And that changed the whole course of my life. From then on I said Fuck the cowboy stuff. I'm going back home, I'm gonna be a scholar, a reader, and a writer.

Did you find later, after that decision, did you find it really hard to have to do other things to survive?

Of course. If you read the books you read what a life I had. How I relied on my wife June to keep me alive. And I did every kind of job, I did a hundred different jobs, and the worst jobs. I was determined, nothing could shake me. Despite the misery I would go on just the same.

214 Conversations with Henry Miller

You were lucky you had such a woman.
Was I lucky! One chance in a thousand. This was an exceptional woman. An extraordinary woman.

I knew someone once, an American woman who said she'd seen you and June in Paris having wild arguments in a restaurant or something.
We weren't having a great time. We were starving to death in Paris every time she came. I couldn't even properly take care of myself and I was a scrounger, a beggar and a liar and a thief, I was everything bad in that period.

Did you used to get angry?
Oh I could blow up. In fact I'm very afraid of my temper. I control myself so that I'm always as you see me now. Serene.

Your books don't give an impression of your having blowups.
I had, oh many many. In fact it would come to blows, yeh yeh yeh. Umn . . . But I hope I have lived that down. I deplore that now. Now I have equanimity, and if I may say I have even serenity. But it's taken all these years.

You mention serenity, and there are references to Zen in your writings. How do you feel about the idea of enlightenment and leaps to insight?
As a matter of a fact I am a great Zen enthusiast. In Zen if you have *satori,* if you reach it, it comes like *that!* Always instantaneous. It isn't a slow evolution. Listen, I will tell you now, I can remember the very day, sometime in the 1930s in Paris, and I had had sort of a hallucination. There was a woman [Madame Blavatsky] who wrote *Isis Unveiled,* the most extraordinary book any woman could have written, like a man's work. She was a Russian. She looked like a *muzhik,* a Russian peasant woman. I had either been reading something of hers or talking about her to somebody who was an occultist. And as a result of that about noontime, I thought I felt her presence in the room. And I'm not inclined to be that way. I looked around and there was nobody of course, but it was very strong, the impression. And the next thing I knew I had had what you might call a *satori* experience. Suddenly I realized that I alone am responsible for all my misery. Not society, not economy,

not my parents, not any other thing. Me. Just me. And the
moment I fully realized that I was like a liberated man. Completely
liberated. Free. Free. Isn't that a strange thing? I took it all on my
shoulders, and felt lightened.

*It must have taken great courage to write the way you have. To
say the things, expose yourself the way you have.*
Oh yes, that I must have had, everybody concedes that. I don't
take credit for it. It was just natural with me. Oh wait a minute,
no I'll modify that. I had to be absolutely desperate before I could
write like that. I had been put right down, to the very bottom,
ignored, and spat upon, and humiliated. Everything wrong happened to me. And my attitude was, I'll get back at you, you
bastards, fuck you. I'll show you who I am.

*The other way to go I suppose is to go with it, get a job in regular
writing on some journal or paper whatever. Go commercial
for survival.*
Oh no, don't do that. Better not to survive. *(He laughs.)* Strange
as that may sound. Because it's really hard to die. You won't die of
starvation. Nobody'll let you starve to death, I found that out.
You'll come damn near it and you'll be miserable, but you won't
starve to death.

*Maybe there are worse-feeling things. I mean, never mind being
poor, what's worse is looking poor!*
You talk a little like Bernard Shaw. He had a detestation of
poverty. Shaw thought it was stupidity to be poor.

If I could give up writing I would, I'll tell you that.
You would huh? Do you really believe that? I don't believe you,
offhand. You wouldn't have travelled all this distance to see me.

*Maybe that's because I can't give up writing. I wish I could
though.*
Yeh. But you can't. That's it. That's the answer. Another thing
is, you know what I always tell anyone who writes and asks my
opinion. I hate to give advice, but I will answer young people who
are writing in this way: If you know what you are doing you must
realize that you are in for ten years before you are accepted in print;

and it'll be another ten years, if you're lucky, before you're
recognized as a writer. Do you see? So it's a terribly long haul.

Is it worth it?
Yes, yes it is. In the end you will, no matter . . . Oh Yes! I
wouldn't change my life for anything. And I tell you, I touched
bottom many times, not once, many times. You know I was a
panhandler. I got to that bad place where at night when I'm married
to this woman who helped me, you know, made me write, and I
wasn't getting anywhere, and we had no money, she goes out,
she tries to rustle up money, and I go out at night when the theater
crowd is coming out of the theater, and they're coming this way
and I'm going against the tide and saying Excuse me can you give
me a dime? And you know that some nights I didn't get a fucking
cent. Not a cent!

*I feel this question is sort of rude. But you know that reading
your books I get the impression sometimes that although you're
very friendly and open, you're saying to all those people you are
borrowing from and staying with and sponging off, You are a
right cunt.*
Oh yes, that's right. I was a superior sort of a . . . an arrogant, I
would say, individual.

But if it's true, that you are saying, say, Sylvester is a right . . .
I told you, I'm a paradox.

How do you feel about yourself?
How do I feel about myself?

When you see this guy who's done and said these lousy things.
I like myself, do you know that? I like myself, I like living with
myself. When I get up in the morning and go and wash myself and
look in the mirror, I say Henry, how are you, you look good! Even
with the decrepitude which has crept over me. Eighty-four years,
infirmities of all kinds.

*I wanted to ask you, do you feel that your attitudes have helped
you lead such a good long life?*
I do think a lot has to do with that. They warn you about germs,
about this and that, but they don't tell you that you should be a

free spirit first of all. If you have freedom, the freedom of spirit,
you'll overcome all those germs and microbes and whatever they
talk about. I think. *(He chuckles.)*

*But it's not easy to keep free. Did you ever worry about lacking
possessions, luxuries? Think damn it, I haven't got a car, I'm
thirty-odd, forty-odd, and I haven't got a house or anything . . .*
Yeh, listen, I must tell you now a very interesting experience. I
was back from Europe. I had been all over and I was back from
Greece, and I'm living in Westwood here in Los Angeles. And
there's a Beverley Glen, a street, and it goes up a mountain. I lived in
that. It was like a lane, and a very wonderful spot. I lived there as
the guest of a man and his wife. I had no car. I didn't have a cent
in the bank, I didn't have a bank account, I didn't even have any
money in my pocket. I was being kept, do you understand. And I
would walk and never think anything about it, from that place, into
Westwood village which was like three or four miles, with a
laundry bag with the dirty laundry over my shoulder, and come
home with shopping for the family. Walking, all the time walking.
Now then . . .

How did you feel about yourself when you had so little?
I tell you I don't change much. I'm so easily satisfied. If I know
that I'm gonna sleep in a bed tonight and that I'm gonna have my
dinner, maybe a glass of wine with it, that's just enough to keep up
my spirits.

What about company?
I can do without company. I always have been able to.

Female company?
That's a little more difficult, yes, but I was always lucky. But I
never finished my story. There's a reason for my telling you this.
And it's a very interesting one. I met by chance, through a French
writer, a Greek woman who was the wife of a shipowner named
Niakos, and she was a millionairess. She was living in Pasadena,
and she heard that I was living here, and invited me to come to
her hotel. They were having dinner outdoors. There was a band and
they had a dance floor, and she was a very charming woman. I
danced with her a few times. And we got to know each other and

she would come in a limousine with a chauffeur to pick me up, drive me around, take me places. But I never attempted to make love to her. I had a very great regard for her. One day she calls me up on the phone. She said, You know Henry, I can't tolerate this idea that you are walking around in rags, and you have no money, and this and that, and no car, and here I am a millionairess. I can afford to do anything. I wish tomorrow that I could meet you, open a bank account, get you a car, buy you clothing, put some money in the bank, all that. And I was overwhelmed. I began to laugh, you know. I said, Look, that's wonderful, give me time to think about it. Because I was too embarrassed, you know. And that night I had a dream. And this is the most wonderful dream I ever had in my life. I dreamt that I talked to God face to face. He was some kind of a big man, I don't know how he looked, but I talked to him. And God said, Henry, I am going to give you everything you wish. What is it you would like, tell me. Anything you wish is yours. And I was so elated that I said Dear God, I said, if you mean that I don't then need anything. And then I woke up. And I phoned her the next day to tell her my dream. She says, That's a marvellous dream. *(Miller breaks off, laughing deeply.)* And I said, Now you won't give me anything. No she said, I respect that. It was so wonderful. Do you understand? It was a wonderful thing, wasn't it? Don't you think? I said to her, Look you've given me a fortune already, by your willingness to do all this. *(A sound is heard in the passage and I look round.)* Somebody there? Do you hear someone? Linda should be around or maybe just came back from the store. Say listen, we've got to begin to think of stopping, you know. I can't go on. I'd like to in a way, I enjoy talking to you.

I could go on like this for hours if it was possible.
You are going back to Wales soon?

I'm afraid so.
You don't have money for travelling around the world is that it? Did you ever try hitchhiking in America?

I tried but I didn't get a lift so I took a bus.
Too bad. Because you can have wonderful experiences, good and bad.

Have you hitchhiked in the States?

I did a lot of it in my time, when I was broke. Or I'd just begin to hitchhike because I was fed up with everything. I'd want to get the hell out of a place. And the guy would stop and say Where are you going? I'd say Anywhere, wherever you are going! And you know that often at the end of a ride when I got out, of course I had been doing a lot of talking, the guy would say Are you sure you are alright, that you can make it? How about this? And he'd hand me a five dollar or a ten dollar bill sometimes. That happened to me again and again. Then others say nobody ever did that to me. Say this is way off the subject, but before you go, if you don't know a certain book I'd like to recommend you read it. I suppose you can get it in England. Its a thin book called *The Marvellous Adventures of Cabeza de I'aca,* by Hamiel Long. Its a tremendous thing to me. I'll write it down for you.

That reminds me. On the letterhead of one of your letters, printed at the foot of the page was a saying in Spanish or Portugese: Valor . . . something pobre . . . san cu.

That was Portugese. And you know what it meant? "When shit becomes of value, the poor will be born without arseholes." Good isn't it? *(He laughs.)*

This book may be a very timely thing for you to read. If you want courage of the first water this will give it to you. You'll never have read of an experience like this. It is a true experience. The book is a transliteration of a letter by one of Cortez's men to His Majesty King Philip of Spain. This soldier was shipwrecked in Florida and lost the whole battalion and crew. And he and another man set out on foot through the jungle and are caught by Indians, and therein begins the story of their adventures. When you are depressed, and you think you've got it bad, take a look at that. Mmn. Yeh.

Did you ever feel like writing for films or TV?

No I never did. It's not in my nature. I have no talent for it. I wish I could in a sense. It's an easy way to make a penny. They pay well, don't y'know. Whereas my books . . . look I have seventeen books by one publisher here in America. You know what my royalties are each year? It doesn't vary. Five to six thousand dollars. For seventeen titles. A yearly royalty!

But your books are in about twenty languages aren't they?
Oh yes. But there are, say, four or five languages in which they're
flourishing. Say, German, French, maybe Danish, Swedish, Italian.

How are your sales in Britain?
Terrible. Terrible.

It's strange, because I could mention your name to anybody.
They know the name. I know. It's the same here. You know
you'd think I'm the best known guy in the world or something, and
everybody thinks I'm a millionaire therefore. Which is so far from
the truth. Listen, when the income tax came, I didn't have enough
money I thought. And at the last minute my accountant makes up
my statement. And he says Henry you don't have to pay a cent.
You overpaid last year. Not only that, I get fourteen thousand
dollars back, because I overpaid. Can you believe that? That was a
stroke of fortune.

Are you writing much these days? Apart from letters.
Oh yes, I'm writing all the time, you might say. For instance did
you see what last came out? This is the last thing that I'm on, and
will be on for another ten or fifteen years. My "Book of Friends."
This is only the first volume of this work. I would give you a copy but
I have only two and they are going to someone in the orient who is
translating me into Chinese.

*Are your writings about sex true, or as some people suggest, like
reviews in British Sunday papers for example, are they just
wish fulfillment?*
No! You know that's typical. That's why the British are my
number one enemies. They are so tight arsed and restrained and
prissy they fart around afraid to let go and they can't believe anyone
else could let go. Every word I wrote was true! And much more,
much more.

*[There followed talk on living writers, which cannot be printed.
Then we are talking about Hemingway.]*

Hemingway in my mind was not the great writer they make him
out to be. He was a craftsman. But he wasn't a craftsman as good
as Somerset Maugham. There was a real craftsman. But if you are

a craftsman you go on turning it out. It gets thinner and thinner.
This French writer I told you about, who I consider a great master,
Delteil, he wrote me a wonderful letter. He had just had a heart
attack and was in the hospital. That's why he wrote the letter,
because he said It's so absurd, that I who consider myself unique
and such a great man, *he* says *(Miller laughs delightedly),* and here
I'm reduced to nothing by a little thing like the heart. And then
. . . Why did I tell you this now, there was a reason . . .

*We were talking about craftsmen and artists, Hemingway and
Maugham.*

Yes, yes, um, oh yes . . . You see, I'm eighty-five and my memory
is getting spotty. I'm getting old. Well, I wrote a little book in French
for the first time not so long ago. And I sent it to Gallimard in
France, the publisher. Claude Gallimard wrote me a letter in *English,*
which he never does, and it begins Dear Henry Miller, I have just
finished your little book. I find it absolutely delicious. Even when
you take liberties with the French language it's full of wit and charm
and invention.

Now he hasn't yet published the book or really done anything
because he's haggling over the advance he should give me. He wants
to give one-fifth of what my agent is asking. Can you imagine? And
here he's got a book on his hands and going with it in the appendix
this letter by the master of the French language, Joseph Delteil.
Now what does this letter talk about? This letter says, he says, Dear
Henry, something like that, So you are writing a book in a foreign
language, a language you don't know—though I did know French
somewhat, or I couldn't have done it—But he said What an adven-
ture, what an opportunity. You can throw everything to the
winds. Fuck the rules, he said. By all means. Bad spelling, no
grammar, do anything you like, it's all yours, it's a playground.
Unfortunately I couldn't take that attitude. *(Miller chuckles rue-
fully.)* I didn't feel as free as that in writing it. I was cautious,
because I am writing in a foreign language. Now I would love one
day to do that in English, to take all the liberties. Only I can't.
I'm conditioned now, you know what I mean? After fifty years of
writing good writing, I can't now suddenly write like an idiot. But
that's what I'd like to do. *(He breaks off, laughing.)* Sounds crazy
doesn't it?

Sounds great. I'd love to do it myself. As far as Hemingway goes though, I find the intensity of much of his work still amazing. The distillation, purity of prose and emotion.

(Laughing.) This is the best I've heard about Hemingway since I know his name, you know that? And I must tell you, as much as I put him down, that first book, *The Sun Also Rises,* had a lot to do with my going to France, it inspired me to go. It shows something doesn't it?

Are they other ends of an extreme, Hemingway's approach and yours?

Yes. He was a very disciplined writer. He was a totally different type physically than I. He was a physical individual, an athlete, a sportsman, a hunter, an adventurer. And though my life is adventurous, its not that kind. I didn't go to Africa. I didn't shoot lions and go in the bull ring and all that.

You rode your bicycle.

Yes I rode my bicycle. Tell me, now you've met me, don't you feel it's better not to see someone whose work you admire?

Why?

Perhaps it's better to keep the idea so the reality doesn't spoil it.

I'm not disappointed if that's what you mean. In fact the reverse. Miller the man seems to me remarkably like Miller the writer.

Really, really, good. By the nature of things there is a separation between the man and the man his writings present. But I try to keep the man and the writer like this. *(He holds up two fingers pressed together.)*

What did I hear about an article by Norman Mailer in a Los Angeles paper on this sort of thing?

Yes. I should like Mailer. I ought to be grateful. He's my number one champion here in America at this time, don't y'know. But he wrote about "Miller the man" and "Miller the writer" as if they are two different people. But I am Miller, and it's me who's writing. The writer had those experiences, is the man in the books . . . Mailer is writing a big book now they say. 500 pages of my writings or something, with his writings about me.[3] How about that, eh? He doesn't even know me and he's writing as if he does. How should I feel about that? This article in the L.A. newspaper, no one could tell what the hell it was from or make it out. It didn't have a proper introduction or end or point. Turned out it was an excerpt from this big book. I don't know why the paper published it. Hmn . . . Listen though, we've got to call a halt. I wanna ask you one thing, I don't wanna embarrass you, do you need a few bucks? I can let you have some money if you need any . . .

NOTES

1. Peter Alexcyevich Kroptokin, 1842–1921. A learned and distinguished man, known for important geographical work involving glaciation and mountains; from the late 1870s till his death in 1921 the foremost leader and theorist of the anarchist movement. By anarchism he meant that all forms of government should be abolished. He wanted to put anarchism on a scientific basis. It is interesting to compare Miller's account of the Big Sur community (in *Big Sur and the Oranges of Hieronymus Bosch*) and Kropotkin's idealistic view of a decentralized, nonpolitical, cooperative society in which people develop their creative faculties without interferences from rulers, priests or soldiers. Kropotkin envisaged private property and unequal incomes giving way to free distribution of goods and services. Each person would be the judge of his own requirements, taking from the common storehouse whatever he deemed necessary. People would do both manual and mental work and division of labor would yield a variety of jobs, resulting in the sort of integrated organic existence that had prevailed in the medieval city.
2. Emma Goldmann, 1869–1940. An anarchist, editor and propagandist, lecturer and literary critic. She was born in Lithuania and grew up there, in East Prussia and in St Petersburg. She emigrated to the United States in 1885. She formed a close association with Alexander Berkman who was imprisoned 1892 for attempting to assassinate Henry Clay Frick during the Homestead Steel strikes. She was imprisoned in 1917 for opposing American involvement in the First World War. Released in 1919, she was deported to the Soviet Union with Berkman and 200 others, but became quickly disillusioned there and returned to Europe. She joined the anti-fascist cause in the Spanish Civil War, and while working on its behalf died in Toronto on 14 May 1940. Miller had met her about 1913.
3. *Genius and Lust: A Journey Through the Major Writings of Henry Miller* (New York: Grove Press, 1976).

Henry Miller Now
Kenneth Turan / 1977

From *The Washington Post* (October 23, 1977), H1, H6–8.
Reprinted by permission of Kenneth Turan.

"When a man has reached old age and has fulfilled his mission, he has a right to confront the idea of death in peace. He has no need of other men, he knows them already and has seen enough of them. What he needs is peace. It is not seemly to seek out such a man, plague him with chatter, and make him suffer banalities. One should pass by the door of his house as if no one lived there."
Typed translation from the Chinese on
  Henry Miller's front door

PACIFIC PALISADES, CA.—Henry Miller is old. Nearly 86 and physically infirm. "I have so many ailments," he says, "it would take an almanac to list them." It doesn't seem possible.

For if Henry Miller's boisterous writings do anything, if "Tropic of Cancer," "Tropic of Capricorn," "Black Spring" and fifty other books have any resonance at all, they affirm living, they reek of life.

"Wild extravagance, a mad gaity, a verve, a gusto, at times almost a delirium," is how his friend Anais Nin characterized his work, and Miller himself says of all he's done, "I think it says primarily 'freedom,' freedom in every respect."

His enormous good humor, barely containable in printed words, his breathless zest for every aspect of existence, for the sexual side especially but really for everything—the scroungers, the lice, the roaches, the prostitutes with wooden legs—it all roars out of his books, a primeval blur of activity. Wrote George Orwell, "The attitude is 'Let's swallow it whole.' " Where could growing old possibly fit in?

"Well, I wouldn't recommend it," Miller says, somehow managing to look impishly attractive in a blue terrycloth bathrobe over pinkish pajamas and white orthopedic shoes. "The time when you

224

begin to fall apart, it's something I never counted on. Up to five
years ago, I was riding bicycles, swimming, playing ping-pong all
day, even in the rain. I played ping-pong with young men and
could beat them. Even the Japanese.''

Yet despite tiring easily now, despite having to move around with
a walker, despite losing sight in one eye and the hearing in one
ear, Henry Miller continues to astound.

"From the neck up I'm all right," is how he put it in his gravelly
Brooklyn voice, but it is more than being all right, it is retaining
all the intellectual vigor, the cascading vitality that was the trade-
mark of his earlier days, it is how he still manages to be a natural
force, quizzical, questioning, "an anarchist, radical to the core,
don't you know" in his own words, occupying his space "with all
the palpability of a huge elm lying uprooted in your backyard" in
Norman Mailer's.

His house is a modest, white two-story building decorated with
black ironwork where Miller, separated from a fifth wife, lives alone
except for a housekeeper, though his son Tony has a house nearby
and visits often. The decor is simple, with posters from films
made of his books as well as copies of the watercolors he did for
relaxation thumbtacked to the walls. And then there is that note
on the door.

"I get visitors all the time," he explains. "What do they want,
they want my spirit. They have read my books, usually, and they
say, 'You had a good time, I am now where you were when you
started, help me, give me $5,000.' Well, I never did this, I never
knocked on doors. So I push them away. I say 'Find out for
yourself, do it yourself, do it the hard way.'

"When I arrived in Paris I didn't even have $10. I suffered greatly
financially, don't you know. I've been so poor that I only started
a bank account when I was sixty. Before that, I carried everything
I had in my pocket. Even now, everyone thinks I'm a rich man, but
I'm not too well off. It 's like pulling teeth to get my royalties. I
don't think money is in my horoscope. Everything else, but not
money.''

Born in Manhattan the day after Christmas, 1891, Miller grew up
in the Williamsburg and Bushwick sections of Brooklyn. His

parents were of German background, his father a tailor, his mother, a person he doesn't hesitate to say, "I hated all my life."

Even in his 30's, when he was home and neighbors called, she would make him put his typewriter away and hide in the closet. "I stood in that closet sometimes for over an hour, the camphor bells choking me," he wrote. "All my life she hated the idea of my being a writer."

"She was a rigid, puritanical woman, we never got along at all," Miller says, still unbelieving. "She never read anything I wrote, and all because I wouldn't become a tailor and take over my father's business."

He turned instead to a series of odd jobs, the most notable being as an employment manager for Western Union, an organization which became the chaotic Cosmodemonic Telegraph company in his books. He even remembers an unfortunate stint working as a night reporter for the *Washington Post* as a change from a dull daytime government job during World War I: "I thought I'd get excitement as a reporter, but I didn't have very good assignments. I quit after three days."

He married in 1917, the first of five times that would leave him with three children, two daughters and a son. His first book, *Tropic of Cancer,* came out in 1934 when he was 43, old for an author. Even at that point, he says, "It's a miracle I found a publisher."

Capricorn followed five years later, and all those other books followed after that, but Miller never escaped being picked at by censorship problems. It was not until 1961, for instance, that the Justice Department ruled that his novels were not obscene after Grove Press, emboldened by its success with D. H. Lawrence's *Lady Chatterly's Lover* brought out *Cancer* and *Capricorn* in paperback editions.

Yet as late as 1965 Miller was still being described as "the most banned author in Australia," six of his books being no-nos there, and in 1967 a magistrate in Lodi, Italy, said that some passages in *Cancer* "surpass the imagination, are unrepeatable and offend decency and morality."

Miller's perennial response was to quote Romans XIV: "There is nothing unclean of itself, but to him that esteemeth anything to be unclean, to him it is unclean.''

Yet perhaps the most charming and surprising thing about Henry Miller at 86 is precisely that he does not dwell on the predictable stuff, that he continues to surprise, continues to be difficult to pin down or predict, a man generically prone to giving unsettling answers to simple questions.

Believer in the self though he is, for instance, Miller did not take kindly to the hippy movement. "They claimed me as one of them, but I had no use for the hippies. I looked on them as a bunch of bums," he says, just like that. "You should do something, work or be creative, not just idle your life away."

Miller is also not totally in favor of the new sexual freedom: "There I take a very conservative view. I believe there are limitations to everything. They shouldn't be dictated by any so-called superior group, of course, but our own sense of decency should lead us to call a halt at certain places." Take that Xavier Hollander.

And no matter what you might have expected, Miller takes a dim view of pornography, of all things, as well. "A lot of books today are horrible, especially the sex books," he says, fiesty. "I never read much erotic literature, except the classics. What's wrong with them? Everything. In the first place it's not literature. It doesn't give any value. It's titillating to teenagers who are still masturbating. I was accused more of obscenity than pornography: I could be bruising, damaging, healing, but not titillating. Today writers are just flirting with sex."

Yes, Miller himself is still writing, having just finished Volume II of a reminiscence called *The Book of Friends*. "It seems like I never tire of writing about my own life," he says, almost twinkling. "It sounds egotistical, but I am the most interesting person to write about.

"I don't have any regular hours for writing. I don't have any regular hours really for anything. I don't ponder over things, wrestle with ideas. I don't follow any program. You write while you're hot and you stop when it gives out, or maybe you hold some for the next day. And now that I really have come to the end of the line, everything I do is gratuitous, something to be accepted as a gift.

"I'm not a Hemingway methodical writer. He made quite a to-do over how it turned out. I am one who does not believe in work, which is what Hemingway did. People consider him so highly. Well I don't consider him highly. He was slave-driving himself."

Miller's other literary opinions are equally unexpected. His favorite American author is Isaac Bashevis Singer—"He's a Jew one hundred and one percent, that's what I love, a man who is one hundred and one percent"—and he doesn't think all that much of Norman Mailer, though Mailer is a fan who recently put together a Miller anthology called *Genius and Lust*.

"I like him very much as a person, he's a charming, seductive individual, but I told him to his face that I find him hard to read. He's a difficult writer. He overelaborates."

As to himself, Miller says simply, and with no trace of anything except honesty, "I'll be very candid with you. I think I rank among the topmost writers of this century. And the others wouldn't be American."

Though perhaps no one else would put it quite that way, Miller has never lacked for literary admirers. Lawrence Durrell wrote that "American literature today begins and ends with the meaning of what Miller has done," and Ezra Pound paid *Tropic of Cancer* the ultimate in backhanded literary compliments by saying "Here is a dirty book worth reading."

And then there was picky George Orwell, who Miller remembers as being quite prepared to fight the Fascists in Spain in a dapper tweed sportcoat—"I told him 'Change that coat, you're going to war, let me give you one of my old corduroys or something"—who called Miller "the only imaginative prose writer of the slightest value who has appeared among the English-speaking races for some years past."

Yet in America, his home, Miller is stuck in most people's minds as the dirty book man, a forbidden, under-the-counter writer, and in recent years even feminists have joined the group taking up cudgels against him, with Kate Millett in *Sexual Politics*, for instance, calling him "a compendium of American sexual neuroses" and worse.

"Well, nothing bothers me too much about what the public thinks, don't you know. I often say that we are living in a world of dead people, dead from the neck up." Miller responds peaceably "In general I would say I'm happy-go-lucky. Durrell used to call me The Happy Rock because I held fast to my views, the waves dashed but they didn't break me.

"And the Zen thing, the philosophy of no philosophy, that helped me habituate myself to accept the blows. I don't say that I'm immune to them, but I don't react or I would be writing letters every week. I used to feel if I had my way I could hang the censors, but I don't think about it anymore. What's past is past, when the curtain falls it falls, and I don't try to raise it, except to talk about happy things."

Happy things for Miller almost inevitably means his years in France. "In America, I was in misery, don't you know," he explains. "I'd written three books, they don't exist anymore, but no one accepted my work. 'Cancer' shows you that, it shows you a man who's an absolute desperate individual, rejected in America for 10 years.

"So at age 40 I went to Europe and really began to live. I dropped all my American ways and became relaxed like the French. I took life easy."

"You take the *clochards,* the bums you see in Paris, the wine bibbers who wear overcoats in the summertime because their probably naked underneath. They're lousy, they live by their wits, it's a mystery how they get their meals, but these people always look happy.

"I've seen couples, a man and a woman, on a bench. He takes a drink, wipes his mouth, hands the bottle to her, and then they begin to talk, just as if they were in some salon. It's another kind of happiness."

If he loved France, the French returned the compliment, just last year awarding him the Legion of Honor. "That was never even noticed in any American paper, while Elvis Presley's funeral, my god it was an event," Miller says, allowing himself a bit of bemused distress. "But that's America for you, they don't even do that for a president.

"My reputation is greater in Europe than America, I'm read by all levels of people there, even old people. Listen, I'll tell you an interesting story. I recently got a letter from an 80-year-old French

woman thanking me for writing *Cancer* and *Capricorn*. She said
they changed her whole life, she wants to live to 180 now, don't you
know. I'd never get that kind of letter from an 80-year-old
American woman, nor would I expect one.''

Miller himself rarely thinks about his old books and never rereads
them, but he has no trouble picking out his personal favorite, an
elegant travel memoir about Greece called *The Colossus of Maroussi.*

"That voyage to Greece was the apex of my happiness, my joy, a
very great eye-opener,'' he says, still wondrous. "What one admires
there is a poor people who are happy, compared to us who are
miserable with our riches.

"In the same way I'm captivated by the pygmies, the happiest,
sanest people on earth. America offered to help them, to come in
with refrigerators or something, but they said, 'We are happy the
way we are.' How many Americans can say that? We wouldn't know
paradise if we had it. We'd have to bring in an ad man.''

Yes, Henry Miller knows he doesn't act or sound very old, but
his ailments allow him no delusions about his lifespan. "My first
operation, five years ago, that put me in touch with death. I never
thought about it till then.

"I don't fear it, sometimes I feel it's time I ought to be there.
Life must be just as good as on the other side. Life goes on, I'm
sure, my intuition, feeling, lead me to believe these things exist.
Otherwise, it's a waste of time to exist. You live a few years,
you're snuffed out, it doesn't make sense.''

People, Henry Miller says, are always wanting to know one thing
about him: all those books he wrote, all those *de trop* adventures,
could they possibly be real?

"I tell them, 'Yes and no.' Distortion is inevitable but in the main
it was truthful. Then they say they envy me, they wish they could
live that kind of life.''

"But when I think of being a panhandler, begging, having nothing
to eat, I don't know whether I'd advise it or not. I attribute my
success to poverty, that spurred me on, but you need a lot of guts.
A lot of it was painful. That's no life for an intelligent man. No
man should be reduced to that, reduced to a bum.''

Yet it was a happy life, all in all, Miller thinks now, despite the bad parts. And anyway, he says with simple understatement, "I'm pretty free of guilt. I've been that way all my life."

But sometimes, "Sometimes I feel like I was an idiot. I had no thought of the future nor did I heed what I was doing. I only did what I was impelled to do." Pause. "I still think that's the best way."

Index